Percy Moreau Ashburn
The Ranks of Death

A Medical History of the Conquest of America

SEVERUS
Verlag

P. M. Ashburn: The Ranks of Death – A Medical
f the Conquest of America
, SEVERUS Verlag 2010.
ck der Originalausgabe, New York 1947.

78-3-942382-28-1
SEVERUS Verlag, Hamburg, 2010

**grafische Information der Deutschen
nalbibliothek:**
eutsche Nationalbibliothek verzeichnet diese
kation in der Deutschen Nationalbibliografie;
illierte bibliografische Daten sind im Internet über
://dnb.d-nb.de abrufbar.

© **SEVERUS Verlag**
http://www.severus-verlag.de, Hamburg 2010
Printed in Germany
Alle Rechte vorbehalten.

Der SEVERUS Verlag übernimmt keine juristische
Verantwortung oder irgendeine Haftung für evtl. fehlerhafte
Angaben und deren
Folgen.

Der SEVERUS Verlag übernimmt keine juristische
Verantwortung oder irgendeine Haftung für evtl. fehlerhafte
Angaben und deren Folgen.

SEVERUS
Verlag

About Percy Moreau Ashburn

Percy Moreau Ashburn was born in Batavia, Ohio, on July 28, 1872. He graduated from Jefferson Medical College (M.D., 1893) and in 1898 he joined the Army. While stationed in the Philippine Islands, Ashburn was a member of the Army Board for the study of tropical diseases and wrote "Elements of Military Hygiene" (1909, 1915). From 1923 to 1927 he taught military hygiene at West Point and in 1927 he was appointed librarian for the United States National Library of Medicine, the world's largest medical library. Here, Ashburn began to read everything about the influence of disease on the early colonization of America. After 4 years of research he wrote "Medical History of the Conquest of America in the Sixteenth and Seventeenth Centuries", which was published posthumously by his son Frank under the title "The Ranks of Death, a Medical History of the Conquest of America" (1947). In 1934 Ashburn accepted the position of superintendent of Columbia Hospital in Washington and remained in that post until a few months before his death on August 20, 1940 in Washington D.C.

Bacon saith that wives are young men's mistresses, companions for middle age, and old men's nurses.

To one who has been for me all of these and infinitely more, and for my children a perfect mother,

I dedicate this book.

P.M.A.

CONTENTS

I	Introduction	1
II	The New World	6
III	Black Tragedy	28
IV	The Medicine of the Conquest	42
V	Famine and Scurvy	56
VI	Shock Troops: Eruptive Fevers	80
VII	Total War: Malaria	99
VIII	Yellow Jack	127
IX	Pale Killers: The Respiratory Diseases	141
X	Sickness in the Noonday: Intestinal Infections and Parasitic Worms	155
XI	The Kiss of Death: Syphilis	175
XII	Skin for Skin: Leprosy, Leishmaniasis, and Trachoma	191
XIII	*Landwehr:* Miscellaneous Diseases	198
XIV	Epilogue	210
APPENDIX A:	Technical Matter Allied with Text	213
APPENDIX B:	List of Citations in Text	250
APPENDIX C:	List of References	268
INDEX		287

Chapter I: Introduction

I WRITE of the effects of disease upon the discovery and early settlement of America, upon the conquest of the American Indians, and, in many places, their total replacement by the white man and the Negro. These effects have been tremendously important, more so in the sixteenth and seventeenth centuries than those resulting from the firearms, the religion, or the general culture of the whites.

Where man goes he carries much from his old environment, especially his language, his habits, his beliefs, his diseases. His new environment has not resulted in similar reactions and his new neighbors have different language, habits, and beliefs. Hence there are misunderstandings, odious comparisons, enmity, conflict, racial antagonisms, and struggles for supremacy.

The weaker party is forced into submission and into an inferior position, and while each borrows or adopts something from the other, the stronger is apt to impose more of its language, habits, and beliefs. The language of the conqueror usually becomes that of power, distinction, and gain, is necessary for advancement in social, governmental, and business lines, and it gradually encroaches upon that of the conquered. Occasionally, as in China and India, the mass and inertia of the conquered are too great to be overcome, and the conqueror is absorbed by the conquered, as has happened repeatedly in China, or he settles to a life of commensalism, as in India, where conqueror and conquered live their separate and mutually helpful lives side by side. Even here, however, the conqueror leaves his mark, and Greek, Mohammedan, and Englishman have all made their impress upon the art, life, and people of India. Such social, political, and economic effects of conquest have received the attention of many writers, the best of all probably Buckle; these have, however, usually neglected or ignored the influence of disease.

In 1909 I was in Liberia, where I saw a minority party, the self-styled Americo-Liberians, in power over a much larger native population, imposing its will in governmental matters, but so enfeebled by sickness as to be able to do no more than hold what it had. Despite the enormous pressure of surrounding barbarism, it clung tenaciously to its civilization and to every outward symbol of it, even to the long black coat and the high hat of ceremony, both utterly useless in that equatorial land except as symbols. I was much impressed by the preponderating influence of disease upon Liberian history.

Service of several years in the Philippines showed me peoples renewing their strength and vigor as they were freed from the incubus of disease, and later service in Panama revealed others emerging from isolation to the full fellowship of nations as the conquest of disease opened a way for them.

The history of medicine has largely neglected the subject of the influence of disease upon history, and has too often been a biographical and bibliographical record of physicians of the past who are monumented by their errors as often as by their real contributions to medical progress. Jones, Ross, and Ellett have presented interesting evidence that malaria was an important factor in the decline of Greece and Rome, but the general historian usually ignores entirely the influence of disease on history. On the other hand, some enthusiastic sanitarians exaggerate it, attributing to the presence of disease events that can be fully accounted for on other grounds. Without any prepossessing opinion, I began to study the effects, if any, of disease upon the early settlement of America.

INTRODUCTION

It was evident that one could not understand what the old writers said of disease unless he understood something of their point of view in regard to it. Although medicine was beginning to throw off the shackles of Scholasticism and to take into consideration more of the observed facts of anatomy, physiology, and disease, it was in the sixteenth and seventeenth centuries still the thrall of Galen and the fantastic humoral theory, and of the Arabians and astrology, and only a few great minds could see facts naked and unobscured. As usual, the popular medicine of the day was far behind the most advanced, and our sources of information are usually non-medical. So a chapter was necessary to set forth the state of medicine of the time. This is the fourth chapter in the book.

It soon became apparent that the Negro brought to America more diseases than the white man, and as he was not a conqueror or a colonist, it seemed necessary to discuss the slave trade in order to account for him and his diseases.

Other outstanding facts were the tremendous mortality attending all efforts at white settlement, and the reasons for that mortality, in nearly every instance deprivation. Then follow the various chapters on diseases among the Indians, some of them, notably malaria, being hitherto unplowed fields.

As information grew, a picture formed, the picture of a race of uncertain origin or origins, isolated for unknown centuries or ages from the Old World, without alphabet or writing, without iron, without draft animals or beasts of burden except for the llama family in Peru, and, *mirabile dictu*, without most of the diseases that now afflict mankind. This race peopled half a world, a continent extending from the cold arctic through the Temperate Zones and the tropics to the cold antarctic, and affording every imaginable sort of physical environment: mild tropic isles, tremendous mountain ranges, high cool plateaus, great fertile valleys, rain-drenched tropical forests, and vast expanses of temperate forests and plains, great rivers and lakes and waterless and barren deserts.

To such varied environments these peoples had reacted for centuries. In the West Indies, with the exception of the cannibal Caribs, they were the simplest, most harmless and innocent of peoples, naked, gentle, unashamed, and friendly. In Peru, Central America, and Mexico they had developed remarkable civilizations, methods of record and communication that were approaches to writing, a skill in handiwork, architecture, agriculture, astronomy, government, and social organization fairly comparable with those of the Old World. In Peru there was the largest functioning example of communism the world has ever seen, with the exception of Russia today. In most of the North Temperate Zone were stone-age savages, cruel and warlike, but not so much so that they were unable to learn much of both cruelty and war after the whites came. It is doubtful if any other savages have ever had so large a measure of respect and admiration from the whites. These various peoples were probably as happy as any, and they were far more healthy than any others of whom we know. Their diseases were mainly such as were due to deprivation and exposure. Death on a wholesale scale came only from war, drought, floods, and famine, on the small scale usually from accidents and injuries, from the mishaps and complications of childbearing, from the sacrifice of captives, from old age. There was no devastating smallpox, measles, malaria, yellow fever, perhaps no typhus or typhoid, almost no tuberculosis, probably no venereal diseases, no disease due to overeating. Maize and tobacco were cultivated nearly everywhere that climate and soil were suitable. Nature was bountiful, and her bounty largely compensated for the lack of iron implements.

If, as in Mexico, the gods were bloodthirsty, so was the Inquisition, which came from Europe to succeed them; if in New England the winters were severe and life hard, they were not made less so by the coming of the Puritan.

Into this Arcadian continent came the white man, thirsting for the riches of this world or the next, sometimes insatiably greedy and cruel, sometimes a zealot, narrow, bigoted, and oppressed by his sense of duty to save souls. The white man was speedily followed by his black slave and white and black brought their diseases. The results I have attempted to set forth in some detail in the following pages. They were tragic beyond my ability to depict them. Arcady was no more. Death stalked from Canada to Patagonia, pestilence walked in darkness, and destruction wasted at noonday. The Indian became a slave or an outlaw, and the followers of the Prince of Peace were the causes of his destruction. They were not such mainly because of their bigotry, cruelty, or evil intentions, but because, beyond their will or even their knowledge, they were the distributors of diseases till then unknown to the Indian, diseases to which he possessed neither natural nor acquired immunity, and to which his unresisting body served for fuel, as straw or fat pine to fire.

This was the greatest mobilization of disease, of its introduction to new and susceptible peoples, the most striking example of the influence of disease upon history, of which we can speak with any certainty, unless the Justinian plague be an exception. It was medical history writ large. Yet it has never before been studied from that point of view; it has received only the most casual notice; it is unknown or unappreciated by those who should know it best, the historians.*

The pursuit of the information quoted has required time and labor, but it has been good fun. A Mexican scholar said after a long discussion, "Señor, you and I are like Don Quixote with his books on chivalry. We suffer from a harmless *locura* [madness] from which we shall never recover, but it is a very pleasant disease." Would that I could communicate it!

---

* Good friends have told me that I have burdened my narrative with footnotes, references, and quotations. I have done so in order to help other workers, and also because I have seen so much of misquotation and misattribution of statements that I wish to furnish proof directly from the sources.

Chapter II

WE CAN find no evidence that there was any high command in Europe that guided and directed the invasion of America. Nevertheless, if one examines the course of the conquest, sets down events and dates, and follows the maps, an extraordinarily clear pattern emerges, so that one seems to detect a guiding force if not a guiding mind.

As though it were done by design, the plans for the conquest of America fell into three great segments, each allotted to one powerful European nation. The onslaught took the form of three spearheads lunging at the American continents. At the north went the French, aiming down the great waterway of the St. Lawrence, following it through the Great Lakes a thousand miles to the western plains, and finding there another great valley, the Mississippi, which in turn led south to the Gulf and so to the sea. When the French voyages and discoveries are traced it is impossible to avoid the feeling that one sees a tremendous encircling movement, first flanking the red man, then swinging behind him, hemming him in and cutting him off.*

---

*It may be that this is too much simplification, since the French at one time established themselves in Florida and were for three centuries active in the West Indies, and since the British swung far north of French Canada in their search for the Northwest Passage and were also active from early days in the West Indies, on the coasts of Central America, and the Spanish Main, and, in the case of Drake, at least, in Pacific waters as well. It is also true that the French established themselves in present Nova Scotia before the St. Lawrence push really began. On the whole, however, none of these

This French attack was streamlined, rather than frontal, following the water. It was also subtle, because the advance guard was commonly the Church, the first emblem the Cross, the message peace, and the immediate result trade. It was the least bloody of all the great invasions. It aroused less hostility than the other main attacks. Its advance was rapid, but always attenuated rather than solid. In 1600 there was a settlement at Tadoussac; in 1608 at Quebec; in 1642 at Montreal; in 1679 at Fort Niagara. In 1680–82 La Salle went down the Mississippi. In 1718 New Orleans was founded, the culmination of a series of posts that stretched up the river, along the lakes, and back to the St. Lawrence and the northern sea. It was a penetration often friendly, generally less troubled than the others, but nonetheless decisive. And wherever one studies it one finds the presence and solemn effects of disease.

At the center came the British. Theirs was a two-pronged attack at first. One point aimed at New England, just south of the French; the other at Virginia and what was later the southeastern seaboard of the United States. Expansion was very gradual. In between the prongs were minor landings by the Dutch and Swedes, so that the whole east coast of North America from Maine to Florida could be said to have been the sector of the North Sea peoples, but the British were the predominant force in this amphibious operation.

This Anglo-Saxon descent differed in several important respects from that of the French or Spanish. Instead of being streamlined like the French, it was scattered and widespread, a broad but shallow inroad along a great coast line. Instead of

facts seems to invalidate the main premise suggested, that the European invasion of America had three great prongs: the French in the north, the British in the middle, and the Spanish in the south. The French landing in Florida was temporary; their struggles, like those of the Dutch, in the West Indies were for the most part quarrels after the invasion proper was completed. The British voyages to the north were exploratory, not military or colonial, for the most part, and their raids and wars in the West Indies were against Europeans rather than Indians.

being overwhelming, sudden, and purely military like the Spanish, it was a kind of slow infiltration. Whereas the Spaniards thought of themselves as conquerors and sought for gold, the British thought of themselves as settlers and sought livelihood and the kind of freedom they desired. Whereas the French and Spanish thrusts were from the beginning high matters of state, the British was conducted to a great degree by private companies of gentlemen adventurers motivated by various aims and ambitions. Both the French and Spanish took the Church in the landing boats; the British came in good part because they wished to leave old churches behind. French and Spanish women came after the men were established; the British women arrived in the first ships and began at once to establish homes.

Important consequences followed from these characteristics of the British invasion. It was much less spectacular, at first apparently less successful than either of the others. Whereas in the first hundred years the French and Spanish had carried their banners and crosses thousands of miles inland and along rivers and coasts, the British had attained a maximum penetration of perhaps two hundred miles. They had established a mighty beachhead, but little more in a military sense, and war still crackled repeatedly along their borders. But they were there to stay; they had settled in. The Spanish seemed to advance like a huge army, horse, foot, and artillery; the French like a highly mobile small force. The British resembled unadorned and unsupported infantry. Like infantry they came ashore and dug in and built pillboxes. Sometimes they lost a pillbox. More often they held it and built another a little farther on and held that and so gradually moved westward, to the command of the ridges. When the waves of the struggle receded there were few Indians left in British-controlled territory, whereas the French and Spanish continued to rule in the midst of the conquered.

And at the south came the Spaniards. Theirs was the first

assault and incomparably the heaviest, most successful, and most ruthless. Spain was at the height of her power and pride. She was formidable in war, insatiable in riches. After her preliminary feeling out of the ground, principally under Columbus and his contemporary adventurers, she established an advance base on Hispaniola (the island of Haiti). This base, Santo Domingo, was the first of many, for the regular Spanish procedure was to build a base, then strike out from it; consolidate the gains; build another base, and so on. A glance at the map and a brief study of the dates will make this clear.

There were five main Indian groups opposing her; the Pueblos in the southeastern (later) United States; the Aztecs in central and northern Mexico; the Mayas in southern Mexico, Honduras, and Guatemala; the Chibchas in Colombia; and the Incas on the ocean slopes from Peru to southern Chile. Of these the Aztecs and the Incas were the most civilized, and the most formidable.

Santo Domingo was established in 1492. Shortly after another base was added in Cuba. Able men and supplies were gathered. Panama was investigated in 1509; Florida in 1518. As early as 1517 Espinosa sailed the west coast of Central America. Then in 1519 Spain struck her first main blow, with a deadly swiftness and intensity seldom equaled, at the very heart of Indian strength.

For she struck at Tenochtitlan (Mexico City) and the Aztecs. Between Mexico and Peru lay the richest, strongest, and best of the Indian kingdoms. The Aztecs and Incas were not savages; they were proud and potent peoples, dreaded in war and masterful in peace. At these two citadels the Spaniards flung themselves, and Cortes in Mexico in 1519 and Pizarro in Peru in 1532 entered into history. Cortes, with five hundred men, eleven ships, thirty-two crossbowmen, thirteen musketeers, and sixteen horses, defeated twelve thousand Indians on the shore at Tabasco, burned his ships, passed mountains higher than the Alps, conquered a great kingdom, humbled a grand monarch, fought a civil war, and established a government that endured from 1523 to 1821.

Again as one examines the details of the Spanish conquest it is difficult to avoid the feeling that one sees a massive military campaign with practically all the present-day elements of strategy and tactics involved. In contrast with the French and British, who struck at the less civilized and less populous Indian nations, the Spanish attacked the most formidable, organized, and civilized of the red peoples. Their goal was not binding a cord around a far-stretching wilderness to draw the cord slowly tight as the French did, nor to infiltrate as the British did; it was the deliberate smashing of central power, the annihilation or dismemberment not of geographical areas, but of governments and leaders. By ripping out the beating heart of opposition they held to kill the whole body and make it fall prostrate. They made spectacular use of their command of the sea.

The general design was remarkably consistent. From the primary base on Hispaniola they moved to Cuba and then to Mexico. From Mexico they sent expeditions south, west to the Pacific coast, northwest, north, and northeast. By 1565 they had mastered most of Florida, had established St. Augustine, and sent expeditions west to the Mississippi valley. From Santo Domingo also they moved to Panama. From there an expedition went north in 1523. Another penetrated to Bogotá in 1538 and the greatest of all to Peru in 1532. From Peru they also reached north to Bogotá and moving south along the coast founded Santiago in present-day Chile in 1541. Meanwhile they had built powerful strongholds along the Venezuelan and Colombian coasts; mighty fortresses such as Santa Marta and Cartagena, which contrasted sharply with French trading posts and British log palisades. By 1538, operating from European bases, they were at Asuncion, far up from the Plata. Buenos Aires was permanently settled in 1580. And far,

far beyond any of these sailed the galleons to Manila and the islands of the East.

It should be noticed that the geographical features of the territories taken by the Spaniards differed from those of the other Europeans. In the first place their lands were mostly tropical or subtropical, which had in itself an important effect in terms of disease. Secondly, whereas North America is a broad continent in which the very fact of distance is critical, Central America is relatively narrow, tapering at one point to a width of about fifty miles. This meant that it was not only relatively easy to dominate the entire middle-American land mass, but also that two oceans were available instead of one, with corresponding freedom of movement. The Spaniards, as indicated, were not slow to take advantage of this.

Of all the conquests, this of Spain was the most speedy, the most overwhelming, the most successful. By 1670 a treaty with England defined the boundaries of New Spain alone (but one of the four great Spanish colonial regions) as stretching from Panama (and including Venezuela and the West Indies) to just south of Charleston, South Carolina; west to Taos in what is now New Mexico; and including both the Atlantic and Pacific coasts between these boundaries.

So massive and conclusive was this onset that it may well have been a principle cause of Spain's rapid enfeeblement and decline. Perhaps such an effort was mortal even to such a great kingdom as Spain, for one may well speculate that nations as well as men have diseases. But that is a matter lying beyond the conquest of America. So far as that conquest is concerned, Spain's effort was decisive.

With the mastery of Central and South America; with the French domination of the St. Lawrence and the Mississippi valleys; with the arrival of the British at the eastern slopes of the Alleghanies, the conquest of America may be said to have been accomplished. What followed was a series of prolonged mopping-up operations; exciting, often desperate; tragic or glorious to the human beings involved, but with the main issue no longer ever in doubt. One could take any one of several dates as marking the end; perhaps the founding of New Orleans in 1718 may serve as a terminal point. Long before that, the eventual outcome was written for all to see. The red man was defeated at every turn; driven, often enslaved, with no hope left but to battle until he was exterminated either by encirclement or the engulfing sea.

Fortunately there were observers among the old Spaniards and others who had the wisdom to mark what they saw and to set it down charmingly. Much that we might wish they had included they left out because it seemed to them unimportant, but they included much that tells us a great deal; much about Hispaniola and Cuba and Mexico and Peru, Virginia, New England, and New France. They did not understand the ways of disease, but they saw its effects and noted them along with the heroism and the danger and their desire for the glory of God and gold.

And they described pleasant lands in which they fought and wrought. Not just wildernesses and realms of terror, but happy, healthful countries, abundant places until the white man came. They all observed the blight that fell so rapidly and for the most part agreed that it was the judgment of God descending on the heathen, and that it was a dreadful thing to witness. It did not occur to them to question such dispensations on the part of One to whom they ascribed the qualities of tender pity, mercy, and forgiveness. They, like other generations, prayed with good conscience when they went to war, and saw in famine, sickness, and poverty only the inevitable tragedy of good patriots trying to do their duty.

They did not know it, but before their eyes was unfolding the whole terrible battle between men an ddisease. Wherever they went men died, and while they naturally noted the military combat, the ways of sword and gun and arrow, far more significant were the casualties who had no wounds, who cared nothing for Spain or the king or perhaps even for a God of whom they never heard, but whose emissaries, many of them kind, well-meaning men, they regarded with an increasing horror.

It will be noted that more medical knowledge of the conquest comes from the Spaniards than from any other source. This was, of course, to be expected. The Spanish had more men involved, encountered more strenuous opposition, and covered more territory than any of the other European combatants. In addition their expeditions often included men who felt under a compulsion to report what they experienced and saw for the benefit of posterity, the information of the king and the church, and, sometimes, the advancement of their own fame. Such men as Bernal Díaz and Las Casas, to name only two, rank high in the list of narrators who have told stories to the world. Men such as John Smith and some of the nameless Jesuits were not unfit to rank with them, but it is to Spain that historians must turn for the fullest accounts of the early stages of the conquest of America.

Díaz and Las Casas are so frequently mentioned in the account that follows that they merit brief descriptions.

Bernal Díaz was an old soldier who, about 1576, when he was eighty-four, wrote a *True History of the Conquest of New Spain*. He had gone to Panama with Pedrarias when a young man in 1514 and had witnessed the quarrel between Pedrarias and Balboa. Returning to Cuba, he joined Cortes on a slave-hunting expedition and was wounded in a fight near Campeche in 1517. When Cortes sailed for his great attack on the mainland in February 1519, Díaz was with him. He fought at Tabasco and on many other fields. He went through all the conquest of Mexico and lived to write about it in one of the most charming of all such accounts. He set down what he saw and what he remembered, seeking to leave the truth behind him.

Bartolomé de Las Casas came to the New World as a layman in 1502, but was so shocked and touched by what he saw of the oppression of the red men that he entered the priesthood and for the rest of his life fought to remedy what he considered a gross injustice. By his faith, works, and character he won respect and in 1515 was given perhaps the noblest of all titles that came from the conquest, that of Protector of the Indians. He left a five-volume *Historia General de las Indias*, which is one of the great sources of knowledge of his time that we now possess.

F.D.A.

The New World

There is abundant evidence that nearly every part of America was healthful and many parts teeming with population when the whites first came. Several accounts of such conditions will be mentioned in subsequent chapters, notably that on malaria, but some will also be mentioned here.

Las Casas (1474–1566), in his efforts on behalf of the Indians, which earned him the well-deserved titles of Apostle of the Indies and Protector of the Indians, probably traveled more widely in Spanish America from 1511 to 1547 than any other man of his day, and he nowhere, so far as I have been able to find, mentions malaria or other disease rendering a region sickly, while scattered all through his writings are praises of the beauty, populousness, and healthfulness of different regions, some of which follow: of Hispaniola, "It is impossible to conceive of a land more thickly populated"; of Tierra Firme, "That country is a beehive of men and it seems that God has made choice of it especially as a place for the multiplication of the human species"; of the Lucayen Islands, "It is the most healthful region of the world"; of Nicaragua,

"The happiest country of the world, a veritable nursery of men"; again of islands and mainland, after praising Hispaniola, "We can say the same as to most of the qualities and characteristics of the neighboring islands, and not only of them but this and much more of the grand and vast mainland which has more than a thousand leagues of coast line already explored, practically all of which, for the above mentioned causes and other particular features, the moderation, pleasantness, softness, healthfulness and clemency of the airs, are most happy dwelling places." Peter Martyr says,[1] "According to his letters and the reports of his companions, all the regions explored by Columbus are well wooded at all seasons of the year, shaded by leafy green trees. Moreover, what is more important, they are healthy. Not a man of his crew was ever ill throughout the whole extent of fifty leagues between the great harbor of Corabaro and the Hiebra and Veragua Rivers." This last sentence relates to Columbus's exploration of the mainland in 1502.

Oviedo says of Honduras:[2] "It is a very healthful and fertile land, with abundance of foods such as maize and many fruits and vegetables, beans of many kinds, and many animals of all the varieties met in other parts of the mainland, many kinds of birds, much honey and wax, and much cotton from which the women make fine cloth." Of the region of Lake Nicaragua he said:[3] "The plains of Nicaragua are among the most beautiful and pleasing lands to be found in the Indies. There is a multitude of people. They have books made of the skins of deer painted in red and black so that they could be read even if there were no writing." Not, apparently, sickly or malarious lands.

In 1602 Captain Bartholomew Gosnold explored the more northern coast, admired and named Martha's Vineyard, and started to make a settlement on Elizabeth's Isle,* but reconsidered and did not. The climate was described as wholesome,

* Cuttyhunk

"the people of a perfect constitution of body, active, strong, healthful and very witty. . . . For ourselves, we found ourselves rather increased in health and strength than otherwise; for all our toyle, bad dyet and lodging; yet not one of us was touched with any sickness."

Contemporaneous writings in regard to the earliest discoveries and settlements in Brazil are as scarce as and no more full in their descriptions of matters medical than those relating to Spanish, French, and English colonies. The most important, from the present point of view, is Carvajal's description of Orellano's voyage down the Amazon, which will be discussed in the chapter on malaria.

However, in 1550 Padre Manoel da Nobrega, head of the Jesuits in Brazil, wrote from Porto Seguro to Padre Simão Rodriguez, his superior in Portugal:[4]

This land, as I have already written to your reverence, is very healthful to live in and we have so proved, and it seems to me the best that could be found, for since we have been here we have had nobody die of fever, but some of old age and many from the French disease. Nothing does good for dropsy because of the moisture of the aliments. The water is very good, the land naturally hot and moist. To keep in health it is necessary to work and sweat as does Padre Navarro. All of the foods are difficult of digestion, but God remedies this with an herb, the smoke from which greatly aids concoction and other bodily ills, and purges the phlegm from the stomach.

The earliest history of Brazil, that of Pero Magalhães, written about 1570, speaks of the great healthfulness of the country and accounts for it as follows: "The fact that it is so healthful and free from sickness is because of the winds that generally blow over it, from the northeast or south, and sometimes from the east or east-southeast. As all these come from off the sea, the air is so pure and well tempered that not only does it do no harm, but on the contrary restores and prolongs human life."

Compare this with the modern statement of M. F. Maury, the great oceanographer: "Now, there is no tropical country in the world which has to windward, and so exactly to windward of it, such an extent of ocean in the trade-wind region. Consequently there is no other tropical country in the world that is so finely watered as is the great Amazon country of South America."

Padre Manuel Rodriguez in 1684[5] summed up the trials, dangers, and hardships to which the Jesuit missionaries on the Amazon were subjected, naming arduous travel by mountain and river, wounds and injuries, fatigue, wild beasts, poisonous serpents, *gegenes* and *rodadores* (two very annoying species of mosquitoes). He also said that the constant heat, humidity, and lack of food caused sickness, but he made no mention of fevers or infectious diseases.

In 1587 Gabriel Soares de Souza described [6] the coast, settlements, and Indian tribes of Brazil from the mouth of the Amazon to the Bahia de San Mathias, south of the Plata in forty-four degrees of south latitude. He made no mention of sickness or unhealthful regions, but said in his introduction: "The land is almost all very fertile, very healthful, cool and swept by good breezes and irrigated by fresh and cool waters." (*"Cuya terra e quasi toda muito fertil, mui sadia, fresca e lavada de bons ares, e regada de frescas e frias aguas."*) He said of the Amazon, "The people call this river the Fresh Water Sea, because it is one of the greatest in the world, and it is thickly populated with settled and well-conditioned people, and according to the information that is available in regard to this river, it travels at least a thousand leagues to the sea; and in it are many great and small islands, almost all populated by people of different nations and customs, and many of them fight with poisoned arrows."

Captain John Smith wrote[7] of the lower 900 miles of the Amazon Valley being very healthful in 1628-29.

Captain North having seated his men about an hundred leagues in the Maine sent Captain William White, with thirtie gentlemen and others, in a pinnace of thirtie tun, to discover further: which they did some two hundred leagues, where they found the River to divide itself into two parts, till then all full of Ilands, and a country most healthfull, pleasant and fruitful; for they found food enough and all returned safe and in good health. In this discoverie, they saw many townes well inhabited, some with three hundred people, some with five, six or seven hundred.

Now, an outstanding fact of the conquest of America, in the West Indies, Tierra Firme (northern South America and Central America), Mexico, Peru, Nicaragua, Florida, Louisiana, Virginia, New England, and Canada, was the rapid diminution or disappearance of the natives, the Indians. The process has been almost continuous under English and American rule, but it was stopped in the Spanish colonies, largely as a result of the efforts of Las Casas. For years he fought zealously for Indian rights. Believing that most of their wrongs came from their assignment to colonists, nominally that they might be taught Christianity, but actually making them helpless slaves, Las Casas went to Spain in 1515 and sought audience with the king in order to help them. The king died before the matter was settled and Spain fell for a time under the regency of two priests, the Cardinal of Spain, Don Fray Francisco Ximenes de Cisneros, archbishop of Toledo, and the Dean of the University of Louvain, who later became Pope Adrian VI. Cardinal Cisneros heard Las Casas and directed that he and Dr. Palacios Rubios draw up a plan to leave the Indians at liberty and well treated. It was decided to put priests in charge of the execution of the plan, and as the Franciscans and Dominicans were opposing one another in the New World, the general of the order of San Geronimo of

Spain was asked to nominate suitable men to take over the work. This was done, although many at court opposed Las Casas as a zealot. The laws were greatly liberalized to protect the Indians, and the Hieronymite friars were sent to execute all that was ordered in regard to them.[8] The immediate effect of this was not great, but it is probably owing largely to this reform that the majority of the people of continental Spanish America are today Indian.

The disappearance of the Indians was viewed in different ways by different nations and different individuals, but in general it may be stated that the better and especially the religious elements of the Spanish and French deplored it and worried about it, while the English, religious or otherwise, seemed to look upon it as an evidence of God's favor to them, His chosen people.

The Canadian priests were deeply grieved by the sufferings of their charges, and profoundly puzzled by the mysterious ways in which God moved His wonders to perform, as to why He should afflict the Indians with disease and death as soon as they embraced His faith and began to go to church. Again and again the Jesuit Relations record such entries as the following: "Disease, war and famine are the three scourges with which God has been pleased to smite our Neophytes since they have commenced to adore him and to submit to his laws. Hardly had they heard of the Doctrine that we preach to them, and commenced to receive this divine seed, when a contagious disease [smallpox] spread throughout these nations, carrying off the healthiest of them," and "Hardly had they left Tadoussac,—where they had listened with love to the Christian truths and presented their children for baptism,—when death fell upon those little innocents, and disease upon a great part of their parents. . . . There is no human eloquence which can persuade a people to embrace a Religion which seems to have for companions only pestilence, war and famine."

Las Casas, intense partisan as he was for fair treatment of the

Indians, at times blamed Spanish mistreatment for practically all of their sufferings and for their rapid disappearance. He unquestionably was a very earnest advocate and he almost certainly exaggerated at times. A letter from Fray Toribio Motolinía to the king, dated from Tlaxcala, January 2, 1555, accuses Las Casas of libeling the Spaniards, saying that he reported only the bad things he could gather up and none of the good, and that even the evils were not always certain or well attested. He states that if the sins and crimes committed in the city of Sevilla were all gathered up and reported for the preceding thirty years, they would exceed all those related of New Spain in the same period. He goes on to say that the natives of Mexico had decreased markedly in the preceding ten years, but that the cause was disease and not mistreatment. Why this should be so is known only to God, Whose ways are hidden from us.

Herrera tries to explain it in the region of Tabasco:

There used to be great numbers of Indians, but by reason of many diseases, and pestilences which they usually have in the province, they diminished greatly, because being sick with measles, smallpox, catarrhs, bloody flux and great fevers, they bathe in the rivers without waiting for the diseases to subside, and so they die. And in accordance with Catholic piety they are not allowed more than one woman, whereas formerly they could have ten or twelve, so the Indians can not increase so much, especially the Chontales.

Fray Motolinía[9] says that God cursed Mexico with ten hard plagues, namely, smallpox, measles, war, famine, oppression in three or four forms, slavery, and work in the mines.

The population of Peru under Incan rule is believed to have exceeded 10,000,000. A census of 1548–53 showed 8,285,000 inhabitants; one of 1791, in the viceroyalty of Quito, equivalent to the present Peru, showed but 1,076,122. The decrease was attributed mainly to disease, especially smallpox.[10]

The Bishop of Santo Domingo, Don Sebastian Ramirez de

Fuenleal, wrote to the king in 1531[11] a letter that sounds like the pious lamentations of the Jesuit Relations in regard to the Canadian Indians:

> But in conclusion I say one thing, which I would have noted by all who may read or hear of it, and it is that this land and all the others which have been discovered or will be discovered are so unfortunate that it is not within the hands of men to be able to give them perpetuity, but rather God permits that the prince and his governors, wishing to benefit, destroy; wishing to enrich, they impoverish; wishing to perpetuate, they depopulate; wishing to give life to the Indians, they kill them; and wishing to increase the King's rentals, they diminish them; so that everything which is done in Spain for the welfare of this land and the natives of it turns to evil, and in all that which they think and do, they err.

The outspoken bishop attributed these contrarieties more to the stupidity of the Council of the Indies than to anything else. In fact, the principal cause lay in the introduction of disease new to the Indians, as it did in Canada.

Oviedo[12] expresses the opinion of the official and exploiting class of Spaniards. Discussing the depopulation of Hispaniola, he wrote:

> All of the Indians of this Island were assigned [*encomendados*] by the admiral [Columbus] to the settlers who came here to live; and it is the opinion of many who came and who speak as eye-witnesses that the admiral found here, when he discovered the islands, a million or more Indians of both sexes and all ages, of all of whom and of those born later there are not now believed to be in this year of 1548 five hundred people, natives and of the stock or progeny of those first ones. For the most of those now here have been brought by the Christians from other islands and from the mainland as servants: for the mines were very rich and the covetousness of men insatiable: some worked the Indians excessively, and others did not give them enough to eat, and in addition to these things, this people is naturally lazy and vicious, poor workers, melancholic, cowardly, vile and evilly inclined, liars and

of short memory and no constancy. Many of them for diversion [*por su pasatiempo*] kill themselves with poison so as not to work, and others hang themselves with their own hands, and others take so many diseases, especially certain pestilential smallpox which prevails generally in all the island, that in a short time the Indians will be ended.

Oviedo discusses other factors influencing the depopulation, but his general conclusion is that God repented having made such ugly, vile, and sinful people and that it was His will that they should die.

That they died in enormous numbers is evident. The West Indian islands in a short time knew them no more. In September 1531, a decade after the conquest, the president of the Royal Audiencia of New Spain wrote to the king that the population of Mexico had diminished one third.[13]

Oviedo's opinions were not greatly unlike those of the English and the later Americans, as evidenced by their conduct.

Increase Mather wrote:[14] "About this time [1631] the Indians began to be quarrelsome touching the Bounds of the Land which they had sold to the English, but God ended the Controversy by sending the Smallpox amongst the Indians of Saugust, who were before that time exceeding numerous. Whole Towns of them were swept away, in some not so much as one soul escaping the Destruction."

One Puritan, quoted by James Truslow Adams in *The Epic of America*, accounting for the epidemic that destroyed the Indians about Plymouth before the Pilgrims landed, wrote that "by this means Christ made room for his people to plant."

Master Thomas Heriot wrote[15] of the Roanoke Island settlement, "There was no town where they [the Indians] had practiced any villany against us but within a few days after our departure they began to dye: in some Townes twenty, in some forty, in some sixty, and in one an hundred and twenty, which was very many in respect of their numbers." There is in this account an unctuous air of saying it served them right,

There has usually been a small minority of persons in the United States striving to see that the Indians get fair play, and that the treaties made with them are lived up to by the whites, but too commonly the view that all Indians were bad, the only good Indian a dead one, seemed to be the rule of action followed.

In the United States and Canada the Indians became miserable remnants. Census statistics do not show that they have decreased numerically, but their social condition is very poor and their numbers have been kept up by interbreeding with the whites. Hrdlicka[16] reported that on careful investigation he was able to find only three possible examples of fullblooded Shawnees, all over seventy years of age, and no fullbloods among the Kickapoos. By this time there are probably no fullbloods among the Shawnees, so those great tribes, although nominally fairly numerous, are really extinct as purely Indian tribes. The *Handbook of American Indians North of Mexico*[17] says, "Another factor of apparent increase is found in the mixed blood element, which is officially counted as Indian, although frequently representing only 1/16, 1/32 or 1/64 of Indian blood . . . The Indian of the discovery was a full-blood; the Indian of today is often a mongrel, with not enough aboriginal blood to be distinguished in the features, yet, excepting in a few tribes, no official distinction is made."

In Spanish America the Indians survived more largely as Indians, but mainly as a conquered and servile race, kept in ignorance and poverty, from which they have only recently begun to emerge. In Mexico the population was divided as follows in 1910:

Whites	1,150,000	or 7.5 per cent
Mestizos	8,000,000	or 53 per cent
Indians	6,000,000	or 39 per cent

and the proportion of whites was decreasing.[18]

Nowhere did the Indians get quite fair play, and in no respect were they greater sufferers than from the white man's diseases, which they had not known before. Not even the white man's drinks or his greed hurt them more.

These diseases were very potent factors in the destruction and subjugation of the Indians, very powerful elements in the conquest and settlement of the land by the whites. Strangely, however, the subject has not been given extensive study or systematic description. Even Gibbon, although he gives a long and graphic description of the Justinian plague, which he says started in Egypt and Ethiopia in 542 A.D. and raged with varying intensity for fifty-two years, spreading to the east over Syria, Persia, and the Indies, and to the west along the coast of Africa and over the continent of Europe, marking Justinian's reign "by a visible decrease of the human species which has never been repaired in some of the fairest countries of the globe," does not imply that it was an important factor in that decline and fall of which he wrote. In fact, while he quotes extensively from Procopius' account of its progress, symptoms, and causes, supposedly "corruption of the air," "the pestilential odor which lurks for years in a bale of cotton," and "swarms of locusts, not less destructive to mankind in their death than in their lives," he classes it with comets and earthquakes as a portent. Certainly, we cannot blame either Procopius or Gibbon for lack of modern knowledge of the epidemiology of plague, but it is astounding that a great historian should not have considered an epidemic that involved the known world, and of which he wrote that "during three months, 5000 and at length 10000 persons died each day at Constantinople; that many cities of the East were left vacant, and that in several districts of Italy the harvest and the vintage withered on the ground," a possible cause of the vast economic and political changes in that Rome of which Constantinople and Italy were the centers, or an important factor in hastening and deepening that period of obscured and forgotten learning that we call the Dark Ages. It must have been important in causing men to forget and neglect the learning and wisdom of the Greeks, the rediscovery of which was so great a factor in bringing about the Renaissance, in leading them into superstition and a blind dependence upon priests, astrologers, and charlatans, in ruining capital and labor and promoting want and distress in comparison with which the present-day worldwide depression is luxury and abundance, in destroying families, institutions, and ideals, in promoting violence and oppression among men.

> Because the good old rule
> Sufficeth them,—the simple plan,
> That they should take who have the power,
> And they should hold who can.

Charles Darwin, great as he was as an observer and collector of facts and marvelous as a synthesist and a deducer of laws, noted two of the facts with which we are dealing, the severity of diseases introduced to newly discovered peoples and the disappearance of one people before another, but he did not quite correlate them, as the following quotations show.* In several places he speaks of the disappearance of the Indians before the Spaniards, but in discussing the blacks of Australia he said: "This decrease no doubt must be partly owing to the introduction of spirits, to European diseases (even the milder ones of which, such as measles, prove very destructive) and to the gradual extinction of wild animals." Then in a footnote, "It is remarkable how the same disease is modified in different

* In anticipation of the criticism that it is improbable that I can have better correlated views on any subject in natural history than could Charles Darwin, it may be stated that the entire subjects of bacteriology and the germ theory of disease have arisen since Darwin wrote of the *Voyage of the Beagle*, and every high-school student now knows more of these subjects than Darwin could have known a century ago, despite the fact that a few great minds had glimpsed the subject as Moses had viewed the promised land, from a mountain height a long way off.

climates. At the little island of St. Helena, the introduction of scarlet fever is dreaded as a plague. In some countries foreigners and natives are as differently affected by certain contagious disorders, as if they had been different animals; of which fact some instances have occurred in Chile; and according to Humboldt, in Mexico." A little further on he says:

There appears to be some more mysterious agency generally at work. Wherever the European has trod, death seems to pursue the aboriginal. We may look at the wide extent of the Americas, Polynesia, the Cape of Good Hope, and Australia, and we find the same result. Nor is it the white man alone that thus acts the destroyer; the Polynesian of Malay extraction has in parts of the East Indian Archipelago thus driven before him the dark colored native. The varieties of man seem to act on each other like different species of animals, the stronger always extirpating the weaker. It was melancholy at New Zealand to hear the fine energetic natives saying that they knew the land was doomed to pass from their children. Every one has heard of the inexplicable reduction of the population in the beautiful and healthy island of Tahiti since the date of Captain Cook's voyages; although in this case we might have expected that it would have been increased; for the infanticide, which formerly prevailed in so extraordinary a degree, has ceased, profligacy has greatly diminished, and the murderous wars become less frequent.

The Reverend J. Williams in his interesting work (*Narrative of Missionary Enterprise*) says that the intercourse between natives and Europeans "is invariably attended with the introduction of fever, dysentery, or some other disease, which carries off numbers of the people." Again he affirms,

It is certainly a fact, which can not be controverted, that most of the diseases which have raged in the islands during my residence there, have been introduced by ships; and what renders this fact the more remarkable is, that there might be no appearance of disease among the crew of the ship which conveyed this destructive importation. From these facts it would almost appear as if the effluvium of one set of men shut up for some time together was poisonous when inhaled by others; and possibly more so if the men be of different races.

We shall have much opportunity to study this picture as an accompaniment of the conquest of America by the whites.

Chapter III

INTO the great struggle between red men and white there was early introduced a new factor of tremendous importance, the black man. With horrifying swiftness the white man's diseases had destroyed the Indians. Everywhere the European went a blight followed, not by his intention, but nevertheless because of him.

In one sense this seemed to the white men of the time a dispensation from heaven, in that it weakened forever the Indians' powers of resistance. But the white man, especially at first the Spanish white man, was not conquering for glory alone or for piety alone; he was conquering for gold and riches. From the beginning he regarded the Indian as a slave, a pagan, a lesser thing to be used. The manner of his usage was cruel and heartless to an extreme; it was also appallingly costly, for in a few years the red man became an almost nonexistent commodity. Desperate in his need for labor, the conqueror saw offered before his eyes a brand-new, accessible, inexpensive, and apparently inexhaustible source of supply, the African Negro.

Few of the European nations are guiltless of shocking rapacity in developing this new treasury of human bondage, but the Spanish and the British excelled in their demands upon it. It is doubtful whether any passages of human history are as tragic and bestial as those of the African slave trade. Even to this day its horrors persist to plague the descendents of the original Christian traders.

From the point of view of the medical history of the conquest of America, the results of bringing the Negro to the New World were far-reaching. Here was a new actor in the drama of disease; a bearer of new and terrible illnesses fatal and debilitating to both white men and red. In those slave ships came more than human cruelty and suffering; there came, too, the seeds of terrible epidemics and pandemics; of accumulative horror and suffering possibly exceeding, at least in bulk, even that of the slaves themselves. And as time went by, everywhere, from Tierra del Fuego to Canada, but particularly in the broad belt from the Plata to the Potomac, the medical consequences of this shocking importation made themselves felt.

Subsequent chapters will deal with numerous vexing questions as to just what diseases can be attributed to the Negroes. There are, however, certain broad principles that may be stated. One is that certain diseases, to which both whites and blacks had a tolerance, were immediately fatal to the red man and that this fact alone may have made the difference between the success and failure of the conquest. In other words, the unfortunate Negro came to America not only as the white man's slave, but as one of his most deadly weapons. A second fact is that the Negro brought with him and embedded in American life several diseases that were just as fatal to the white man as to the red, and that this probably resulted in a very considerable slowing up of the process of conquest. A third fact is that these diseases, because of the Negro, became endemic to the New World and have been important factors in its history ever since, so that the primary fact of the conquest itself gave birth, as always happens with the prime facts of history, to innumerable other consequential facts which are still of major importance in America today and which probably are of much greater concern to many millions of Americans than such matters as the tariff or states' rights or the relationship of labor to capital or any number of other topics of deep import that are dealt with in the pages of the history books.

F.D.A.

Black Tragedy

The introduction of African slaves to America was a fact of tremendous importance to the medical history of the conquest and the continent. Not only did the Negroes bring with them all of their superstitions, their magic, voodooism, and ignorance, but even more important, they brought their diseases, and as will be shown in succeeding chapters, we probably owe to them some of the most serious diseases the Western world has known.

Slavery followed the first settlers within a few years. It was introduced into the West Indies in 1501 or earlier. In that year "a royal edict permitted negro slaves, born in slavery among Christians, to be transported to Hispaniola. Thus the royal ordinances of Spain authorized negro slavery in America. Within two years there were such numbers of Africans in Hispaniola that Ovando, the governor of the island, entreated that the importation might no longer be permitted."[1] It does not seem probable that such numbers of slaves were really "born in slavery among Christians," and direct importation from Africa may have begun in 1501 or 1502.

The first slaves on U.S. territory were sold in Jamestown, Virginia, in 1619, when John Rolfe wrote: "About the last of August came in a dutch man of Warre that sold us twenty Negars." Slavery was introduced into New York in 1626 and into New England in 1637. No effective settlement was made in Louisiana until about 1700, and I have no record as to the date of the first introduction of slaves, but in April 1719 one shipment included 250 Negroes, and from three hundred to four hundred a year were taken in for several years thereafter.[2]

As early as 1448, the control of the African slave trade was granted by the King of Portugal to Prince Henry the Navigator, in recognition of this prince's promotion of the exploration of the African coast and of his Christianizing zeal. The African explorations and Prince Henry's enthusiasm were the results of the proselyting to a greater extent than of the commercial spirit, and it was partly this fact that led the popes to sanction Portugal's claims.[3] The maintenance of a monopoly was not popular with either Portuguese or foreigners and the effort to maintain it weakened Portugal.

As the Indians died off in Spain's American possessions, Negro slaves were wanted there in larger numbers.*

The number of Negroes introduced into America was very large, although the total is unknown. When one recalls that the traffic lasted for three centuries, and that all of America south of Canada was supplied with slaves, such items as the following are very suggestive. As early as 1522 slaves were being taken to Cuba by the shipload, one load of three hundred being landed at Santiago that year.[4] In 1763 the English seized Cuba and in five months thereafter they introduced 10,700 Negroes at ninety pesos per head. Up to this time 60,000 had been introduced. Thereafter the rate was more rapid, 41,000 being imported in the next twenty-seven years. Thirty-two thousand of these were landed at Havana.

In 1799 the Portuguese were credited with taking 18,000 of the 70,000 slaves carried away from the coast of Africa each year.[5] The trade was always one of high mortality among the whites engaged in it, of frightful mortality to the blacks. From the documents collected by Donnan I have tabulated the mortality of slaves on the voyages for which the data for figuring

* Las Casas, great philanthropist as he was, was in part responsible for Negro slavery in America. He recommended it because he thought the Negroes more hardy than the Indians and able to withstand the hardships that were destroying the latter. What they really withstood better were the newly imported diseases. Other nations, France, England, and Holland, entered the trade, which later assumed enormous proportions and had important effects upon the policies of the nations concerned.

it are mentioned, finding that for the sixteenth, seventeenth, and eighteenth centuries it averaged over 30 per cent. Whether or not there was a selected publication of documents showing a high mortality I do not know, but I have not seen evidence of it.

In addition to this heavy mortality on the trip across the sea, there was a heavy mortality of slaves in caravans and in camps in Africa and still others died after landing in America. The slaves dying in Africa could influence America only by the diseases they passed on to fellow slaves before their deaths. Phillips[6] states that the mortality among new Negroes in America was from 20 to 30 per cent in the three or four years after they landed. It seems doubtful if one fourth of the slaves captured by raiders in Africa survived to render service of value in America.

Although a number of books on the diseases of slaves were written in the eighteenth century,[7] they shed little light on the question as to what diseases the Negroes brought with them. Nevertheless, it is interesting that the diseases treated of in these books are mostly the same as gave the great mortality or required treatment on the slave ships or on the west coast. Dazille said that diarrhea and dysentery were common and deadly, worms and venereal diseases very common. He also speaks of peripneumonia as serious, and abscess of the lung frequent. Yaws were common.

James Thomson said dysentery, worms, and dirt eating (hookworm cachexia) were common, as was smallpox, despite the fact that the Negroes practiced inoculation, calling it "buying" the disease. A low nervous fever (probably typhoid) was very serious, lockjaw common, yaws common, and syphilis rare.

The "Professional Planter" described the same diseases as Thomson but said that dysentery caused one half of all deaths among Negroes. He also gave an excellent description of the severe cachexia of *mal d'estomac* or dirt eating, a severe and

BLACK TRAGEDY

fatal affection. It may be noted here that such advanced cases of hookworm infestation would not have been purchased in Africa, but mild cases could not be recognized.

Sigaud states[8] in 1844 that slaves from the coasts of Cabinda, Angola, Benguela, and the eastern part of Africa brought to Brazil and disseminated there scurvy, itch, ophthalmia, smallpox, yaws, and dysentery, and that these diseases are the inevitable accompaniments of the traffic. He also said that the Negroes suffered much from certain diseases characteristic of their race, such as leonine leprosy, mal d'estomac (hookworm cachexia), and nervous diseases, under which he included functional as well as organic disorders, for example hysteria and tetanus.

Southey[9] tells that dysentery was introduced to the Indians of Piratininga in 1562 by Negro slaves.

Donnan says, "Our records of the slave trade shed little light upon the manner of people enslaved, their origins, and the differences among them, save when such points were translated into pounds sterling," and she might well have included their diseases. The slave ships carried surgeons, but their principal function was to examine the slaves offered for sale as to their ages, general fitness, and strength.

When these slaves come to Fida, they are put in prison all together, and when we treat concerning buying them, they are all brought out together in a large plain; where, by our chirurgeons, whose province it is, they are thoroughly examined, even to the smallest member, and that naked too both men and women, without the least distinction or modesty. Those which are approved as good are set on one side; and the lame and faulty are set by as invalides, which they here call mackrons. These are such as are above five and thirty years old, or grey-haired, or have films over their eyes: as well as those which are affected with any venereal distemper, or with several other diseases. The invalides and the maimed being thrown out, as I have told you, the remainder are numbered, and it is entered who delivered them. In the meanwhile a burning iron, with the arms or name of the companies, lyes in the fire: with which ours are marked on the breast.[10]

From such surgeons we can expect little, and we obtain even less.

However, mortality was directly translatable into pounds sterling, and from the reports of factors, agents, ships' captains, and supercargoes we can glean quite a good idea as to what caused the principal losses of slaves, losses which constituted "a great detriment to our voyage, the Royal African Company losing ten pounds by every slave that died, and the owners of the ship ten pounds ten shillings, being the freight agreed on to be paid them by the charter-party for every negro delivered alive ashore to the African company's agents in Barbadoes."

Apparently the most frequent and deadly disease was dysentery. Practically always when the high mortality of a voyage is attributed to named disease, dysentery is mentioned alone or as one of the principal causes. Smallpox is also mentioned as much dreaded, and in many instances the mortality is related to want or spoiled provisions. When smallpox broke out before the ship sailed, the slaves were landed for such time as the epidemic raged and the ship was cleaned, at least in reported instances, as the disease was much feared by the American Spaniards. The Negroes also had worms and were sometimes treated for the trouble.

White dysentery is spoken of as extraordinarily fatal. The ship *Hannibal*, captain Phillips, in 1693 was two months and eleven days between São Thomé and Barbados, in which time she lost 14 sailors and 320 Negroes.

The distemper which my men as well as the blacks mostly die of, was the white flux, which was so violent and inveterate, that no medicine would in the least check it: so that when any of our men were seized with it, we esteemed him a dead man, as he generally proved.* The negroes are so incident to the smallpox, that few ships that carry them escape without it, and sometimes it makes vast havoc and destruction among them: but tho' we had 100 at a time sick of it, and that it went thro' the ship, yet we lost not above a dozen by it.

The opportunities afforded by slave ships for the spread of infectious diseases such as these could not be surpassed. The slaves were terribly crowded, lying in close physical contact over the decks, part of the time chained. They had little opportunity to keep clean; slave ships were notoriously stinking and the slaves ate in groups of ten from common bowls, using their fingers, or sometimes wooden spoons. A Parliamentary record shows that the British vessel *Brookes*, of 320 tons, was authorized under the regulating act to carry 454 slaves, yet by using all available space and allowing but six feet by one foot four inches of deck for each man, five feet ten by one foot four for each woman, five feet two by one foot two for each boy, and four feet six by one foot for each girl, she had room for only 451.[11]

When the disease spread and the consequent losses of money were great, all were worried. It was elicited by suit in court that under such circumstances Captain Luke Collingwood, of the *Zong*, having lost sixty slaves and many others sick, threw overboard 133 living sick, jettisoning them to save the rest of the cargo, and incidentally shifting their loss from

* Just what Captain Phillips meant by "white flux" is not clear, but the word white suggests the absence of blood. A very deadly diarrhea without blood in the stools, "so violent and inveterate that no medicine would in the least check it," suggests cholera, but there is no other evidence of the occurrence of that disease. Another possibility is that this white flux was amoebic dysentery, as this type is often characterized by the passage of much mucus and relatively little blood. The objection to this is that amoebic dysentery is much less likely than the bacillary to occur in explosive epidemics, but in the special instances that may have been the result of repeated and massive infections under conditions of great hardship and severe deprivation.

the company, which stood all losses for deaths from sickness aboard ship, to the insurance companies.[12] The underwriters lost the suit and had to pay for the slaves, Lord Mansfield stating that "The matter left to the jury was whether it was from necessity: for they had no doubt (though it shocks one very much) that the case of slaves was the same as if horses had been thrown overboard."

Dr. Schotte is quoted elsewhere as saying that slaves brought to the coast from the interior of Africa often developed scurvy on the way. It is probable, however, that slaves clearly suffering from this disease were not purchased by the whites. I have seen no mention of scurvy on the slave ships, but many things to suggest that it occurred from time to time. Most important of such things were the length of the oversea journey, varying from four weeks to as many months;* the slaves' diet, which will be discussed later; and the fact that slaves often reached the dealers in Jamaica and Barbados in very poor condition, for which they were fed upon fresh meat and green vegetables to bring about recovery. Another suggestive fact is the statement that the Portuguese, who were said to have a smaller mortality among their slaves than the other nations, "when they put them on board . . . that they may come safe and sound to their intended ports, they provide medicines, especially lemons and white lead to use against the worms." This mention of white lead suggests the explanation of the disease dry bellyache, for the prevention of which the slaves were given melegueta pepper. Dry bellyache was probably lead poisoning due to the use of lead given for the treatment of worms.

The slaves' diet was usually such as would produce scurvy. The standard and common items were rice, beans, corn, palm

---

* The Dutch ship *St. Jan* left Mina on March 4, 1659, making land at Tobago in October, "the greater part of the slaves having died from want and sickness, in consequence of such a long voyage, so that we saved only 90 slaves out of the whole cargo" of 219.

oil, suet or lard, salt, melegueta pepper, and an occasional small issue of tobacco and of rum, trade brandy, or other spirits. The ration necessarily varied with time and place of supply, and accounts show the purchase at times of salt meat, salt fish, yams, bananas, dried plantains, peas, vinegar, biscuit, oranges, lemons, and coconuts. "Mercator Honestus," in a defense of the slave trade written in the *Gentlemen's Magazine* in 1740, spoke of the ration as a pint of corn and a herring. James Barbot wrote in 1700, "We messed the slaves twice a day . . . the first meal was our large beans boiled, with a certain quantity of Muscovy lard. . . . The other meal was of pease or of Indian wheat, and sometimes meal of Mandioca, boiled with lard or suet or grease by turns: and sometimes with palm oil and malaguette or Guinea pepper."

Captain Phillips, of the *Hannibal*, wrote of his slave passengers:

Their chief diet is called dabbadab, being Indian corn ground as small as oatmeal . . . and after mixed with water and boiled well in a large copper furnace, till it is as thick as a pudding, about a peckful of which in vessels is allowed to 10 men, with a little salt, malagetta and palm oil to relish. . . . Three days a week they have horse beans for their dinner and supper . . . these beans the negroes extremely love and desire, beating their breast eating them and crying Pram! Pram! which is very good! They are indeed the best diet for them, having a binding quality, and consequently good to prevent the flux, which is the inveterate distemper that most affects them, and ruins our voyages by their mortality.

It is occasionally noted that slaves died of "the lethargy," which was probably African sleeping sickness, or trypanosomiasis.

It is obvious that the slave traders themselves recognized that they were importing dysentery, smallpox, and intestinal worms, but not at all evident that they attached any significance to the fact except as these things affected their profits.

A Negro landed and sold gave them no further concern. Although the surgeons rejected Negroes in whom they recognized venereal disease, there must have been then, as today, many cases of such disease that could not be recognized by inspection.

There is no evidence that the traders knew that they were also bringing in malaria or yellow fever, or that they would have cared had they known it. As a matter of fact, it is improbable that they could have recognized these diseases in the Negroes, and certain that they would not have recognized either Negroes or whites as carriers of them; but they did recognize that the white mortality from fevers was high. For instance, in 1551–52 Captain Thomas Windham visited Benin and Guinea, the former proving very deadly to his men. Of seventy leaving England, scarce forty survived. Both the captain and the pilot died.

In 1562 John Lok lost half his men from sickness on the Gold Coast.

In 1600 John Barbot wrote:

> The air of this river [Old Calabar] is very malignant, and occasions a great mortality among our sailors, that makes any long stay. I remember, that my first voyage into Guinea, being in the frigate called the *Sun of Africa*, I met at sea, crossing the line, an English flyboat, bound for Nevis, but first for Prince's Island, which had but five men of all the crew able to hand the sails, having been ten months in Old Calabar, to purchase about three hundred slaves, of which one-third part, or better, were then dead tho' they had been but three weeks from that river.

It was noted in the same year by Captain Phillips that "Our factory [at Whydah] . . . stands low near the marshes, which renders it a very unhealthy place to live in: the white men the African company sent there seldom returning to tell their tale."

In 1732 the ship *Mary* lost 20 of her complement of 27 sailors, as well as 141 Negroes.

From the time of our first knowledge of it to very recent years, the west coast of Africa, particularly from the Senegal River to Angola, the location of much the greater part of the old slave trade, was known as the white man's grave, and English army service there carried an increase in pay and in leave privileges as a partial compensation for the increased risk. Within the past century, when diagnosis has been more reliable, the principal cause of disability and death has been malaria. Dysentery has also been very important, and most tropical diseases have been more prevalent there than in other parts of the world. Investigations in recent years support the belief that the coast was also the home of yellow fever, much of which may have been mistaken for malaria.

Sir Robert W. Boyce has argued well that yellow fever has probably always been endemic on the west coast although not recognized, being usually considered malaria. He says that mild forms of the disease are very common. "A very large proportion of the 'remittent' and 'bilious remittent' fevers of West Africa today are the well known mild forms of yellow fever. The African native is as saturated with yellow fever as he is with malaria, and his escape from severe yellow fever and its very frequent occurrence among the whites is proof of this contention." [13]

In view of the immense volume of the slave trade during three centuries of popular and medical ignorance of hygiene and epidemiology, it would have been nothing less than a miracle had the diseases of the west coast not been imported to America. That miracle did not happen and succeeding chapters will set forth good reasons for the belief that many of them were so introduced.

A period of quarantine or separation of newly imported slaves was practiced to prevent the spread of their diseases. It is a certainty, however, that this could not prevent the introduction of diseases that had periods of latency, such as malaria, sleeping sickness, amoebiasis, hookworm infestation, leprosy, filariasis, Guinea worm, yaws, and syphilis. It could not exclude mosquitoes carrying the yellow-fever germ. One of the diseases named, sleeping sickness (trypanosomiasis), was missed because the tsetse fly, its insect host, does not occur in America. Yellow fever may have been absent for the first century and a half of Spanish settlement because of the absence of the mosquito that transmits it.

Let us remember too that it was because of the introduction of diseases to which the Indians had no immunity and the Negro had much that the Indian disappeared from many parts of America and the Negro took his place. This was certainly true of the West Indies, Brazil, and much of the coast of tropical and subtropical America, probably true of our own slaveholding states. In the highlands of Mexico, Colombia, Peru, Bolivia, above the levels at which malaria and yellow fever occurred, the Indian survived and became the peon, the unskilled, servile, and exploited laborer. These highlands now have some malaria, but the available records indicate that it is of recent introduction and that it was not present for a century or centuries after the conquest. Even yet it is not so common as in the lowlands. The Indian might have done the same in our southern states had their geography been the same, had malaria and yellow fever not found suitable environments in conditions that favored cotton, sugar cane, indigo, and rice. He was not displaced by the Negro in the northern states or Canada because servile labor was never economically necessary or strongly arguable in those parts.

Of course, the Negro is today found in all parts of the continent, but he constitutes the majority or a large part of the population only in regions that have known malaria and yellow fever. Had it not been for these diseases and eruptive fevers we should probably have no Negro question in the

United States today. African slavery cost incalculably more than the pounds and shillings, pesos and dollars paid for the slaves, more than our Civil War, and America is still paying for this sin of our fathers, long after they and generations of their descendents have passed from the scene.

Chapter IV

IN FEW respects has modern man departed further from the practices and beliefs of his not very remote ancestors than in his conception of and dealing with disease. There are two worlds of medicine: that before, let us say, Pasteur, and that since his great discoveries.

It is not merely that vocabulary and knowledge have changed; the whole manner of thinking is different. And the changes are so far-reaching, their implications so large, that one must be wary of interpreting the observations and conclusions of the old doctors and writings in modern terms.

Yet all our knowledge of the medical history of the conquest comes from men who wrote in their terms with their meanings and not in our terms with our meanings. We cannot hope to decipher their record unless we understand their premises and their ways of thought. We cannot blame them for omissions that they never conceived as requiring inclusion. We cannot blame them for not diagnosing what they never believed existed. If we examine their tenets and their practice it becomes clear why in their time disease was a much more serious and constant threat to life and endeavor than it is in ours; we can understand why, in such and such a case, this undertaking failed or that succeeded, apparently because of the will of God.

F.D.A.

The Medicine of the Conquest

The medicine of the America of the conquest was less learned than that of Europe at the same time, was far behind the best, still further from good. It could not rise above its sources, which were mainly in medieval and ancient Europe. No leader of medicine, no great contributor to it in the sixteenth or seventeenth century ever saw America. A few physicians of New Spain, men sent out officially by the government to study, write, or teach, were probably as good as the almost best in old Spain. Very few physicians of education went to the English or French settlements of the seventeeth century. Those few wrote very little; what they wrote related more to colonial affairs than to medicine. However, the historians and lay writers of the period reflected at least the popular medicine of the day, and from them we get practically all of our information bearing on medical aspects of the conquest. It is probable that then, as now, popular medicine was far behind the most advanced medicine of the day, so we cannot expect from it anything more helpful than plain statements of facts observed. Any attempt to explain too much or to use medical language confuses more than it helps. Bearing these facts in mind, let us examine briefly the state of medicine in Spain and England in the centuries of their colonization.

SPANISH MEDICINE IN THE SIXTEENTH CENTURY

The two centuries that witnessed Spain's rapid rise and beginning fall, the fifteenth and sixteenth, are known as the centuries of the Renaissance. In general, and for most of Europe, it was in truth a time of rebirth in the spiritual and mental sense, a time of freeing spirit and mind from the bonds of Scholasticism and dogmatic theology, a time of resuming independent thinking and experimental research such as had not obtained since the oblivion of Greek culture. The fall of Constantinople in 1453 and the reintroduction of Greek learning and literature through the Byzantine refugees had started men on unorthodox trains of thought. The discovery of printing in the middle of the fifteenth century began to expedite the diffusion of knowledge at a rate never previously possible. The Reformation came at about the same time and set men to thinking of religion for themselves and to arguing and fighting for their views. Then, before the end of the century, came the great Portuguese and Spanish voyages of discovery, the opening of a new world, the substitution of sea routes for caravan routes in trade with the Orient, the decline of Venice, Genoa, and the Italian control of Oriental trade, the shifting of trade to the West, and the rapid rise in wealth and power of Spain. However, Spain rose in power largely in spite of the Renaissance, rather than because of it. Her rise was due mainly to the immense new wealth and the opportunity for physical adventure, exploration, and conquest furnished her by the New World, not so much to freedom of mind and spirit. In Spain, more effectively than elsewhere, authority and orthodoxy succeeded in curbing mental explorations by the "bold, skeptical, inquiring and informing spirit" that was the most outstanding characteristic of the Renaissance. The instrument that served to accomplish this was the Spanish Inquisition. Religious in origin and benevolent in intent, this institution became, largely through excess of zeal, but partly because put to political rather than religious uses, an instrument of cruelty and oppression, an obstacle to progress, a main support to a dying Scholasticism, a stimulus to religious bigotry. But it kept Spain Catholic, made most of the American continent the same, and was a very important fact in history.

Partly because of it, Spanish medicine did not have much

part in the rejuvenation that occurred in Italy and most of Europe. When Leonardo da Vinci, Michelangelo, and other artists were by their studies and their art proving Galen's ideas of anatomy largely erroneous, while Michael Servetus* was being burned with the book in which he stated the facts as to pulmonary circulation, while Fracastorius was writing clearly and intelligently of contagion and Paracelsus was combating Galen and studying the alchemy that became chemistry, while Ambroise Paré was writing in the vernacular and being abused for it, and was applying good common sense to surgery, Spanish medicine was still bound in the swaddling clothes of Scholasticism. It is true that Vesalius, an anatomist of light and learning, was at the court of Spain, but he was a foreigner and out of his element, and he had ceased to produce. His *De humani corporis fabrica libri septem* is considered a foundation stone of modern science, but he had completed it before he was thirty years of age and long before going to Spain. When he became a courtier he ceased to live as a scientist.

European medicine in general at the time of the Spanish conquests was not much ahead of that of the Arabians of some centuries earlier, some of whose works were but recently translated. The works of Rhazes (850–923) were relatively new, his description of smallpox being first translated in 1498. The *Liber Regius* of Ali Abbas (994) was first published in 1492 and Avicenna's *The Canon*, a system of medicine, was first printed, in Hebrew, in 1491. In Spain, perhaps even more than in the rest of Europe, the greatest medical authorities were still Aristotle, Hippocrates, Galen, and the Arabians,

* Michael Servetus or Miguel Serveto, a Spaniard, was burned at Geneva by Calvin, after first being convicted and burned in effigy by the Catholics at Vienne, from whom he escaped. His death was in no way related to his discovery of pulmonary circulation, but that discovery was published in his *Christianismi Restitutio*, for the writing of which he was tried, convicted, and burned as a heretic.

See "Michael Servetus–Discoverer of the Pulmonary Circulation of the Blood" by John C. Hemmeter, *Janus*, 1915, XX, 330–64.

and medical lore was still largely deductive reasoning from false premises. The observation of facts was not allowed to invalidate orthodox beliefs. An example of this attitude applied to general history, rather than to medicine, is the definite statement of the licentiate Montesinos, in his history of ancient Peru, that the Peruvians came from Armenia; because all men were descended from Noah, who had landed in Armenia and settled there after the Flood. As that land became overpopulated, Noah's descendants scattered to the parts of the world best suited for their occupancy, and the sons of Ophir chose Peru. Montesinos thought Noah, as a navigator, might have visited the land earlier and might have advised his descendants in regard to it. That all men were descended from Noah was a premise founded on Holy Writ and one not to be challenged. If its correctness were granted, the subsequent reasoning was not bad. Another interesting example is Fernando Colón's statement[1] that his father, Columbus, recognized the mainland to be *tierra firma* and not an island because Esdras had said in his fourth book that six sevenths of the surface of the earth was land and only one seventh water. Having seen so much water, Columbus doubtless believed that the earth had no room for more, in view of what the Scripture said.*

The statements of Aristotle, Hippocrates, and Galen re-

* At the time of Columbus's voyages there were in use four books of Esdras. The Council of Trent (1545–63) rejected parts of these and adopted for the use of the Catholic Church the two books of Esdras, one of them also called the book of Nehemias, now found in the Douay English version. The Protestants later adopted as apocryphal the two books of Esdras found in the old English Bibles, but rejected yet other parts, so that the Douay and the King James versions each contain two books of Esdras, and these differ radically in the two versions. The statement cited by Columbus is found in II Esdras 6, 42, of the Apocrypha of the King James version. "Upon the third day thou didst command that the waters should be gathered in the seventh part of the earth: six parts hast thou dried up, and kept them, to the intent that of these some being planted of God and tilled might serve thee."

ceived much reverence from the educated physician, while the uneducated one, and there were many such, was at best a dabbler in magic, a herbalist, or a horse leech.

The following is an example of the medicine and public hygiene of the day. Writing for the Cabildo officials of Panama, Andres Cortes, procurator general, petitioned the king as follows, under date of April 12, 1600:[2]

> This city and province are very unhealthful because of the intemperence of heat and moisture, for which reason one lives here with much risk to his health and many people have tried and still try to go to other places to live, as they have done for the past six years, because of the numerous and grave diseases which have newly developed, such as sore throat, smallpox, abscesses, boils, typhus fever, all acute diseases from which many people of all sorts have died; and the causes of these new diseases being sought by the doctors, they found them to be caused by the wine which is brought here from Peru.

Wherefore the officials besought the king to prohibit the importation of Peruvian wine and to permit only that of Spanish wine. Attached to this petition was a certificate from two medical men to the effect that the said wine of Peru, being of a hot and moist nature, while the climate of Panama is also hot and moist, causes many ardent and putrid fevers, pain in the side, bloody stools, rheumatism, and other hot and moist diseases, as it boils in the veins, comes in contact with the brain, and causes the diseases named above, and boils and smallpox and measles and hoarseness. José Gabriel Navarro[3] draws the following gloomy picture of the medical man of the period of the viceroys in South America, a time later than the conquest:

> Medicine was not in the required program of the American colleges and universities. Why? Because at that time, like the arts and mechanical work, medicine was considered a plebeian art proper

for mulattoes and unworthy of gentlemen. For the latter were the dignities of doctorates of canons, of law and of theology; for the former the comedy of feeling the pulse and so earning the miserable pay which was given them. Because of the dishonor of medical practice, our predecessors could not beg and receive their reward without taking the pulse, feeling the sick person and seeing him intimately, smelling his humors and assisting him to the hospital. An autopsy was the very culmination of baseness and humiliation. As a natural consequence of these antecedents the physician was an inferior being, who scarcely filled a place between the barbarous tooth-puller and the bloodletter.

It was only toward the end of the sixteenth century that the Pope, Sixtus IV, authorized the study of anatomy on the cadaver.

It must not be understood from what has been said that Spanish medicine alone was slow in advancing. In this century the professors of the Sorbonne bitterly assailed and opposed Ambroise Paré, the chief grounds for their opposition being that he was ignorant of Latin, and therefore wrote in his native language, that he used common and even obscene words, and that he ligated blood vessels, contrary to the teachings of Galen and the Arabians. Even in the following century, Harvey met with violent opposition when he published his *Exercitatio anatomica de motu cordis et sanguinis*, despite the facts that he wrote in Latin and proved his thesis. Jean Riolan (1577–1657), physician to Louis XIII and the queen mother, was a true Scholastic when he contended that if Harvey's dissections did not really agree with Galen's teachings, then the structure of man had changed since Galen's day, for it could not be admitted that the latter had erred. Guy Patin, the most famous medical man of Paris at the time, said that Harvey's description of the circulation was "paradoxical, useless, false, impossible, absurd and harmful." *

* For further description of Spanish and other medicine of the period see Appendix A, pp. 213-24.

ENGLISH MEDICINE OF THE SEVENTEENTH CENTURY

Inasmuch as we shall deal with English settlements made in the seventeenth century, a brief survey of English medicine of that period is indicated. It was a great century in history and science, a century of rebirth and progress, the century of Galileo, Kepler, Newton, Descartes, Malpighi, and Leeuwenhoek. In England it was ushered in by the spacious days of great Elizabeth, and the English names of Shakespeare, Milton, Bacon, Newton, Harvey, Cromwell, and Hampden adorn it.

The greatest medical event of the century was Harvey's description of the circulation of the blood in 1628, after the settlement of Britain's colonies in America was well under way. There were two or three epidemics of plague in London during the century, and malaria was both endemic and epidemic in England.

English medical practice advanced toward common sense under the leadership of Thomas Sydenham (1634–89), and the observation of facts began to outweigh medical orthodoxy. Although Sydenham's views on the epidemic constitution of years suggest medieval thinking, they were really the result of Hippocratic teachings and of independent, even if erroneous, reasoning upon his own observations. Sydenham was preeminently a clinician, noted for knowledge of disease as seen at the bedside and for his ability to describe and to treat it. To him we owe our first or best early descriptions of scarlet fever, sweating sickness, hysteria, gout, and chorea, and in another chapter we shall see how acute was his observation of malaria. What he saw he interpreted and described according to the vision and good sense of Thomas Sydenham, and whether or not it agreed with Galen's teaching seems to have worried him not at all.

He led English practice into the ways of sound thought and

gave it that practical utility that still distinguishes it. However, it must not be understood that he was not influenced tremendously by Galen. The humoral theory constituted his approach to all diseases, and was used in explanation of all, but when his facts did not accord with the theory, they still remained facts and he would state them and say that he could not explain them.

But not every English doctor of his day, in fact none other, was a Sydenham. Galen was not to be ousted in a day and astrology was still going strong. According to Herringham,[4] medical education in England in Harvey's day was a national disgrace. Degrees were granted for cash or favor, there was no recognition of the natural sciences, such as chemistry, botany, and even anatomy, and the duty of the Queen's Reader in Physicke at Cambridge was "to read and interpret Hippocrates and Galen in such sort as shall seem meete for his auditory."

However, John Mayow (1643-59) discovered oxygen, which he called the "nitro-aerial" constituent of air, and gave a really good description of respiration and the part played in it by this substance. These descriptions attracted little attention at the time, but they stand as clear evidence that Harvey was not the only English physiologist whose originality, clarity, and activity of thought marked that great century.

It was not until the latter half of the eighteenth century that any clinical instruction was given in London.

In the seventeenth century Robert Boyle, likewise a physician, founded the Royal Society, became its first president, and carried on investigations that rank him as a founder of English chemistry.

However, the English and French kings and pretenders were still touching for scrofula or king's evil at this time, and Valentine Gratrakes, a soldier of Cromwell's army, rose to wealth and fame by reason of the cures he wrought by laying on of hands, as have many others since his day. And 'tis true, 'tis pity, that in this century Le Sage and Molière so pictured medical ignorance and pretense, in *Gil Blas* and *Le Malade imaginaire*, as to win immense applause, and we have reason to fear that the painful and shameful pictures were but too real; were caricatures but, like most successful caricatures, were founded on fact.

NEGRO AND INDIAN MEDICINE

There are yet two other sources that could and undoubtedly did influence medicine and disease in all American colonies, the Indian and the Negro. The more helpless and ignorant men are in the face of natural events, especially sickness and disaster, the more prone they are to appeal in a desperate sort of way for supernatural help, divine, diabolical, mysterious, or magical. It is within the memory of men living today that quacks posing as Indian herb doctors were financially successful, that voodooism still influenced the conduct and happiness of thousands in America, that school children wore bags of asafetida to protect them from sickness, that old gentlemen wore rings made from horseshoe nails or carried buckeyes in their pockets to ward off rheumatism. Bad as was medieval medicine in Europe, that of the Indian and the Negro was sometimes worse. The savage Indians and the Negroes contributed little or nothing of value to any branch of medicine, and from them we received a mass of superstition and ignorance that reinforced and strengthened what we had brought from Europe, a heritage that still plagues us.

Because the Aztecs and the Incas had made considerable advances in civilization, it might be supposed that they had valuable information to add to the sum of European medicine, but there is little or no evidence that such was the case.

Inca Garcilaso (*Comentarios reales*) gives us an almost contemporary account of the state of Peruvian medicine at the time of the conquest. He states regretfully that the Peruvians had no knowledge of astrology, but says that happily they used bloodletting and purging. They bled from the arms and legs but did not know the niceties of the art, "nor from which vein blood should be taken" for a particular disease. They merely opened one near the seat of trouble. For severe headache they bled at the junction of the eyebrows and the root of the nose. In place of a lancet, they used a sharp stone point bound in a cloven stick. This point they placed over the vein, gave the stick a tap, and so opened the vein, they thought, with less pain than from a lancet. They knew nothing of the humors (lucky people) nor how to tell about them from the examination of the urine. They took purges when they felt tired and heavy but were in good health, not when they were sick. Garcilaso himself tried the popular purge and gives a graphic description of its powerful effects. One felt and looked as though he would die, was dizzy, faint, and helpless. He cast off whatever humors were in him, the evacuation being in both directions, by vomit and stool. Worms and any other vermin that may have developed in the body were expelled, but after the storm the patient was a new man, willing to eat anything, ready for a fight or a frolic.

There were no doctors, but some midwives and herbalists, and these ordered the bleedings and purgings for the royal and noble families. The common people treated themselves or, like beasts, had no treatment. As for nursing children, when they became sick with fever they were washed in urine in the morning, and if the urine of a child was available, they were given some to drink.

When a child was born, the umbilical cord was cut at a finger's length and when the stump had dried and fallen away it was carefully preserved and was given to the child to suck when it did not seem well or had a coated tongue. Only the child's own cord had any curative virtues. Others were useless.

The Peruvians knew not how to take the pulse or to give

clysters, and they applied ointments and plasters seldom and only for slight things. After a person had yielded to sickness and gone to bed, no treatment was given. They understood the medicinal virtues of milk and of the resin of a tree that they called *mulli*. This had an admirable, almost a supernatural, effect on wounds. There was a plant called *chillca*, the roots of which, heated in an earthen vessel, were used to strengthen the gums. The hot root was bitten in two and kept in contact with the gums until it cooled. Next day the gums were white as if scalded, and for two or three days only spoon food could be eaten. At the end of that time the burned flesh fell away and strong, red flesh was seen beneath it.

They made much use of the plant called tobacco, taking it in powder into the nose in order "to discharge the head." The virtues of this plant were so highly appreciated in Spain that it was called *yerba santa*, holy plant. There was another plant, called *matecllu*, which was very good for the eyes. It was chewed and the juice put into the diseased eyes in the evening, and the chewed plant itself laid on the lids as a poultice and bandaged in place. During the night it would relieve pain, remove obscurities, and heal injuries. Garcilaso says that he himself placed it on a boy whose eye was about to come out of his head, and was so inflamed it looked like pepper and the white and dark parts of it could not be distinguished. The eye was already half out on the cheek. After the first night it was back in its place and after the second it was sound and well. Garcilaso afterward saw the boy in Spain and he said that that eye was better than the other.

The Incas knew only vegetable simples, no compounded medicines. Of natural philosophy and astrology they knew nothing.

Since that time, the Spaniards have experimented with many medicinal substances, but principally maize, and this was due to the fact that the Indians had told them little about it but they had themselves philosophized in regard to what they saw, and had thus found that maize, in addition to being so useful as a food, is also of benefit in disease of the kidneys, the pain of *ijada* [appendicitis], stone in the bladder, retention of urine, pain in the bladder and urethra. And this is to be noted, that few or no Indians are found to have any of these diseases, because of their common use of a drink made from maize, and many Spaniards having such diseases therefore use much of that same drink.

Ondegardo[5] tells us that "there are also Indians who treat diseases, men and women called *Camasca* or *Sincoyoc*, and they give no treatment that is not preceded by sacrifice and search for omens, for they say that the office of curing was given them in dreams, somebody who felt their need appearing and giving them the power. So they always sacrifice to these beings when they treat the sick."

There were also midwives and they said that the office was given them in dreams, by those who appeared and gave them the power and the instruments. They knew how to treat the pregnant woman so as to guide the child or even to kill it in the womb by artifices that they knew, taking pay for this.

There were others who cured broken bones and during the treatment they made sacrifices and used words, ointments, and other superstitions. "If an Indian woman bear two children and be poor, she thereafter acts as midwife, making sacrifices, fasts and ceremonies in her labor. Whoever had had a broken arm, leg or other part which healed in less than the usual time was regarded as a master for the cure of such injuries. There were also persons who feigned such injuries and claimed that they had been healed very quickly, and the people, regarding that as a miracle, hastened to such persons for treatment." Ondegardo adds that it is only the poor and needy who employ such persons, the rich and powerful having those who give a reason and origin for each thing.

Peruvian medicine is not going to help us.

The preceding review of medicine up to and during the

THE MEDICINE OF THE CONQUEST

period of settlement of America gives an idea of the obscurity and confusion of medical thought at that time, of the muddiness of the source from which our clearest information and descriptions should have come. However, we get very little in regard to medical conditions in America from the doctors. Our very best sources of information are such plain and uneducated men as Bernal Díaz del Castillo, Captain John Smith, Governor William Bradford, and the Honorable George Percy, men who knew nothing of medicine, who had to use plain and simple words because they had no others, whose minds were not shrouded nor their eyes blinded by a useless scholasticism.* From them we get statements of fact that we can understand and that throw a real, if often feeble, light on the diseases and deprivations that they faced. Unless it were a Sydenham, it is possibly as well that the doctors were not present or were silent.

* In a sense it is very unjust to speak of these men as uneducated. They all spelled terribly, but that was the custom of the time in both English and Spanish, and to a lesser extent in French. But Governor Bradford "attained unto a notable skill in languages. The Dutch tongue was become almost as vernacular to him as the English. The French tongue he could manage. The Latin and Greek he had mastered. But the Hebrew he most of all studied, because, he said, he would see with his own eyes the ancient oracles of God in their native beauty." And he was a splendid governor for thirty-two years and was doubtless more than any other one man responsible for the success of the Plymouth plantation.

John Smith's works show him to have been a man of wide knowledge of the world and one possessed of a good literary style, as well as one of decisive action and a real leader of other men.

Bernal Díaz del Castillo was over eighty and nearly blind when he dictated his *Historia Verdadera de la Conquista de la Nueva España* to a priest in Honduras, but he revealed a prodigious memory and a fine sense of proportion, and told a fascinating tale. Whether he or the priest was more responsible for the fine prose style of his history is not known.

Despite all this, these were not schoolmen, and from the standpoint of the medicine and probably of the doctors of their times, they were uneducated. But they had acquired from the "university of hard knocks" a kind and degree of education for which we should be very grateful.

Chapter V

Thus far we have dealt with diseases in terms of generalities. We have shown how, in the large, they exerted a wide influence on the whole course of the conquest. Now we must examine them in more detail, seek for their nature and their specific effects and manifestations.

The main impact of disease was from east to west. The white man, with his unwilling ally the Negro, had a larger and altogether more formidable arsenal of maladies than did the red man, and therefore most of the story must deal with what could be called the offensive illnesses, rather than defensive.

Yet there were defensive ones, too; not as spectacular as the others, in fact often not regarded as diseases at all, but in their own more quiet and deliberate way just as effective. There were two great branches of these relentless hosts. The first was famine and the second was scurvy. They were besiegers, engineers; not shock troops. It is to be noted that neither was presented to the invader by the Indian. He, poor savage, may not even have had in his possession a major communicable sickness! So that nature, as though in pity at the unequal armaments, dropped into the scale on his side twin grim and relentless devastators.

Everywhere the white man went these pallid, patient specters followed him, waiting in expectant insatiety until their time came. Sometimes they nestled beside him at sea, sometimes on the land. The red man never repelled a landing on his shores in force, but time and again while he hovered impotently in the forests, the hills, or the bayous, he saw invisible famine or hungry scurvy settle quietly down upon his enemies, saw them sicken, dwindle, and die, and finally creep away a remnant, or sometimes, as perhaps at Croatan, vanish as though they had never been. These two may have been, for all their mild aspect, the most effective illnesses of all, because they needed no host for transmittance, they recognized no immunity, they had no respect for climate or race, and they moved slowly, not violently (that might have been more merciful), with a day-by-day weakening relentlessness. And sometimes it seemed they did not wish to kill outright, but having exhausted a man, left him easy prey for other, more ferocious, things, building up in his soul and body the kind of helplessness that walked in Russia after World War I and will walk again in many parts of the earth within the next few years, as it has been walking steadily and stealthily over a sick earth during the recent war.

F.D.A.

Famine and Scurvy

The early settlement of America was marked by great mortality among both whites and Indians. The Indians suffered chiefly from communicable diseases which were quite new to them and frightfully devastating. The whites, on the other hand, met practically no new diseases, but they met and fell before the effects of deprivation.

Starvation and scurvy were their great enemies. The reasons are not far to seek. Life was then everywhere hard and precarious as compared with our times. Agriculture was primitive and famine rather frequently recurrent even in Italy, France, and England, then the most advanced countries of Europe.

As compared with our own day, methods of food preservation were almost nonexistent. Meat was salted, but the only other foods that could be carried on long voyages were the dried grains, peas, and beans, dried fruits, and salt, oil, and vinegar, as well as cider, wine, beer, and brandy. Dried fruits were not common articles of sea ration. Fresh fruits, vegetables, and meats were practically unknown at sea.

Ships were small and poor and always crowded; the trip from Europe was of uncertain duration but always long, and rations had to be carried to cover a period until food crops could be raised, and these often failed because of adverse weather conditions, flight of natives, poor European labor, too great interest in gold hunting, unfamiliarity with season, or other reason. At the best, the margin of safety was small, as it was stated as an evidence of Virginia's fertility that one man could cultivate enough corn for five persons.[1]

As examples of how the iron men (and women) who made the adventurous trip in these centuries lived when they had rations, a few instances may be cited. Captain John Smith, who was the greatest English authority of his day on the subject of colonization, recommended [2] the following "victuals for a whole year for a man and so after the rate for more,

> "8 bushels of meale
> 2 bushels of pease
> 2 bushels of otemeale
> 1 gallon of aquavitae
> 1 gallon of oyle
> 2 gallons of vinegar."

Oviedo tells us[3] that when Simón de Alcazaba set out from the Guadalquiver on May 24, 1534, to pass through the Strait of Magellan and make settlements between there and Peru, the ration provided was ten ounces of biscuit daily for each man, three *azumbres* (about six quarts) of drink for ten men, the drink consisting of more than half water and the rest cheap wine, and some days less of biscuit but a small bit of salt meat or two or three sardines.

Du Tertre tells us[4] of a French colony on the island of Guadalupe that "It may be said that the sufferings of this colony began on shipboard, the meat and meal were spoiled and so little cider had been taken aboard that in the midst of the voyage it had to be diluted half with sea water, which caused an unbelievable disturbance in all the passengers and a heat of the entrails so violent that many of them died as soon as they got ashore."

In addition, the adventurers took great chances. When Henry Morgan cut away from supplies at the Chagres River, on his way to sack old Panama, he carried one day's rations and his men were six days without food and marching through jungle before they reached the plains near the town and could kill cattle and eat them before attacking.

When Pánfilo de Narváez left his ships for the exploration of Florida, his men carried two pounds of biscuit and half a pound of bacon each. The few survivors wandered for some ten years.

When gold was discovered in Matto Grosso in 1734 there was a gold rush. The gold was so plentiful that for the first year every slave commonly returned three or four *oitavos* a day; it lay upon the surface of the ground. "But the thoughtless adventurers had made no provision for supporting themselves in the wilderness. . . . The gold which they gathered was expended upon provision: all was not enough, and most of them literally died for want of food."[5]

The fifteenth, sixteenth, and seventeenth centuries, although they knew nothing of either calories or vitamins, and did not always know the cause of scurvy, did know starvation and scurvy in the flesh as they have since rarely been seen in the Western world, as no future century should know them.

It may be our personal ignorance of these diseases that leads modern writers to take fifteenth-century descriptions of famine and scurvy and on the basis of some single symptom mentioned, such as yellow color, sudden death, or fever, translate the account to one of typhus fever, yellow fever, malaria, or almost anything else that may intrigue the interpreter's fancy. Such ignorance is of happy social significance, but it may lead and sometimes has led the historian astray. It is therefore worth while to pause to review the clinical aspects of starvation and scurvy, to view them through the eyes of men who knew them intimately and too abundantly.

It is possible to give very modern descriptions of starvation, written by accomplished medical men of modern education and large experience. It is well that we refer to these descriptions later when we read that the starvation at Isabela, at Darien, in Honduras, at Jamestown, Virginia, or elsewhere is being interpreted as typhus, malaria, yellow fever.

Major General Sir Patrick Hehir, Indian Medical Service, who was the chief medical officer of the British and Indian forces during the siege of Kut, describes the effects of chronic starvation as experienced there. The siege lasted 148 days (December 1915–April 1916). After the first month the garrison was on reduced rations, the British receiving eventually only 1850 calories per man and the Indians 1110 calories. Toward the end of the siege it was recorded that "on an average fifteen men are dying daily: of these, five a day are dying of chronic starvation, and ten with chronic starvation with diarrhoea, bronchitis or some other simple malady supervening. The present condition of nutrition and health of the average man of the garrison is physiologically highly unsatisfactory. His stamina is greatly lowered, his resistance to disease-causes considerably reduced, and should he suffer from any disease, such as pneumonia or bronchitis, fever from any cause, dysentery, or severe diarrhoea, it will greatly tax his vital powers."[6]

Everybody lost weight, usually from 10 to 15 per cent. Most were giddy on exertion, their temperatures and pulse rates subnormal; there was a tendency to sleep much. During the last month of the siege the men could keep at work for only short periods between rests. The tour of sentry duty had to be reduced to one hour, as the sentries would faint if not relieved often. Many Indians returning from work in apparently good condition were found dead the following morning. Such deaths were due to exhaustion of the vital processes from starvation. Men in such debilitated conditions could stand little in the way of disease and an attack of simple diarrhea or a cold, which would have been overcome in a day or two at the beginning of the siege, was apt to end fatally in March or April.

The principal diseases and most frequent intercurrent causes of death were diarrhea and dysentery, believed to be due to starvation alone. These continued to appear after the men reached prison camp and were receiving enough food. The condition is a part of every lasting famine in India. It was noticed in hundreds of Indians that there is a stage in the course of starvation from which recovery cannot occur, regardless of feeding and care. Apparently all capacity to assimilate food is lost; the glands and tissues engaged in digestion and assimilation have atrophied and ceased to function. The writer cautions as to the necessity for great care in treating the effects of starvation and in allowing a return to ordinary food. "Death frequently occurs in those who after forced abstinence of some duration suddenly and completely gratify their hunger.* [7]

* George R. Minot, on reading this chapter, made the following comment: "I think it should be made clear that although starvation and scurvy were great enemies, there are many individuals who do not have scurvy, but who may be starved. Indeed, one may see at the Boston City Hospital scurvy almost any week of the year, except in the summer, in individuals who are not starved and also in individuals who are starved. I think it would be worth while to indicate that scurvy is a nutritional deficiency due to a lack of adequate amounts of vitamin C throughout the body and so forth."
—F. D. A.

Concerning scurvy I shall first quote from an acute seventeenth-century observer who was thoroughly familiar with the manifestations of the worst forms of the malady but did not know its cause. Torquemada,[8] who wrote in 1611, described the trip of an armada of three ships sent by the Viceroy of Mexico, the Conde de Monte-Rei, for the exploration and conquest of California. The expedition sailed May 5, 1602. By December 29 it had many sick and it sent back an appeal for help. Torquemada continued:

It seems to me that it would not be out of place to discuss here what that disease was which the people of this Armada had in common. I wish to give an account of it, for it is the same which commonly affects the sailors in this region who are coming from China to New Spain, and from which most of those aboard the ships usually die. At this latitude there blows a thin and cold air which pierces thin or feeble men, and I understand that it must carry some pestilence: and if it does not carry it, then with its subtlety, and rarity, it causes it in those fatigued, feeble and thin bodies, which have suffered so long.

First of all, there is a universal pain in the whole body, and one is so sensitive and touchy that everything which touches him causes such pain that he cries out, and he can not rest nor get a bit of ease: and after this his whole body, especially from the waist down, is filled with mulberry colored spots, larger than coarse mustard seed: and after these follow bruises of two-fingers breadth and more, which are of the same humor and color as the small spots, and are developed below the bend of the knees and which extend from the middle of the thigh to the knee, and these are as hard as stones and the legs are embarrassed by them so that they can not extend, nor flex, but the legs must remain crippled in the state in which this accident catches them, without being able to move, nor to go from one place to another without very great pain, and these spots spread as if they were spots of oil on fine cloth, so widely that all the calf of the leg and thigh are violet and purple: and after this, this evil humor spreads throughout the whole body, and more to the back than elsewhere, and there are terrible pains in the loins, back and kidneys, so that the miserable body can not be moved except at the cost of pain and groans, which are so cruel that all would think it a very good fate to die rather than suffer them.

Because of the miserable condition of the bodies, which are as though all inflamed: and of the extreme sensibility which these sick feel in their persons, so that the clothing placed upon them seems to tear out their lives: and as they can not move nor turn on one side or the other, they cry to Heaven: and if the healthy ones come to help them and wish to aid, on feeling them approach, their cruel pains redouble, so that the greatest help one might give them would be to let them alone and not touch them, not even the bedclothing. And this was not all that this pestiferous humour caused in these human bodies; for it caused other accidents even more insufferable than those described: and this was that the gums became swollen, above, below and inside, and they increased so that the teeth and molars could not be brought together and the teeth were so bared of flesh and without protection, that in shaking the head they were shaken out: and there were persons who in spitting the saliva which came into the mouth would spit out teeth two at a time. For this reason they could not eat, except liquids such as paps, biscuit and water, almond cream and other such things, which could be drunk: with the result that the sick became so weak that, lacking the natural strength, they were as dead but conversing: and all by the mercy of Jesus received the sacraments of Penance and Extreme Unction, at least, when there was no occasion to give them the Viaticum. This is the disease which touched all and that which took from this life those who on that voyage gave their lives to their Creator and Redeemer.

James Lind, surgeon in the British Navy and father of modern naval medicine, in 1754 published an excellent *Treatise on the Scurvy*, which showed his large experience with the disease and his knowledge of its cause, prevention, and cure. He said that the first indication of it is a change of color in the face. "Scorbutic people for the most part appear at first of a pale or yellowish hue, which becomes afterwards more darkish or livid." There is soon a universal lassitude, a stiffness and feebleness of the knees, early fatigue, and shortness of breath. The breath becomes foul, the gums livid, spongy, and putrid. Hemorrhage may occur in many parts, from mucous membranes and under the skin, into muscles and joints. Wounds become ulcers, old scars break down and ulcerate, and the ulcers become foul and fungous. Even slight bruises degenerate into such ulcers. These ulcers are easily distinguished from all others. "Whatever former ailment the patient has had (especially rheumatic pains, aches from bruises, hurts, wounds, etc.) or whatever present disorder he labours under: upon being afflicted with this distemper, his former and old complaints are renewed, and his present malady, whatever it may be, rendered worse." Pain is nearly always present and severe, especially in the back and limbs, and is aggravated by motion. There is often pain in the chest. Fever is not usually present, but is so occasionally. Besides being spotted by subcutaneous hemorrhages, the legs may be greatly swollen.

Use of the limbs may be lost because of contractures of muscles and tendons and swelling and pain of the joints.

Patients are apt to die suddenly upon being moved. The teeth become loose and may fall out. Hemorrhage may prove fatal. General oedema and oppression in the breast may also cause death.

Dr. H. R. Carter, in his excellent book on yellow fever, expresses the opinion that scurvy cannot occur on land in the tropics because of the prevalence of green food, a statement that cannot be accepted without modification. Sieges, fear of an enemy, or other cause may prevent utilization of food at hand, and not all green material is edible or would be eaten. In addition we have clear accounts of scurvy in Louisiana in summertime.[9]

Donald Monro[10] wrote, "Though scurvy is most frequent in cold countries, yet it ought to be observed, that a want of

FAMINE AND SCURVY

fresh vegetables is capable of producing it in every climate on the face of the globe." Dr. J. P. Schotte[11] said:

> The slaves, therefore, which are brought there [to Senegal from the interior] being unaccustomed, for the most part, to eat victuals seasoned with salt, the masters of the vessels take the greatest care not to give them free indulgence in the use of it, but allow them only a trifling quantity, in order to accustom them to it by degrees: and the same precaution is observed, when they are put on shore at the island of Senegal, till they are transported in an European vessel to the West Indies. This method is pursued in order to prevent the scurvy, which experience has taught the traders the free use of salt will produce in these people; for whenever it happens, through the neglect or carelessness of those who have the inspection of their victuals, that they indulge too much in it, they are soon seized with this horrid disease, of which they seldom or never recover.

The high incidence of scurvy in the Union Army during our Civil War came in July or August in the years 1862, 1863, 1864, and 1865.[12]

Let us dismiss any thought that scurvy could not occur on land in the tropics in the earlier centuries, although admitting that it was much more likely to occur in cold countries.

So narrow was the margin of safety that separated sufficiency and famine among the northern Indians that they doubtless suffered from the latter many times before the coming of the whites, as they did afterward. Champlain describes vividly such a famine among them in 1608–9. We have a clear and lucid record of a great famine in Mexico in 1454 and for two years thereafter.[13] This was due to a drought of three years' duration. Montezuma bought up food from fertile provinces and fed his people as long as possible, after which great numbers died and others wandered away to sell themselves or their children into slavery that they might live. This is mentioned here for the reason that this mortality has been attributed by writers to typhus and also to yellow fever. Duran's description is definite and ascribes it to famine due to drought. He does state briefly that some fell sick (*"Empecó la gente a desfallecer y a andar marchita y flaca con la hambre que padecian y otros ā enfermar"*), but he describes no symptoms, and sickness of one sort or another is a part of group starvation, as we have seen above.

Every one of Columbus's four voyages to America was threatened with starvation on occasions. On the first voyage, shortage of provisions was one of the reasons for the budding mutiny which was cut short by the discovery of San Salvador. On the second voyage there were several narrow escapes. On July 16, 1494, the Admiral's ship was struck suddenly by a storm off the coast of Cuba and was almost sunk. Quick action in lowering sail and getting out anchors saved it, but "the people were unable to get out the water with the pumps, because they were so afflicted and weak from lack of provisions, for they had nothing to eat but a pound of rotten biscuit and a glass of wine for each day." On the return voyage to Spain in that year, there was such shortage of food that the ration was cut to six ounces of bread, and some of the crew wished to kill the Indians who were being taken to Spain, so as to save what they would eat.

Before Columbus's arrival at Puerto Bello on his fourth voyage, the meat and fish brought from Spain had all been eaten and "there were worms in the biscuit and, so help me God, they would wait until night to eat the dust fragments [*mazamorra*], so as not to see the worms that were in it; but there were some who were so accustomed to it they did not try to get rid of the worms when they saw them, because if they stopped to do this they would lose their supper." [14]

On his first voyage Columbus built a fort and established a colony, which he named Navidad, on the island of Hispaniola, now Santo Domingo. When he returned on his second voyage

FAMINE AND SCURVY

all members of this colony were dead. Inquiry elicited evidence that they had been killed by Indians, but famine may have been a factor. Columbus then established a second colony, which he named Isabela, which soon suffered severely from famine. All of the old chroniclers (Las Casas, Oviedo, Herrera, Fernando Colón, etc.) and Christopher Columbus himself attributed the sickness and death solely to famine. Modern writers have read into the record an epidemic disease, especially yellow fever. Las Casas and Oviedo[15] held diametrically opposed views in regard to the Indians, but they agreed in their accounts of the famine at Isabela being brought on first by the spoiling of rations brought from Spain and later by the Indians' plan to plant no crops that year, with the idea of getting rid of the Spaniards. They expected to be able to live off the country, but a greater proportion of them died than of Spaniards, possibly because, as Las Casas said, they did not understand the Spaniards, who are more inflexible when hungry and harder from suffering. ("*Cuanto más hambrientes tanto mayor teson tienen y mas duros son de sufrir y para sufrir.*") This incident is mentioned in the chapter on yellow fever.

There was another famine among Spaniards in Hispaniola in 1502, among men newly arrived with Nicolas Ovando, the new governor. Herrera says that more than a thousand died.[16]

The great sufferings of the parties of Ojeda, Nicuesa, and Balboa on the Caribbean coast of Panama, at Nombre de Dios and Darien, were due to famine.

In the introduction to the translation of Andagoy's work there is quoted a letter from Balboa, dated January 20, 1513, to the king, in which he said of Darien, "We were then reduced to such extremity that, if succour had been delayed, it would no longer have been necessary. For no remedy could then have delivered us from the consequences of famine: and in our great need we lost 300 of the men we found here [Darien] of those I commanded, of those of Uraba under

Alonzo de Ojeda and of those under Diego de Nicuesa at Veragua." The same letter tells something of the hardships of exploration, which added to the death rate:

> The country is difficult to travel through, on account of the numerous rivers and morasses and mountains, where many men die owing to the great labor they have to endure. . . . Your Royal Highness should not imagine that the swamps of this land are so light that they can be crossed easily, for many times we have had to go a league, and two and three leagues, through swamps and water, stripped naked, with our clothes fastened on a shield on our heads, and when we had come to the end of one swamp we have had to enter another and to walk in this way for two or three to ten days. . . . Up to the present time we have valued the eatables more than the gold, for we have more gold than health, and often have I searched in various directions, desiring more to find a sack of corn than a bag of gold.

These rather long, though relatively few, extracts from writings about Darien are given because the facts of the great mortality there, the later great prevalence of malaria, and Pedrarias' abandonment of the place on the alleged score of unhealthfulness permit an apparently strong argument for the presence there of pre-Columbian malaria. But not one of the early writers mentions tertians, quartans, quotidians, or chills and fever.

Nombre de Dios, not far from Darien, is in the same status. Nicuesa's men there died of hunger, although at the time when he discovered it Columbus had called the place Puerto de Bastimentos (Port of Provisions), "because all the surroundings and the small islands were filled with cultivation and maize plantations," [17] a state of affairs indicating a numerous and healthy population.

The later suffering of the Pedrarias expedition at Darien was due to *modorra* and to hunger. Andagoya, who was of the party, does not name modorra, but says the deaths were due

FAMINE AND SCURVY

to hunger and sickness.[18] He states that Pedrarias arrived at the end of July 1514 at Darien, where he was received by the people who were there and where he landed all his troops. The settlement was small and the resources of the land but few. The provisions on board the ship were disembarked and divided among all the people. The flour and other stores were injured by the sea, and this added to the evil nature of the land, which was woody, covered with swamps and only thinly inhabited. These things brought on so much sickness among the people that they could not be cured, and in one month seven hundred men died of sickness and hunger. Bernal Díaz del Castillo was a member of this expedition, and, as usual, his description merits consideration. He wrote, "At that time there was a pestilence from which many soldiers died and all the others were sick and we had bad sores on the legs." The prevalence of ulcers on the legs suggests that there may have been scurvy as well as starvation.

The conquest of Tierra Firme (northern South America and Central America) was marked by numerous defeats by famine. Cannibalism occurred in the expedition under Julian de la Cosa in the region of Cartagena, in an expedition led by Felipe Guitierrez, governor of Veragua, and in some others.

In May 1535 Governor Jorge Espira set out to explore his province. At Cariga, in July, more than half of his 371 men were left behind sick because of poor food ("*y la connida no acostumbrada a ellos y de otra calidad que la de España*"). In October he went back for them and found them improved by reason of having had much game, deer and wild hogs. They may have had scurvy. For two years they kept on, but when they returned to Coro there were but 134 men left and they had eaten all of their dogs and most of their horses.

Gonzalo Ximenes started to explore the Rio Grande in Venezuela in April 1536, with 500 foot and horse marching and other forces in boats. At Opon there remained only 170 foot and horse, all the others having died on the road "as much from hunger as because most of the people were newly arrived from Spain." [19]

The famine encountered by Cortes on his Honduran expedition and in the party that he relieved at Nilo is discussed in the chapter on malaria, and the great famine in Nueva Galicia in the chapter on dysentery. Icazbalceta tells us[20] that in 1550 Dr. Pedro Arias de Benavides disembarked in Honduras, and that of seventy-six passengers on the ship with him, seventy died in the short space of one week of a disease called *la chapetonada*, a name derived from *chapeton*, a term there applied to newcomers. Trying to identify this disease, I find *chapetonada* given by Cardenal [21] as meaning "the change of climate"; in other words, it was the newcomers' disease in Peru also. What could it be? Quite possibly it was the result of overeating by people half starved on the long voyage. The following facts support such an opinion:

(a) Those cited above in regard to slow starvation.
(b) The length of the sea voyage and the character of the rations issued at that time often resulted in partial starvation.
(c) Very few infectious diseases have an incubation period so short and are themselves so severe as to permit of such a mortality as that cited above, within a week after infection. Cholera is a possible exception, but there is no reason to regard these instances as cholera. Certainly malaria, yellow fever, typhus, smallpox, or meningitis could not have done so. On the other hand, the outbreaks were attributed to change of climate, not to contagion, pestilence, or fever, and there is no mention of any prevalence of the disease before disembarcation.

Pizarro's conquest of Peru was almost prevented by starvation. It was first undertaken in 1524, although not accomplished until seven years later. In November of the former year Pizarro, Almagro, and Luque sent out the first expedition under command of Pizarro. It went to the Rio Biru, where Andagoya had previously explored, reaching there short of rations. Almost no food was found and the suffering was great. Pizarro and part of his men remained there, and sent their ship back to the Pearl Islands for provisions.

"When Montenegro returned, 27 soldiers were already dead, and because their deaths were due to lack of food, they called the place the Port of Hunger." [22]

The conquest of Peru was marked by many experiences of famine. At Popayan in 1539 there was a great lack of food, and the Spaniards went twenty or thirty leagues for maize, because the natives did not cultivate the land, hoping thus to drive out the Spaniards. Spaniards and Indians ate weeds, lizards, serpents, locusts, and other unclean things, and the Indians ate the flesh of other Indians. A great pestilence followed and many thousands died.

"And it was a pity to see the roads full of dead Spaniards, Indians and Negroes, some eaten by the living. Some Spaniards drank the blood of their horses and when they killed one they would sell a quarter for three hundred pesos . . ." [23]

In the same year an expedition under Pedro Ancurez lost nearly one half of its men from hunger.[24]

The settlers of the Plata River regions had the usual experiences. In 1526 Sebastian Cabot attempted a settlement, which was a failure and had to be abandoned in its third year. "They were in great need of the necessities of life. They ate only herbs, because the Indians would not let them get out to fish, and killed those who did go out, and also those who sought herbs and roots if they went inland at all. So that already the Indians had killed 75, without counting those who died of sickness and hunger." So the expedition returned to Spain, "to the loss of its backers and without honor or accomplishment." [25]

In August 1535 Don Pedro de Mendoza led another expedition consisting of twelve ships and two thousand men to the Rio de la Plata. Thirteen hundred men died, yet the survivors praised the healthfulness of the land and said the deaths were due to lack of food.[26]

Herrera says of this same expedition that the Spanish at Buenos Aires indulged in cannibalism, eating two men who were legally executed.[27] From November 2, 1541, to March 9, 1542, Álvar Núñez Cabeza de Vaca was marching overland from Brazil to Ascension, about a thousand miles, and in January his party was near starvation and was saved by the discovery that the joints of the canes through which they were cutting their way contained large white worms of the size of a finger, so fat that they fried well, and upon these the party subsisted for some time.[28] Sigaud indeed states that a favorite dish of the Malali Indians in Brazil is the *bicho da Taquera*, a large white worm found in the interior of the bamboo when this is in flower.

At the end of the sixteenth century, Hendrick Ottsen sailed from Holland to Africa, Rio de Janeiro, and the Plata, putting in at the last-named region in search of *"orangie appelen"* with which to treat the scurvy, which, together with starvation, eventually cost the lives of thirty-seven of his forty-two men. He was captured by the Spaniards, who were themselves in such desperate condition that their governor wrote, "The people are shoeless, their clothing is washed all winter without soap, there are no vinegar, sugar, almonds, honey, linen, cloth, leather, nor anything else.—Consequently, it is necessary that these things come to the port or that the land be abandoned." [29]

Gonzalo Pizarro's party on the upper Amazon underwent great sufferings from hunger after it was abandoned by Orellano, as described in the chapter on malaria. Oviedo places the number of deaths among the 176 men at something between 76 and 87, while Herrera described the party's trip as a tri-

FAMINE AND SCURVY 73

umph of mind, valor, and constancy, for never had men suffered so much.*[30]

Seven of the fifty-seven men who accompanied Orellano died of starvation and the whole party was near the same fate several times.

There are very many other instances of famine and starvation in the Spanish annals, but it is not necessary to mention more.

An attempt to establish a Scotch settlement on the Isthmus of Panama at the end of the seventeenth century was defeated mainly by famine. On July 26, 1698, twelve hundred men, among them three hundred youths from the best families of Scotland, sailed from Leith under the leadership of William Patterson, to establish settlements on the Isthmus. They landed at or near the old Spanish settlement of Acla on November 4, having lost fifteen men on the way out. They founded a settlement, which they named New St. Andrew.

Their provisions, supposed to be enough for eight months, gave out in as many weeks. Fishing and hunting were precarious and the colonists were soon on the verge of starvation. Sickness followed and many died, "and the survivors were only kept alive through the friendly services of the Indians." In June 1699 the settlement was abandoned. Four hundred persons died on the trip home.

Eight weeks after the abandonment of the colony two ships arrived with supplies and three hundred recruits. These were taken to Jamaica. Shortly after, another expedition of thirteen hundred men was sent out in four ships. The ships were hastily fitted out and during the voyage one was lost and the others scattered. Many people died on the voyage and the others

---

* "*Finalmente, Goncalo Picarro entro en el Quito, triumfando del valor, i sufriminento, i de la constancia, recto, e immutable vigor del animo, pues Hombres Humanos no se halla, haver tanto sufrido, ni padecido tantas desventuras.*"

reached New St. Andrew broken in health and spirit. Meanwhile two sloops arrived with provisions but the supply was small, so five hundred of the party were sent back to Scotland at once.

In February 1700 Captain Campbell arrived with a company of three hundred soldiers who had served in Flanders. The Spanish besieged them.

For six weeks the Scotch sustained a siege, and when their ammunition gave out they melted their pewter dishes and fashioned them into cannon balls. At length provisions ran short and the Spaniards cut off their water supply. A surrender became inevitable. Campbell with a few comrades escaped on board his vessel and made his way to New York and thence to Scotland. The rest capitulated on condition that they be allowed to depart with their effects, but so weak were the survivors that they were not able to weigh the anchor of their largest ship until the Spaniards generously came to their assistance. All but two of the vessels were lost: only thirty of the men succeeded in reaching home, and after the loss of more than two thousand lives and several millions of money, the Scotch abandoned further attempts at colonization in Tierra Firme.[31]

What proportion of the two thousand deaths was due to famine and what to infection is not known.

Louisiana gives a history of several periods of suffering from famine, one at Biloxi in 1720. "As for the Concessionaires, they remained at home, where they fared none too well, reduced as they were to a few beans and a small quantity of peas. To crown their troubles there arrived a ship-load of negroes who were distributed to those who could feed them. At length the famine became so great that numberless people died, some from having eaten plants which they did not know, and which instead of prolonging their lives, killed them, others from having only oysters which they gathered at the shore. The greater

FAMINE AND SCURVY 75

part of those who were found dead near piles of shells were Germans." [32]

The Huguenots of Florida suffered from famine in the summer of 1565. "The effects of this hideous famine appeared incontinently among us, for our bones began to cleave so near unto the skin that the most part of the soldiers had their skins pierced through with them." [33] By August 28 the colonists were ready to abandon the settlement because of famine, when a relief expedition under Captain Ribault arrived.

The settlement of Virginia was delayed a full generation because of famine, and the real settlement at Jamestown was almost defeated by the same cause. The first exploration with intent to settle Virginia was sent out in 1584, under Sir Walter Raleigh's patents from Queen Elizabeth. It named the land in her honor but did not actually leave colonists. In the following year, however, Sir Richard Grenville, an associate of Raleigh's, left 108 men to establish a colony on Roanoke Island. In 1586 Sir Francis Drake, on his way home from raiding Santiago in the Cape Verde Islands, Santo Domingo, Cartagena, and St. Augustine, put in at Roanoke Island and found the colonists greatly distressed by reason of hunger. He offered them passage to England and they were all glad to accept it.

Yet Ralph Lane, who had been left in charge of the settlement, wrote of it: "It is the goodliest soil under the cope of heaven: the most pleasing territory of the world. . . . The climate is so wholesome that we have not one sick since we touched the land." [34]

That same year fifty more men were left on the island, but when relief was sent to them the following year (1587) all had disappeared, only the bones of one man being found. At this time 115 more men were left on the island. In 1589 three ships sailed under command of John White to assist the colony, but they found nobody. The fate of the 115 men was never learned.

Again in 1609 the little colony was near starvation, and mutiny was also threatened. Captain John Smith met both by announcing, " 'This salvage trash you so scornfully repine at, being put in your mouthes, your stomachs can digest it: and therefore I will take a course you shall provide it. The sick shall not starve, but equally share of all our labors: and every one that gathereth not every day as much as I doe, the next daie, shall be set beyond the river, and forever bee banished from the fort: and live there or starve.' This order, many murmured, was very cruell. But it caused the most part so well [to] bestir themselves that of 200 men (except they were drowned) there died not past 7 or 8." [35]

The Pilgrims fared no better than the papists and the wicked. Governor Bradford tells us:[36]

But that which was most sadd and lamentable was, that in 2. or 3. month's time halfe of their company dyed, especialy in Jan. and February, being the depth of winter and wanting houses and other comforts, being infected with the scurvie and other diseases, which this long vioage and their inacomodate condition had brought upon them: so as ther dyed sometimes 2. or 3. of a day, in the foresaid time: that of 100. and odd persons, scarce 50 remained. And of these in time of most distress, ther was but 6. or 7. sound persons, who, to their great comendation be it spoken, spared no pains, night or day, but with abundance of toyle and hazard of their own health, fetched them wood, made them fires, drest their meat, made their beads, washed their loathsome cloaths, cloathed and uncloathed them: in a word did all the homely and necessarie offices for them which dainty and quesie stomacks cannot endure to hear named: and all this willingly and cherfully, without any grudging in the least, showing herein their true love unto their friends and brethren. . . . The disease began to fall amongst them [the crew of the *Mayflower*] also, so as almost half of their company dyed before they went away, and many of their lustyest men, as the boatson, gunner, 3 quarter maisters, the cooke and others. . . .

The spring now approaching, it pleased God the mortalitie

FAMINE AND SCURVY

began to cease amongst them, and the sick and lame recovered apace, which put new life into them.

This was almost certainly scurvy.

The colony fared well during the following summer but the arrival of a shipload of immigrants without food in September necessitated half rations for all for the next six months.

Plymouth was again in peril of starvation in 1623, and a day of thanksgiving was set apart in gratitude for relief from it. Bradford tells of it thus:

I may not here omitt how, notwithstanding all their great paines and industrie, and the great hope of a large cropp, the Lord seemed to blast, and take away the same, by a great drought which continued from the 3. weeke in May, till about the midle of July, without any raine, and with a great heate. . . . Upon which they sett a parte a solemne day of humiliation, to seek the Lord by humble and fervent prayer, in this great distress. And he was pleased to give them a gracious and speedy answer. . . . For which mercie (in time conveniente) they also sett aparte a day of thanksgiving.

Bradford also tells of the Massachusetts settlement planted by Mr. Wesson in 1623: "Many sould away their cloathes and bed coverings: others (so base were they) became servents of ye Indians, and would cutt them woode and fetch them water, for a cup full of corne: others fell to plaine stealing, both night and day, from ye Indians, of which they greevosly complained. In ye end, they came to that misery, that some starved and died with cold and hunger. One in gathering shell-fish was so weak as he stuck fast in ye mudd, and was found dead in ye place."

Scurvy was furthermore present "among those who came from Leyden . . . in the ships yt came to Salem" in 1629.

Jacques Cartier's expedition to the St. Lawrence suffered severely from scurvy in the winter of 1535–36, which they passed on the St. Charles below Quebec, and his description of the disease in sixteenth-century French is graphic and excellent.[37] He relates that there was much sickness among his men from November to April. They were living in their ships, which were banked in ice and snow and lined with ice four fingers thick. The disease began first among the Indians of the neighboring town of Stadacone, on the site of the present Quebec. Fifty of them died. The French, thinking the disease contagious, prohibited visits from the Indians, but the disease attacked them. By February there were only ten well men among the 110 French; of Cartier's men, eight had died and hope had been abandoned for fifty more. An autopsy was performed on one body, Philippe Rougemont, a sailor, in the hope that the nature of the disease might be learned. The image of the Virgin was carried in procession with chanting and prayers for divine intercession, but by April there had been twenty-five deaths. Then Cartier saw an Indian, whom he knew to have lost his teeth and to have been very sick with the disease, apparently quite cured of it. Cartier asked how he had been cured and was told of the virtues of a certain tree, the leaves and bark of which when prepared as a decoction and drunk was a specific. The Indians called the tree *ameda* or *anneda*. It was apparently pine, spruce, or fir. The French used it as directed and were all cured of all their diseases, one man of syphilis of six years' standing. We have been told before that all diseases are aggravated by scurvy and it is not improbable that many might be cured, in appearance at least, with the cure of complicating scurvy.

This outbreak was an important factor in delaying the French settlement of Canada for sixty years. Cartier went home in the spring of 1536, abandoning one of his three ships because of lack of personnel to work it. Another expedition, under Sieur de Roberval as lieutenant general of the king and Cartier as captain general and master pilot, attempted a settlement during the years 1541–43, and after its failure all attempts were abandoned until Champlain's day.

FAMINE AND SCURVY

Champlain discusses the occurrence of scurvy at Quebec in the hard winter of 1608–9.[38] Eighteen persons were attacked by it and ten died, as well as five others from dysentery. Champlain says that the season for the disease was January to April, and that it came from eating too much salt food and dry vegetables, "which heat the blood and spoil the interior parts." He thought that certain earthy vapors also infected the air. His people were well dressed, warm, and well nourished (not hungry), but they had too much salt food. He also said that spring was the time of recovery.

He had heard that the Flemish had found a singular remedy for the disease but he did not know what it was. As Lind says[39] that the Dutch had known the virtues of orange juice for two hundred years, it was probably of this that Champlain had heard rumors.

Scurvy was a frequent scourge of the missionaries and settlers in Canada. Although the Jesuit Relations rarely use the word, they several times describe sicknesses that must have been scurvy. Riddell says[40] that the disease was called *mal de terre* and *les pourpres*. We find it mentioned under these terms in the Jesuit Relations. The editor of the usually excellent English translation of their great work apparently regarded scurvy as an infection, as he wrote,[41] "The climate of Miscou, although now salubrious, seems to have been at that early time, full of danger to Europeans: the island was repeatedly swept by the scurvy, which was usually fatal." Of course this fatal scurvy was due to lack of adequate amounts of vitamin C, easily obtained from many foods, especially fresh foods.

Who went adventuring to the New World in the sixteenth or seventeenth century always risked his life, and his greatest risk was that he should lose it through insufficiency or total lack of food. War, cannibalism, torture, fire, and flood were minor risks.

Chapter VI

No greater contrast could be imagined than that between the illnesses primarily operating against the white man and those which he unleashed against the red. With the coming of the Negro there were more diseases, both for and against him, but he had a goodly supply of evils to which he had full claim.

Chief among these ranks of death were three dreadful killers, the shock troops of the conquest. Famine and scurvy were slow and placid, but these three white man's diseases were swift, violent, mutilating. Their very character made one think of the shock and terror of war. They struck a man as he was struck in battle, painfully and without warning. Even as he fell, his comrades fell beside him, dying or maimed. But it was worse than battle, because night was as dangerous as day and there was none of the excitement and panoply of ordinary wars. Nor was there any respecting of persons; the strong man succumbed as readily as the weak; neither cowards nor brave men were safe. The very aspect of these diseases was often fierce. They killed swiftly, with agony often, but if they did not kill they disfigured and scarred; they left men ugly and blind; they inflicted raw wounds and foul stenches; they left men bloated or discolored. They were altogether terrible and their names were, in order of frightfulness, smallpox, typhus, and measles.

Smallpox has been curbed in North America today so that

SHOCK TROOPS: ERUPTIVE FEVERS 81

we forget what a wild and reckless killer it is. For centuries it had been endemic in Europe. The child who grew up to full adulthood without having had it was possibly as rare as the modern one who grows up without benefit of measles. Its control has certainly been one of the factors that has made possible the tremendous increase in European and American population in the last century. It was a killer without subtlety or compassion. Hundreds of years of exposure had given the Europeans a comparative tolerance to it, as we are comparatively tolerant of measles, but to the American Indian it was death, with no reprieve. It was a weapon more effective, of greater range, of surer aim than any rifle or poison gas ever devised. It was, as has been said, captain of the men of death. And, befitting its position, it had a kind of independence, a harsh integrity. It did not depend on tiny insects, or crouch in filth, or wait for hunger and weakness. It was bold and overbearing and appeared to ride on the wings of the wind. One cannot know for sure its whole effect on the conquest, but one may say with certainty that the whole story would have been different had smallpox not been present.

Typhus, second of the three terrors, is the one whose introduction by the Europeans is most disputed; in fact, it is the only one about which serious dispute seems justifiable. The author, after examining the evidence, takes the position that the Europeans did bring it with them. It was not as handy a weapon as either smallpox or measles because it was as dangerous to the whites as to the reds, but, since there were more reds than whites and since they had, if anything, even less tolerance than the whites, it wrought great havoc among them and was as grim a by-product of war then as it is today. Where poverty and hunger and inadequate housing and clothing go, with poor sanitation, there goes typhus. It needs the aid of the louse and the rat (or some other host), and since these are most friendly to man when his bodily needs are greatest, it has for long generations been an ever threatening plague to armies and populations beset by war or stunned by wars that have gone by.

One need not be astonished at finding such a familiar malady as measles listed as the third public enemy. Diseases, like men, pass through phases. Some of the most vicious citizens after days of shocking violence and behavior settle down in pleasant communities of peaceable men and women and as time passes become first tolerated and then accepted as part of community life. So with diseases and so with measles in particular. The evidence is overwhelming that to a people who have not acquired tolerance measles is even today a terrible scourge. And the red man in America was completely and hopelessly intolerant of this companion to European civilization. It was not so frightening as smallpox and was called by its victims "little" as contrasted with "big" skin sickness, but it was colorful enough; it spread like fire in a dry forest and everywhere it marched in the front ranks.

F.D.A.

Shock Troops: Eruptive Fevers

SMALLPOX

It was almost the end of the eighteenth century (1798) when Jenner observed that cowpox or vaccinia afforded protection against smallpox. Prior to that time the only real protection against the disease was to have an attack of it, and as it had been learned that cases caused by inoculation were usually mild, resort to that measure had been increasing for many years. The disease was everywhere and, like measles with us,

SHOCK TROOPS: ERUPTIVE FEVERS

it was especially a disease of childhood, as the large majority of persons reaching adult life had had it. It was a principal cause of death.

This was true during the fifteenth, sixteenth, and seventeenth centuries, when the early white settlements were being made in America, and where the whites went smallpox followed. Where smallpox went the Indians died in swarms. In the West Indies, Central America, Peru, Mexico, New England, and Canada, the story was much the same, so far as the ravages of the disease were concerned. Exact figures cannot be given, but smallpox always killed many more Indians than did firearms. At some times the proportion probably rose to a hundred or even a thousand to one. Bernal Díaz de Castillo wrote his history of the conquest of Mexico partly to correct the exaggerations of Gómara, saying that had the Mexicans been tied, Cortes' little army could not have killed so many as Gómara claimed. But smallpox could.

The conquest of Mexico is one of the most dramatic and astounding events in all history. That a handful of men, possessed of firearms and horses it is true, but depending mainly on the sword as a weapon, should have conquered a great empire of brave people considerably advanced in civilization would pass belief if the facts were less well attested. But it is less remarkable than the ordinary reader of Prescott thinks it, if we consider how smallpox aided. Of this Díaz del Castillo tells us[1] that Narváez, who landed in May 1519, hoping to supersede Cortes, "brought with him a Negro who was in the smallpox, an unfortunate importation for that country, for the disease spread with inconceivable rapidity, and the Indians died by thousands of it. . . . Thus black was the arrival of Narváez and blacker still the death of such multitudes of unfortunate souls, which were sent to the other world without having an opportunity of being admitted into the bosom of our holy church."

The disease spread all over the country and it interfered

with the assembling of the Mexican armies. The successor of Montezuma died of it.*

Díaz thus described the condition in the last portion of the city of Mexico held by the Indians at the time of the surrender in August 1521. "The streets, the squares, the houses and the courts of Talteluco were covered with dead bodies: we could not step without treading on them, and the stench was intolerable. . . . Accordingly they were ordered to remove to the neighboring towns, and for three days and three nights all the causeways were full, from one end to the other, of men, women and children, so weak and sickly, squalid and dirty, and pestilential that it was a misery to behold them."

López de Gómara thus describes the outbreak:[2]

This war [between Narváez and Cortes] cost Diego Velazquez much money, Pánfilo de Narváez his honor and an eye, and the Indians many lives, not from wounds but from disease, and it was thus. When Narváez' people landed there was among them a negro with the smallpox, which he communicated to the house which they had at Cempoallan, and then one Indian to another: and as they were very many and slept and ate together they spread it so much that it went through the land slaying. In most houses everybody died, and in many towns the half, as it was a quite new disease for them. . . . And those who survived were such, from having scratched, that they frightened those who saw them, with the great and numerous pits which they had on face, hands and body. Famine came upon them because, having no mills, the women were unable to grind the grain between stones and many

---

*Montezuma, the Aztec emperor at the time of the arrival of the Spaniards, was made captive by them through treachery and died a prisoner. He was succeeded by his brother Cuitlahua. Within four months he died of smallpox, but not before the Spaniards had been defeated and driven from the city. Cuitlahua was succeeded by a nephew, Guatemozin. It was he who headed the last desperate defense against Cortes and his Indian allies. Prescott describes him as a sort of Indian Hannibal, devoted to hatred of the Spaniards as the other Hannibal to hatred of the Romans.

SHOCK TROOPS: ERUPTIVE FEVERS

died of hunger. Unburied bodies stank so that houses were pulled down over them to cover them. The Indians called the disease *huizanatl*, which means *gran lepra*. From this, as from a very notable event, they thereafter numbered their years. It seems to me that they here paid for the bubas [syphilis] which they communicated to our people.

Shattuck estimated the number of victims at three and a half million. All of the other early historians agree with Díaz and Gómara as to the terrible epidemic begun by the Negro landed by Narváez.

Narváez had sailed from Cuba and one of his Negro slaves had taken the disease from that island. Cuba had probably received it from Santo Domingo, where there was a terrible epidemic in 1518 or 1519. Of this, Las Casas wrote, "I do not believe that there remain alive a thousand who escaped this misery, of all the immense multitude of people that was formerly in this island and which we had seen with our own eyes."

In a letter addressed to the king by the Frailes Geronimos under date of January 10, 1519,[3] they expressed the opinion that about one third of the natives of Hispaniola and of Puerto Rico had already died of smallpox and that it was extending to other islands, but that very few Spaniards had been afflicted and none had died. The disease reached Tierra Firme (the mainland) the same year, 1518–19, and seriously interfered with the plans of the Frailes Geronimos to Christianize and settle the Indians in towns. Herrera said that because of it, of their changed manner of life, their natural weakness and complexion, there was a great diminution of them, although the padres never failed to go to their aid and to care for and treat them with the greatest care and charity. "There died an infinity of Indians." As usual, the immense Indian mortality from a disease that scarcely affected and did not kill the Spaniards was attributed to feebleness of constitution, "complexion," and to bathing during the disease. Actually it was due to the fact that smallpox was a new disease to them, one against which they had no sort of immunity, while every Spaniard in the New World had probably had the disease in childhood.

In another place[4] Herrera, after speaking of the laziness of the Indians, their addiction to the vice of the flesh, and their drunkenness, which caused many diseases that destroyed them, added, "and so few of them are alive, and smallpox finishes many of them, especially the women, but nobody born in Spain becomes sick with it. For which reasons the lowlands [*"la parte Maritima"*] of New Spain are almost deserted; and in the islands of the Gulf of Mexico there are no natives."

So common was smallpox in Spanish children that Ruy Díaz de Isla cited as remarkable the fact that he knew a man who had not had it until after his twentieth year. "Avicenna says that smallpox and measles are an ebullition of the blood and that smallpox is caused by residual blood in the veins which we bring from the wombs of our mothers, of the menstrual blood in which we are engendered, and that each of us according to his nature finds himself strong enough to cast out and get rid of these remains at the age of two or four or ten years. But I have seen a man more than twenty years old with smallpox, and he had never had it before."[5]

The first great epidemic of smallpox in Peru after the conquest occurred in 1533, but there is much reason to believe that there was an earlier one about 1519 or 1520, and some writers state that it was from this disease that Huayna Capac died about ten or eleven years before the conquest. Although the Spaniards had not then penetrated the country, they had explored the coast and had dealings with the natives as early as 1514 and 1515, and Andagoya explored it with the object of settlement and conquest in 1525. Pedro de Cieza de León said that more than two hundred thousand Peruvians died in the

SHOCK TROOPS: ERUPTIVE FEVERS 87

smallpox epidemic that killed Huayna Capac.[6] Probably this was an extension of the same epidemic that ravaged the West Indies, Tierra Firme, and Mexico. There was another great epidemic in Peru in 1538.

Sigaud wrote (*Du climat et des maladies du Brésil*) of smallpox in Brazil, "Smallpox is the disease which makes the greatest ravages among the Indians; it is usually confluent and the epidemics observed since the early years of the discovery of Brazil show that it is almost always mortal. The epidemic of 1563, which began in the island of Itaparica, extending from there to San Salvador and the whole province of Bahia, destroyed 30,000 Indians and six colonies founded by the Jesuits." There were other great epidemics in the following century; in 1621 along the Amazon, in 1642 in Pernambuco, in 1669 in Rio de Janeiro and south of there, in 1666 from Pernambuco to Rio. Sigaud speaks of smallpox as a scourge imported from Africa.

French settlement of Canada began in 1535 under Cartier, and fishing was pursued actively by the French from that time, but Champlain, who really made the colony, did not go out until 1603. The Jesuit missionaries went in 1611 and there are scattered papers about events from 1610, but the Jesuit Relations proper do not begin until 1632. The Indians began to diminish from the early years, but from 1635 onward there are numerous mentions of the ravages of smallpox. Very few French contracted the disease, probably because, like the Spanish and English, they had had it at home in childhood. Father le Jeune wrote of "the great epidemic which has slain nearly all these peoples, without getting any hold on the French," and others made the same observation.

Indian intertribal relations were also affected by smallpox in such a way as to have real historical significance. The Jesuit Relations of about 1645 tell us of the downfall of the Hurons and other Indians allied to the French in Canada.

88 THE RANKS OF DEATH

Hardly had they heard of the doctrine that we preach to them, and commenced to receive the divine seed when a contagious disease [smallpox] spread throughout these nations, carrying off the healthiest of them. No sooner had disease ceased its ravages than war—which had previously been so much to their advantage that they had become masters of their enemies' country, and had defeated them everywhere, commenced, and has since continued to be so disastrous to them that they have lost all their best warriors, have been driven from their country and at present can do nothing but flee from the cruelty of the Iroquois.

The smallpox did not seriously affect the Iroquois until later. In August 1684 a French expedition under De la Barre, against the Iroquois, failed because of disease and famine.[7] The disease was probably smallpox, as it was then prevalent among the French Indians.

The settlement at Plymouth, hard as it was and great as was the mortality, might well have been impossible had the Indians been capable of resisting it. Increase Mather tells[8] that an exploring party found the country empty until it reached a place called "Patuxit, where there were a multitude of Indians, but they were all dead of the Plague which had been there a few years before." And Governor Bradford wrote[9] that the Indians were "not many, being dead and abundantly wasted in the late great mortality which fell in all these Parts about three years before the coming of the English; wherein thousands of them dyed." This plague was probably smallpox in 1617, as Captain Dermer in a letter to Reverend Samuel Purchas wrote of "The Sores of some that had escaped, who described the Spots of such as usually die." English and French fishermen had touched on the coast occasionally for some years, it had been raided for slaves by a man named Hall, and Captain Gosnold visited Martha's Vineyard in 1602, so smallpox could easily have been introduced. Or it may have come overland from Canada.

It is possible that an Indian war was averted by the smallpox

SHOCK TROOPS: ERUPTIVE FEVERS

in 1631, as Mather tells us that "About this time the Indians began to be quarrelsome touching the Bounds of the Land which they had sold to the English, but God ended the Controversy by sending the smallpox amongst the Indians of Saugust, who were before that time exceeding numerous. Whole Towns of them were swept away."

A vivid picture of the ravages of this disease among the Indians and the absolute or relative immunity of European settlers to it at that time is the following from Bradford, in regard to the Indians about the Connecticut River settlement in 1634:

This spring, also, those Indians that lived about their trading house there fell sick of ye small poxe, and died most miserably: for a sorer disease can not befall them: they feare it more than ye plague: for usually they that have this disease have them in abundance, and for wants of bedding and lining and other helps they fall into a lamentable condition as they lye on their hard matts: ye poxe breaking the mattering, and runing one into another, their skin cleaving (by reason thereof) to the matts they lye on; when they turn them, a whole side will flea of at once, (as it were) and they will be all of a gore blood, most fearfull to behold; and they being very sore, what with could and other distempers, they dye like rotten sheep. The condition of this people was so lamentable and they fell downe so generally of his disease, as they were (in ye end) not able to help one another: no, not to make a fire, nor to fetch a little water to drinke, nor any to burie y dead; but would strive as long as they could, and when they could procure no other means to make fire, they would burne ye woden trayes and dishes they ate their meate in, and their very bowes and arrowes; and some would crawle out on all foure to gett a little water, and some times dye by ye way, and not be able to gett in againe. But those of ye English house, (though at first they were afraid of ye infection.) yet ceeing their woefull and sad condition, and hearing their pitifull cries and lamentations, they had compastion of them and daily fetched them wood and water, and made them fires, gott them victualls whilst they lived, and buried them when they dyed. For very few of them escaped; notwithstanding they did what they could for them, to ye haszard of them selvs: The cheefe Sachem him selfe now dyed, and allmost all his freinds and kinred. But by ye marvelous goodness and providens of God not one of ye English was so much as sicke, or in ye least measure tainted with this disease, though they dayly did these offices for them for many weeks together.[10]

MEASLES

Measles was not so constantly and universally present as smallpox, or else it did not excite so much comment because it was less revolting.

It is well known, however, that among peoples to whom it is new it always creates great havoc, as has happened in much more recent times than those of the early settlement of America. In 1846, after an absence of sixty-five years, the disease was introduced into the Faroe Islands, and 6,000 out of a total population of 7,782 were stricken with it, 102 dying.

Introduced into the Fiji Islands by H.M.S. *Dido* in 1875, measles swept away 40,000 of the 150,000 inhabitants.[11] When introduced into the Sandwich Islands, it killed about 40,000 of the 150,000 inhabitants.

Many great and very fatal epidemics of disease in early American settlements are so poorly described as not to be identifiable, and some of them may have been measles, but there are some definite statements as to the ravages of this disease.

Fray Toribio de Benavente Motolinía[12] names it, with smallpox, among the ten great afflictions of Mexico, and says that eleven years after the epidemic of *gran lepra* in 1519–20 there came a great epidemic of measles like it in severity. The Indians called this the year of *la pequeña lepra*. Probably the same epidemic extended to Honduras and Nicaragua, as both Oviedo and Herrera describe it as very destructive in those provinces in 1532, Oviedo saying that half of the population died of measles and other diseases. Herrera is more definite in naming the other diseases. His statement is:

At this time there was such a great epidemic of measles in the Province of Honduras, spreading from house to house and from town to town, that many people died; and although the contagion also touched some Spaniards who were there, none of them died. ... This same disease of measles, and dysentery, passed on to Nicaragua, where also many Indians died. ... And for two years there was another very common disease of pain in the side, and of the stomach which also carried away many Indians.

Herrera also records an epidemic of measles occurring at the same time as a plague of locusts in Peru, in 1540. Sigaud says[13] that measles claimed almost as many victims from the Indian tribes of northern and central Brazil as did smallpox. In 1749 an epidemic of measles ravaged the tribes on the Amazon. It continued during the year 1750, and the mortality in that time was estimated at thirty thousand. In many tribes the disease killed five hundred to six hundred people.

Père le Jeune (Jesuit Relations, 1635) tells of an epidemic of measles among the Canadian Indians in 1635. It was also communicated to the French, "but, thank God, none died." Riddell says[14] that a great measles epidemic was reported by Gouverneur de Denonville in 1687.

It is to be remembered also that, although only large and early epidemics of these diseases are discussed here, they have acted continuously upon the Indian race from the days of the conquest until the present, have been persistent causes of invalidism, death, and destruction.

Livingston Farrand brings this out strikingly:[15]

The lack of immunity against infections and epidemic diseases must be laid to a different source. These came from the whites, and the Indians have not yet acquired the racial immunity. As a consequence, measles, scarlet-fever and smallpox have a mortality among the aborigines which greatly exceeds that among the whites —a single epidemic of measles will sometimes almost extinguish an Indian village or tribe. Whether or not epidemic diseases of any sort existed before the coming of the Europeans is doubtful.

SCARLET FEVER

I have seen but one reference to an epidemic of scarlet fever in the history of the early settlements and that was in the Jesuit Relations of 1710 and was for some unknown reason translated to "purple" fever. The almost complete silence in regard to this disease is not surprising, as scarlatina, although well described by Sydenham in 1675, was not commonly recognized as a distinct disease until a considerably later date. Garrison[16] notes as historically important the mention of the disease in London in 1739 and 1770 and in St. Albans in 1749, yet it was probably always present after 1675, if not before.

TYPHUS FEVER

Typhus fever, which in those days was known in England as jail fever, famine fever, and ship fever, and in Spain as *tabardillo* or *tabardete*, a louse-borne disease a good deal like typhoid fever, with which it was always confused until well into the nineteenth century, was brought from Europe to the West Indies, Mexico, and Peru, to Canada, and to New England. It is probable that typhoid fever was also introduced, but there are no such clinical descriptions in the early histories as will permit us to distinguish it from typhus, although some of the descriptions of typhus are pretty good. A number of epidemics characterized by passage of blood from the bowels and by nosebleed have been described, but not so clearly as to indicate that they were typhoid rather than dysentery or typhus. Flores says that typhus is represented in the Aztec picture writing by an Indian with severe nosebleed. A number of very

SHOCK TROOPS: ERUPTIVE FEVERS

severe epidemics were described by the Spaniards, and also by the French in Canada, as characterized by nosebleed as the most striking symptom.

Hirsch[17] states that the earliest European references to typhus having a degree of definiteness date from the eleventh century. He cites an epidemic in 1083 in the monastery of La Cava, near Salerno, and others in Italy and in Bohemia in the same century, and says that toward the end of the fifteenth century the disease was widely spread in many countries of Europe. It was epidemic in Spain in 1489–90. Villalba says of this epidemic[18] that it began in Spain during the civil wars in Granada in 1489–90, and was a *"calentura maligna punticular,"* a malignant fever with punctate eruption, which was brought from Cyprus by soldiers and contaminated both the Christian and Saracen forces. It spread from the camps of Granada to the army of Don Fernando the Catholic, which army lost 20,000 men in 1490, of whom 3,000 were killed by the enemy, while 17,000 died from disease and exposure.

Juan de Aviñon[19] spoke of tabardillo being very prevalent in Seville in 1393, along with smallpox, measles, and fevers due to bad blood.

Fracastorius gave a good description of the disease and made special mention of severe nosebleed, which he thought should have been very beneficial, as he regarded it as an evidence of nature's effort to throw off the disease. In practice he found it a bad sign if relief did not follow promptly, "for I have often seen cases where three pounds of blood burst from the nostrils, yet the patients died soon after." * [20]

His observations on the epidemiology of the disease are very interesting in view of our present-day knowledge that the disease is louse- and flea-borne. He said that it was contagious,

---

* Farfan regarded moderate nosebleed as a good sign, saying, "The sixth and last prognostic in this disease is that he who is well purged from his belly or whose bowels move (spontaneously), who has a copious sweat or a moderate nosebled will recover by reason of any one of these things."

but that it did not infect quickly or by means of fomes, or at a distance, but only from actual contact with the sick. "Few women died of this fever, very few old men, almost no Jews, but many young people and children, and they were of the best families. This is contrary to what happens in true pestilent fevers, which chiefly attack the common people." Familiar exchange of lice and repeated opportunities to acquire immunity from mild attacks probably were or had been so much more common among the Jews, the old, and the poor than among the young and the noble as to account for these differences. It is likewise probable that it, like smallpox, was then so common as to be pre-eminently a disease of childhood, and that most older people were immune, in Italy as in Spain, because of previous attacks. Fracastorius allows us to infer as much when he says, "The reason why this contagion attacks children and young people rather than others, is that in them there is more and wetter blood, and with that kind of blood this contagion has analogy."

Sahagun was apparently describing typhus when he wrote:

At that time [i.e., about the time of the introduction of smallpox] there also began in the country of Amaquemacan Chalco the disease called *cocoliztli*. It began in the month of August and was not at first very severe; it was especially grave during September, when it spread during the whole month. So long as this epidemic lasted the greenish fever prevailed: blood came from the mouth and from the nose and caused death: There was no remedy, so a great number of people died throughout all of New Spain. . . . It froze during fifteen days of September and all through October: and the mortality reigned at the same time.

Herrera has already been quoted as saying that cocoliztli meant any great epidemic. Juan de Cárdenas describes under the term a disease characterized by severe nosebleed and great injury to the liver, but attacking only Indians, not Spaniards.

SHOCK TROOPS: ERUPTIVE FEVERS

It is not possible to say definitely that the cocoliztli of Sahagun and of Cárdenas was typhus, but it is almost a certainty. Doubt of Reko's diagnosis of diphtheria is abundantly justified. The Spanish could not have been uniformly immune to diphtheria. All Spaniards would have been and probably were practically immune to typhus from having had attacks, as were most Russian soldiers at prison camps in World War I.

Reko quotes Torquemada as saying that one epidemic of typhus fever killed two million people and Alegre as saying that it destroyed two thirds of the population of Mexico.

León[21] quotes an eyewitness of the epidemic as saying that Viceroy Enriquez made a record of the deaths from typhus in 1576-77 and that they exceeded two million.

A number of writers (León, Reko, Flores, etc.) state that the disease was known before the arrival of the Spaniards, and the bases cited for the opinion are usually the Aztec name for the disease, *matlalzahuatl*, and the conventional picture of the Indian with spots and nosebleed, proofs that seem insufficient, as the Indians, not knowing Spanish, were obliged to indicate new diseases and objects in their own way.

The disease was introduced into New England and New France several times as ship fever, a disease that took heavy toll from many ships, but it did not become a fixture and endemic, unless in the form of typhoid fever. This, although a totally distinct disease, of entirely different cause and method of transmission, was confused with typhus until after the close of the first third of the nineteenth century. Typhus has also been known in Peru since the sixteenth century, but it has not caused such extensive epidemics as in Mexico.

From the time of the conquest to the present, the history of typhus in Mexico has been unbroken. It has been constantly present and from time to time it has occurred in great epidemics. It is almost unknown in the low, hot, moist coastal regions, where little clothing is worn and where that which is used is often washed, and the bodies are bathed daily; it is always present in the dry, cold uplands, where wool is worn, water is scarce, and bathing infrequent.

Of the very numerous epidemics of disease mentioned in the Jesuit Relations as destroying the Indians, most were probably smallpox, even though the descriptions are often so meager as to leave the matter in doubt. The following examples are apparently typhus or ship fever. In September and October 1637 three priests, Chastellan, Dominique, and Jogues, were sick with "burning fever or purple fever" (*"une fièvre pourpreuse"*); both suggest typhus.

On June 22, 1646,[22] there was reported the arrival of three canoes of Algonquins, who said that a disease that caused vomiting of blood had destroyed a good part of their tribe. (*"Une maladie qui faisait vomir le sang avait perdut une bonne parti de leur nation."*)

On September 5, 1660, the ship *St. André* landed 130 passengers. Nine or ten had died on the trip of a contagious fever.

Three years later the ship *La Justice* arrived with more than one hundred sick; many of them died.

Although Governor Bradford did not name typhus, it (including typhoid) was probably the disease that he mentioned several times as infectious fever.

Of the Salem plantation in 1629 he wrote, "It was before noted that sundry of those who came from Leyden came over in the ships yt came to Salem, wher Mr. Endicott had cheefe command; and by infection that grue among ye passengers at sea, it spread also among them ashore: of which many dyed, some of ye scurvie, others of an infectious feavors, which continued some time among them (though our people, through God's goodness, escaped it)."

He also writes of an infectious fever in 1634, "of which many fell sick and upward of 20 persons dyed, men and women, besides children. . . . This disease also swept away many of ye Indians from all of ye places near adjoining." *

ERYSIPELAS

During our Civil War, erysipelas was classed among the common eruptive fevers, and it was far more common than at the present time. Its nature, now known to be that of a streptococcic infection of the skin, was not then understood. I have found no evidence upon which to base an opinion as to whether it was indigenous or imported to America, no mention or description of a disease in an early settlement that I can identify as this. Ruy Díaz de Isla wrote of it as a late manifestation of syphilis.[28] He probably used the term to indicate a red, painful condition of the skin, and not in its present more specific sense. Erysipelas was described by both Hippocrates and Galen and was well known to the physicians of the Middle Ages and the Renaissance, being then often called *sacer ignis* or sacred fire. If it had been known, or at any rate at all common, in the new world, it would seem that it should have been mentioned by some of the old chroniclers. The absence of such mention suggests its absence.

Although malaria and yellow fever later proved greater troubles to the low, warm parts of America, it was the eruptive fevers, especially smallpox, that in the sixteenth century most hurt the Indians, actually exterminating them in the West Indies and other places. Against this disease the whites and blacks usually possessed the immunity conferred by previous attacks acquired either by natural infection or by inoculation. It was wholly new to the Indians. They knew neither how to avoid nor how to treat it, and, as Governor Bradford said, they died like rotten sheep. This, probably more than any

* For further discussion of typhus and other eruptive diseases in early America see Appendix A, pp. 224–8.

other single factor, opened the way for the Spaniards, the English, and the French to possess the land, and made an opening and a need for the Negro. Smallpox was the captain of the men of death in that war, typhus fever the first lieutenant, and measles the second lieutenant. More terrible than the conquistadores on horseback, more deadly than sword and gunpowder, they made the conquest by the whites a walkover as compared with what it would have been without their aid. They were the forerunners of civilization, the companions of Christianity, the friends of the invader.

Chapter VII

WITH the Negroes came another champion. Their title to him has been disputed, some claiming that credit should either go to America or at least be divided between America and other continents, especially Africa. Again the author's conclusion, after careful study of the evidence, is that this disease was brought to America during the conquest. However it was brought, even if it existed before the invasion, there can be no doubt that it was present during a great part of the conquest; that its presence exerted a profound influence on the course of events and on subsequent history; and that the Negro was the primary carrier and spreader. The name of this champion was malaria.

Few diseases are as widespread as this and perhaps none holds more undisputed sway or is such an absolute monarch once in power. The eruptive fevers flame and burn out. Even smallpox, for all its deadliness, strikes but once and that swiftly. It wrestles with its victims and destroys many of them, but on those that do not die in the struggle it confers perpetual immunity. Not so with malaria, for though malaria kills its multitudes wantonly at times, it prefers enslavement. It masters whole populations insidiously, weakening them and taking away the vigor and joy and drive of life. And, lest they forget who is master, it returns again and again, showing its power at recurrent intervals, so that the conquered walk in abiding weakness and fear, gradually losing incentive and hope.

Malaria, if it lacks the ferocity of smallpox, lacks also some of the latter's bold integrity. It seems a strange thing that such a power on the earth, such a great tyrant and oppressor of mankind, should depend for its very existence on stagnant pools and should need as its agent a fragile and stealthy insect. Yet it is so. The tiny anopheles mosquito, with its lancet smaller than the point of a pin, is all that has stood between mankind and freedom from this old misery, but of this neither the conquerors of America nor the conquered knew anything and the pale monarch found new broad worlds to conquer.

It is fascinating to speculate on how malaria first arrived. Perhaps nearly simultaneously in several ships; perhaps in several Negroes in a single ship; but it would have taken just one poor slave and one hungry anopheles anywhere on the shores of the New World to set in motion the whole tragic course of the disease. If there had not been a single other evil consequence of Negro slavery, mankind would have paid in full for wickedness.

And here we encounter fully for the first time an aspect of the conquest extending far beyond the conquest itself. It has been said that no great historical event can be isolated; each has its consequences and its implications for future time. Nowhere is this more true than of disease. Broadly speaking, the illnesses of the conquest fall into three great groups: first, those that exerted a large effect on the conquest itself; second, those that, although having little contemporary effect, came and were planted during the conquest and have had great effects, socially and economically and medically, since then; and lastly, those that were important both during the conquest and after. To the third group belongs malaria. As the story goes on we shall see that there were other diseases, in both the second and third groupings, that must be given thoughtful consideration.

In the case of malaria, for example, its spread through the Negro to both whites and reds had a large general effect, at least in the later stages of the conflict. There is considerable reason for believing that as the eruptive fevers demolished effective resistance by the Indians in the front lines, so malaria, working among the civilian population as well as among the warriors, increasingly weakened both the will and the ability to resist further or to support the war. It is, of course, dangerous to attempt too strict a comparison between the conscious, cold-blooded planning of Hitler's Nazis for the conquest of Europe and the blind gropings of fate through disease in America, but nevertheless the same main elements were present in each. First the assault, air-borne, water-borne, land-borne, and the smashing of front-line resistance. Then, as say in Poland, with the destruction of the Polish army and government, a slow but steady wasting and demoralization of the whole population; a process by which in the long run the inhabitants of the country were given just three alternatives: to stay and perish; to stay and be a subject race; or to escape leaving all possessions and affections behind in the hope of finding shelter elsewhere.

This was the effect of malaria on the peoples of the New World. During the conquest it had a certain impartiality, to be sure. Many times it drove out the white garrisons as well as the natives, enfeebled and decimated the victors as it had the vanquished. For generation after generation it continued a menace; an unseen, highjacking gangster of a thing, forever demanding tribute and extorting fear. To the whites it was a far more deadly and costly enemy than all the Indians put together.

And finally, in this connection and as one of the diseases within the third group mentioned above as well as the first, it brought in its train a very important result so far as the Negro was concerned. Malaria undoubtedly contributed largely to the extermination or emasculation of the red man and it is at least questionable whether it would have done so had not the black man brought the disease. By the same token, the black man's relative toleration of malaria meant that he could, and did, serve admirably as a substitute laborer for the white master. Had he not brought malaria with him he would not have been needed so sorely; had he not been needed the slave trade would never have reached such proportions as it did; and had the slave trade been limited the whole course of American (and possibly African) history might have been changed. But he did come, or was brought, in vast numbers; malaria became established in most of the New World and dominant in much of it.

It will appear that from now on the story of this book changes its aspect somewhat. Hitherto we have dealt largely with broad trends, generalizations. Increasingly the tale will consist of detective stories. We shall begin with the evidence of dark deeds, of murder done in the grand manner, and our task will be to find the culprits. It will be a matter of discovering clues, following them, putting them together, thinking, speculating, weighing, until we can return an indictment that will pass any district attorney. Occasionally we must admit that we cannot prove a case against some disease of very thug-like and antisocial aspect, and we will let him go unindicted, but with reluctance, as one who may not have been guilty of the particular crime, but who is untrustworthy just the same.

At times the following of clues becomes detailed and laborious. It is necessary to consider words, meanings, little specks of blood, small tokens of evil imbedded in recorded circumstance. Some of it will be clearer and more interesting to the medical man than to the layman, but it is all part of the medical history of the conquest of America, and to anyone, professional or amateur, it is fascinating investigation. There is the corpse, there are the witnesses, there is adventure, there is desperate crime among the most innocent-looking characters, and, usually, there are the murderers themselves, waiting at the end of the trail. Some of them are still at large.

F.D.A.

Total War: Malaria

Malaria is a disease of such subtlety that if unchecked it may debilitate a people and lead to its degeneration, ruin a nation, and jeopardize or destroy a civilization. There is some evidence that "the glory that was Greece, and the grandeur that was Rome" succumbed to it. W. H. S. Jones, in his *Malaria in Ancient Greece*, and Jones, Ross, and Ellett in *Malaria, a Neglected Factor in the History of Greece and Rome*, present scholarly studies to prove that the disease entered Greece in the fifth century B.C., brought in from Asia by slaves or soldiers, and Rome in the second century, introduced by Hannibal's soldiery; that it eventually became endemic in both countries and caused such degeneration of the populace as to affect harmfully the national spirit, and that this was an important factor in national decadence.

There are a few fair spots in the tropical and subtropical worlds, Hawaii and some other Pacific islands, where malaria has not yet obtained a foothold, but in most parts of the Torrid and Temperate Zones it is only too well known, and it is one of the great slow killers and disablers of mankind. At times it shows wide epidemic extension. This is apt to occur when war, famine, and other great calamities make life harder for the already poor. Beeuwkes tells us that, during the Russian famine of 1921–23, millions of cases of malaria occurred and the disease spread all over the country, even the form of it that occurs usually only in the tropics being seen as far north as the Arctic Circle.[1]

The disease is firmly entrenched in tropical and much of temperate America, although now rare in the northern United States and Canada, where it once was common. Barbieri tells us[2] that it has for many years been a barrier to the current of immigration to the Argentine, discouraging the foreign workman from settling in sickly regions, and it has impressed its characteristic stamp on the inhabitants of such regions, crushing their activities, depressing their intelligence, debilitating their constitutions, making them indifferent and apathetic. On the other hand, Hirsch states (*Handbook of Geographical and Historical Pathology*) that Uruguay and the eastern provinces of the Argentine are free from the disease, although swampy, a statement suggesting the absence of a suitable anopheline carrier.

Celli says[3] that the history of malaria is confounded with the economic life of peoples inhabiting the regions where it prevails, and that the notable difference between the north and the south of Italy depends largely upon the different distribution and intensity of malaria.*

The three great indigenous civilizations existing at the time

---

* The reclamation of the Roman Campagna and the Pontine Marshes now in progress is most interesting. Extensive ruins, as well as written history, show that these regions were once populous and rich. Then for centuries they reverted to pestilential wilderness. A century ago Charles Dickens described the Campagna as dismal, desolate, and unpopulated save by rare, savage, and miserable shepherds. Gibbon, discussing the state of Italy under the Lombards, wrote:[4] "The Campagna of Rome was speedily reduced to the state of a dreary wilderness, in which the land is barren, the waters impure, and the air infectious."

Today Rome is a beautiful city, "Roman fever" a legend, and the Campagna and the Pontine Marshes are again beginning to blossom with rich crops and pleasant homesteads, as the result of mosquito control and antimalarial work. To one having a knowledge of the facts, this is one of the interesting and beautiful sights of that land of interest and beauty.

On the other hand, the comparatively recent extensive epidemic of the disease in Ceylon (*Time*, January 14, 1935), like its epidemiology in Panama, shows how, even today, great epidemics may be brought about by factors affecting the balance between mosquitoes and their natural enemies. The Ceylon epidemic was caused by drought in a normally wet country. In Panama the most common cause of epidemics was the drying of swamps by large hydraulic fills incident to canal construction. Very often the cause has been the formation of puddles, streams, and swamps where there were none before.

of the conquest of America, the Mayan, the Aztecan, and the Incan, disappeared within a relatively short time and their peoples fell to the condition of peons and serfs. Progress of archeological investigations is now giving us an ever increasing knowledge of their former greatness and admiration for their accomplishments before they knew the whites.

In view of these facts, it would seem a matter of great historical interest whether or not malaria existed in America before the whites came or was introduced later. Strangely enough, the subject has not been carefully investigated. A number of writers have expressed opinions in regard to it, but so far as their writings show, they usually did so without careful investigation.

KNOWLEDGE OF MALARIA NOW AND IN THE SIXTEENTH CENTURY

At the present time we know that malaria is caused by the growth in the blood, in the red cells only, of certain protozoan parasites known as plasmodia, which are introduced by the bites of infected mosquitoes of certain species, all belonging to the subfamily *Anophelinae*. In these insects the plasmodium undergoes an important and invigorating phase in its life history, that of sexual reproduction. It undergoes an asexual multiplication in the human body, but that does not render it transmissible from man to man except by transfer of blood, a method now used in the fever treatment of general paralysis. For its continuance in nature, malaria requires the presence of anopheline mosquitoes of the proper species, and these require access to infected human blood and an environment affording a sufficient degree and duration of warm weather and enough of water to permit their breeding and survival. Malaria is usually readily identified by the demonstration of the parasite in the blood, much less reliably by the therapeutic effects of quinine, an alkaloid of the cinchona plant. There are three varieties of plasmodium, the simple tertian, the quartan, and the tropical or subtertian, each producing a specific type of fever. The disease is usually characterized by paroxysms of chill, fever, and sweat that recur with such definite periodicity and such clear-cut intermissions as to set it in a class by itself.

Except for the occurrence of intermittent or periodical fevers, known as quotidian, tertian, and quartan according to their occurrence daily, once in two days, or once in three days, the medicine of the sixteenth century really knew nothing of malaria, although it was very common in Europe. Morejon[5] says that malaria has always been endemic in Spain and the most frequent and common disease in the peninsula, and that Mercado (Mercatus), a Spaniard, was the first to show that some intermittents are pernicious, the rest of the world having accepted without question the Hippocratic axiom that all kinds of intermittents are good, and believed them not mortal.

Many of the early explorers described the America of their days as very delightful and healthful. Several such descriptions of places now notoriously malarial have already been quoted.

PANAMA

So great was the popular fear of yellow fever and so deadly had it often been to visiting whites in Panama, that most people think that it was the greatest obstacle to the construction of the canal. However, it is probable that malaria not only killed more people in nearly every year of Spanish-American history after its introduction, but that it did more to impair labor, than did yellow fever. It is true that there was a heavy mortality among the Spaniards on the isthmus in the early days, but this has been accounted for in preceding chapters. I have found no mention by any early writer of disease in

Panama in the first generation after its discovery that can be identified as malaria.

MEXICO

Next after the isthmian region, the best places to claim pre-Columbian malaria would probably be Honduras and the Mexican gulf coast near Vera Cruz, now highly malarious, and such claims have been made. Dr. Otto Effertz has reported in recent years that from 50 to 90 per cent of Mexican Indians of the gulf coastal regions die of malaria, and that he had been in several Indian villages where an epidemic of malaria had already destroyed 10 per cent of the inhabitants. Yet that same region was thickly populated and healthful at the time of Cortes's landing. The best evidence that it was not malarious is the fact that Cortes and his men remained there from March to August, the very worst season for malaria, before starting for Mexico, and neither Cortes in his letters to the king nor Bernal Díaz del Castillo nor Gómara in their histories of the conquest makes any mention of sickness among the men, although two of these writers were present (Gómara probably obtained his information from Cortes) and wrote at length of the experience. And the subsequent accomplishments of the little army indicated health, strength, and almost unbelievable vigor, not the invalidism of untreated tropical malaria.

Francisco A. Flores[6] states that malaria existed in ancient Mexico and that the Mexicans had words for quotidian, tertian, and quartan fevers, but he does not cite a reference to support the statement. Molina,[7] in his Spanish-Mexican portion, gives no equivalent for *paludisme, fiebre intermittente, terciana, quartana, cuartana,* or other special fever. In his Mexican-Spanish section he gives *viptlatica*, cited by Flores, as meaning "every third day," but the next word given means "every third year," which makes it difficult to say that the first word meant tertian malaria.

However, it is possible to quote Flores against himself in regard to the significance of this word, for he says in his discussion of syphilis, which he thinks was *not* of American origin, "The mere existence [of the name of a disease] in the language means nothing, for all the things brought in by the conquest were named, as they became known to the natives, with names formed according to the peculiar genius and ideology of the idiom."

Victor A. Reko[8] states that malaria, amoebic dysentery, and leishmaniasis were all known to the ancient Mexicans, and that Bernal Díaz del Castillo states that Cortes, on his march into Honduras, lost many men from them. Actually, Bernal Díaz does not mention or suggest any of these diseases, and the word *atonahuiztli*, cited by Reko as meaning malaria, is given by Molina as meaning *calentura con frio*, fever with chill, but that is a symptom occurring in many diseases, including the great epidemics of the early days of the conquest, typhus and smallpox, so it cannot be accepted as proof of the existence of malaria. Moreover, the fact that Molina's dictionary was published half a century after the introduction into Mexico of Negro slaves destroys any value that the word might be supposed to have as proof of the existence of malaria at an earlier period. Reko further says that Bernal Díaz del Castillo stated that he and Cortes both had malaria on the Honduran trip. Careful search has failed to reveal any such statement. Old Bernal did say that both Cortes and he were sick. As for his own sickness, the writer very definitely states that it was *calentura*, which is any fever, and that it was due to sunstroke. ("*Estuvo yo muy malo de calentura y del gran sol que me habia entrada en la cabeza, porque ya he dicho que entonces habia recio sol.*") And of Cortes's sickness he says, after describing the great labors and great hunger Cortes had long suffered, "He was so thin that it made us sad to see him, because, so far as we knew, he had been about to die of *calentura* and of the sadness [worry] that he had within him, and even at that time he did not know a thing good or ill of what was going on in Mexico: and others said that he had been so near dying that they had made him a Franciscan habit to be buried in: and then he went afoot with us to the town and put us up and we supped with him: and there was poor cheer, as we scarcely had enough even of cassava." *

Cortes wrote to the king (*Carta quinta*), "It is impossible to express what I felt at seeing myself so helpless, for I was almost without hope and thought that none of us could escape dying of hunger; but our Lord God, who always has charge to help us in our needs and has many times saved me to continue in your majesty's service, despite my unworthiness, sent a ship . . ."

Although malaria now exists in Mexico City and is very prevalent and sometimes severe in the state of Morelos, there is good evidence that it is of relatively recent origin and spread in both places.[9]

PERU

Many parts of Peru are now highly malarious. Victor C. Vaughan says,[10] "There has been some discussion as to whether malaria existed in the western hemisphere in the pre-Columbian days. The general belief is that it was introduced into the West Indies and North America by Europeans. However, this can hardly be true in the case of South America, from which country the most valuable discovery ever made, so far as the

---

* "*Y estaba tan flaco, que hubimos lastima de verle: porque, segun supimos, habia estado a punto de morir de calenturas y tristeza que en si tenia, y aun en aquella sazon no sabia cosa buena ni mala de lo de Mexico: y dijeron otras personas que estaba ya tan a punto de morir que le tenian hechos unos habitos de San Francisco para le enterrar con ellos: y luego a pie se fue con todos nosotros a la villa, y nos aposento y cenamos con el: y tenia tanta pobreza, que aun de cazabe no nos hartamos,*" etc. This description can no more justify a diagnosis of malaria than one of typhus, walking typhoid, dysentery, tonsillitis, or any one of a dozen diseases.

restriction of malaria is concerned, has come." Vaughan was, of course, referring to cinchona, or Peruvian bark. This is analogous to the argument used in the sixteenth century that syphilis must have originated in the New World because God had there created the remedy, the blessed guaiac.

When the Panama Canal was opened, Guayaquil, a part of ancient Peru, was considered a pesthole and a constant menace to the Canal Zone. It has since been cleaned up and modernized and is regarded as a "clean port," although still having much malaria. In the middle of the sixteenth century Guayaquil was a health resort. Herrera wrote of it that the water of the river, having so many roots of sarsaparilla in it, was very good for the French disease and similar troubles, and that many people went there to recover their health. Monardes discusses the virtues of the Guayaquil River at some length and says that "in eight or nine days they [the visitors] are well of all those diseases which are cured by sarsaparilla; and of many others which it would take too long to name. Suffice it that nobody goes there who does not return well, however grave disease he have, except acute fevers; but in this or other acute disease the cure does not occur, but in all others the effects are marvellous." It was evidently a healthful place.

Barbieri said that the ancient Peruvians knew malaria as *el chuchu* and that they also knew the specific virtues of cinchona. He cites no authorities for the last statement, and it was impossible to verify it.

All the references to *chuchu, chucha,* and *chucho* that I have found seem to derive from Garcilaso,[11] who tells us of it as the cause of death of Huayna Capac, the last great Inca emperor before the coming of the Spaniards. He says, "Huayna being in the kingdom of Quito, one day toward the end of his life entered the lake to bathe, for his recreation and delight; from whence he came out with a chill, which the Indians call chuchu, which is to tremble, and as the fever, which they call *rupa,* (the r soft) which is to burn, overcame him and as he got worse and worse the following days, he felt that his disease was mortal, as for some years he had had warning of it through the magicians. . . ."

The description is brief and, while it might relate to malaria, being merely a description of chill followed by fever which after a time proved fatal, it could as well relate to pneumonia, typhoid, typhus, or any of numerous other diseases, including Carrión's disease, Oroya fever, the peculiar fever of modern Peru (*el fiebre del pais*), which we know existed also before the conquest. Pedro Pizarro, who bears the same relation to the conquest of Peru as Bernal Díaz del Castillo does to that of Mexico, that of a soldier of the conquest, who knew how to write vivid prose, attributes Huayna Capac's death to smallpox, which he says was epidemic among the Indians before the conquest.[12] This is quite possible, as there had been exploration to some extent along the coast for fifteen years before Pizarro began his conquering march from the sea.[13] Pedro Cieza de León (1519–60)[14] and Herrera[15] also say that the death was due to smallpox. Gamboa says[16] that "the Inca was taken ill with a fever, though others say it was smallpox or measles," but he adds that when Ninan Cuyoche was to be notified of the succession, he *also* was dead of the smallpox. Tello says that the death has been variously attributed to smallpox, measles, verruga, malaria, and typhus.

Garcilaso[17] mentions malaria and connects it with chuchu in another place, where he deals with Peruvian medicine. "They call the chill of a tertian or quartan Chuchu, which is to shake; fever they call Rupa, the r soft, which is to burn: they greatly fear such diseases because of the extremes, now of cold, now of heat." * This use of the terms tertian and quartan does suggest that the diseases existed in Peru, but it really means only that Garcilaso knew them, as he had to

* "*Al frio de la terciana o quartana llamen Chuchu, que es temblar; a la calentura llamen Rupa, r sencilla, que es quemarse: temian mucho estes tales enfermadades, por los estremos, ya de frio, ya de calor.*"

know them, from his long residence in Spain. And what he says is merely a repetition of what he said in regard to Huayna Capac's death, that a chill is called chuchu and the fever following it rupa. The fear of a chill followed by fever could easily have come from experience with Oroya fever, pneumonia, septic infection, and many diseases other than malaria. As a matter of fact, the chill and fever of malaria are usually less feared by the sufferer than are most diseases. It is a case of familiarity breeding contempt, but familiarity with pneumonia or Oroya fever does not have that effect. Garcilaso simply applied the terms chuchu and rupa to the respective features of malaria as seen in Spain. He makes no mention of cinchona or any other drug for the treatment of chuchu, although he devotes a chapter to medicinal plants. What has been quoted from Garcilaso is the entire evidence which I have been able to find in favor of pre-Columbian malaria in Peru.

THE AMAZON VALLEY

There is another incident in connection with the Peruvian conquest that should have brought out malaria had it then existed in America. Toward the end of 1541 Gonzalo Pizarro started from Quito with a large command to discover fabled El Dorado and the forests of cinnamon. The party reached the upper or Andean part of the Amazon, experiencing great hardships and famine. A boat was constructed and Francisco de Orellano was sent down the river in search of food, accompanied by fifty-three others. Whether Orellano seized the opportunity to obtain an independent command and make an important exploration, as Pizarro reported to the king, or was, as he himself claimed, unable to reascend the river because of the current, he decided to descend it to its mouth, leaving Pizarro and the larger command stranded, not only without food but also without powder or crossbows, all of which were in the boat. A priest, Fray Gaspar de Carvajal, was of the party with Orellano, and he wrote a full account of the trip. The party embarked from Pizarro's camp on January 2, 1542, and their first stop was at a place called Yurara, where they remained until February 1, after which they experienced great hunger. At Aparia they built another boat. Here it was necessary for each worker to have another man stand by and fight away the mosquitoes while he worked, and all had to sleep covered for protection. They passed Lent here, a period of forty-one days. After this they slept in the boats, which they usually tied up at night. On May 29 they reached the Rio Negro. The riverbanks were nearly always thickly populated and most of the Indians hostile. Carvajal tells of towns extending for two, two and a half, and five leagues along the river, and of one stretch of eighty leagues where the towns were nowhere separated by a greater distance than a crossbow shot. He also mentions repeatedly the vigor and fine physical condition of the people met, especially of the Amazons.

The party reached the Atlantic in August, having lost three men killed by Indians and seven by starvation, but the rest of the party got through safely. *There is no mention of fevers.* It is doubtful if it would have been possible at any time in two centuries past for fifty men to traverse that territory, being almost eight months in the Amazon Valley without quinine and often without food, at war and pestered by mosquitoes, without a heavy mortality from malaria. Not only was the escape of the Spaniards significant, but the fact that they found the riverbanks so thickly populated from the Rio Negro downward is about as much so.

There were other voyages down the river in the seventeenth century. Twenty years after Orellano's trip, General Pedro Orsuña made the journey with an army, but he was a rebel attempting to set up his own kingdom, and when he reached the sea by that mouth of the Amazon nearest to Trinidad he was captured and executed for treason.[18] I have seen no account of sickness in his command.

In 1637 two Spanish priests and six soldiers made the trip and were so pleased with it that they asked the Portuguese governor of Pará to help them return the same way. A large Portuguese command under Captain Pedro Texeira was sent up the river under the guidance of the Spaniards. Texeira established a colony on the river but he and a considerable part of his command went on to Quito, where they were received with wonder and acclaim. Two Spanish priests, Padre Cristóbal de Acuña and Padre Andrés de Artieda, were ordered by Chinchon, the viceroy of Peru, to accompany the Portuguese on their return trip down the river and then to proceed to Spain and make full report to the king. Fray Acuña wrote a full account, which was printed in 1640. The party was ten months in making the trip and Acuña makes no mention of any disease experienced.

In comparison with these early accounts, let us consider recent reports by well-trained and highly competent medical investigators. Councilman and Lambert say:[19]

> It is a solitary region. . . . The usual estimate of the population is one to the square mile, but there is no accurate knowledge of the population. . . . It is possible to travel in a steamer for an entire day without seeing a human habitation. The population is on the highway of the watercourses. . . . The people seen presented the indications of ill health; the nutrition was poor, there was evident anemia and lack of energy. . . .
>
> Malaria in chronic form is extremely prevalent in the Amazon Valley, both in the cities and in the sparsely settled districts along the rivers. It is the cause of much poverty and misery, and is one of the chief causes of the country's lack of development. . . .
>
> In Para in 1909 there were 1159 deaths from malaria, and taking the average mortality of 2.89 per cent, this would give 40,100

cases, or one to every four and a half inhabitants, which would certainly seem excessive.

Strong and Shattuck wrote:[20]

The Brazilian Commission of 1913, in referring to the unhealthy conditions that prevail in the territory in the neighborhood of the Rio Branco, and of the ravages of disease in these regions, state that there has been a total depopulation of many of the small towns that formerly existed on the banks of these rivers. Our observations would tend to support this statement. Towns formerly of some prosperity and said to have a population of several thousand, are now in ruins or consist of some half dozen to a dozen more or less delapidated dwellings. . . . The most insalubrious situation of some of these villages, the great prevalence of disease among the few inhabitants who remain, and the entire absence in these regions of anyone in robust health, further support the idea that the great majority have either been driven away by disease or have perished from it. This view is also in accordance with information that we obtained by questioning the remaining inhabitants or those who had previously visited these localities.

Generally speaking, the inhabitants living upon the river banks show evidence of either acute or chronic disease or the effects of having suffered from such disease. Portions of Amazonia today constitute some of the most unhealthy and most dangerous regions to reside in, from the standpoint of health, that exist in the tropics. . . . Chagas pointed out that the Valley of the Amazon is, without doubt, the region of Brazil where malaria has its most severe types and is most intense. . . . LeCointe states that malaria constitutes the principal obstacle to the penetration of man into the interior of the country. . . .

On the lower Amazon, the Rio Negro and the Rio Branco up to Vista Alegre, we never visited a locality in which we did not find individuals suffering from either acute or chronic malaria, though in some localities the rate of infection was of course higher than in others. It was at Vista Alegre that a number of the members of the expedition became infected with the disease and that one, Dr. Koch, succumbed.

THE USE OF CINCHONA

As for the use of cinchona, we have no information in regard to it for a full century after the conquest of Peru, and the contention by several writers that the Indians had knowledge of the great blessing for all that time and kept it secret because of their hatred of the Spaniards seems fantastic in view of many known facts. Among such facts are these: that the Indians gave up everything else they had in order to procure Spanish favor; that they never stood wholly together and some of them always favored the Spaniards; that many of them were the offspring of Spaniards and Peruvians, and in a century some of these should have learned the secret; that Garcilaso was of noble Spanish and royal Inca blood and in touch with the Incan nobility, and he assiduously collected everything he could find that might serve as source material for the history of pre-Columbian Peru and the Peruvians, including all he could find of Peruvian medicine and materia medica, yet he never learned of cinchona; and that the Indians in the neighborhood of Loxa, whence the secret was supposed to have been revealed, knew nothing of the use of the bark in Humboldt's day.[21] Markham agreed with Humboldt, and these two carefully investigated the matter on the ground and reported most fully in regard to it. Both thought it more probable that the Jesuits first learned of the drug in the course of their examination of all the plants of the country, and that cinchona received particular attention because of its bitterness.

MALARIA IN FLORIDA AND LOUISIANA

To the sixteenth-century Spaniard, the name Florida meant all the territory of the present Florida, Georgia, and South Carolina, and the territory west to the borders of the Mexico of that day, a very indefinite area, but all claimed for Spain.

TOTAL WAR: MALARIA 117

Ponce de León, Pánfilo de Narváez, and Hernando de Soto were the early explorers. Ponce de León's expedition was defeated by famine and Indians and he himself died of an arrow wound. Narváez' expedition landed on the gulf coast of present Florida and became lost. The survivors marched west, some of them eventually reaching Compostela, Nueva Galicia, in western Mexico.

De Soto is known to have marched from the present Florida into South Carolina, across Georgia and Alabama, probably into Tennessee, across Mississippi and the great river, and for some distance into Arkansas. He found the country well populated and many tribes hostile. His trip lasted four years before he died, and much of it was warfare and hardship, with starvation imminent at times. After his death, his men made boats and descended the Mississippi and then followed the coast to Mexico, where 311 out of the original 600 arrived safely in September of 1543.[23]

These are tales of great adventure, but not any such tales of terrible malaria as our own army records tell of the same regions three centuries later. A century ago the mortality in such southern posts as Fort Gadsden and Baton Rouge was frightful. A similar prevalence of malaria in De Soto's day must have destroyed his army in less time than it wandered in those regions.[24] The conclusion that health conditions, especially as related to malaria, had changed tremendously in two centuries is inevitable.

The Huguenot and Spanish settlements in Florida and South Carolina in the sixteenth century occasionally exterminated one another on religious grounds and, as usual with settlements of the time, they had their experiences of famine. This caused the abandonment of the first Huguenot settlement. The account of the second expedition, which settled on the river of May, mentions,[25] in addition to famine, "many dangerous diseases due to putrefaction in the air from decomposing fish, so that most of the men fell sick," but they all recovered. Later Laudonnière developed a *continued* fever that lasted for weeks, suggestive of typhoid. There is nothing to suggest malaria, among either the Huguenots or the Spanish.

VIRGINIA IN THE SEVENTEENTH CENTURY

Virginia was defined by Captain John Smith as a "country in America, that lyeth between the degrees of 34 and 44 of the north latitude. The bounds therof on the East side are the great Ocean. On the South lyeth Florida: to the North nova Francia. As for the West therof, the limits are unknown." So it may have been larger than Florida, but the early history of it is, for our purposes, mainly the history of the present state of the same name. The principal information in regard to it is collected and published with the writings of Captain John Smith.

The first permanent settlement was at Jamestown in 1607, although it was effected by the sixth expedition sent from England. In December 1606, as the result of much urging by Captain Gosnold, who had already explored the coast farther north, an expedition was sent out from England by way of the West Indies, landing at half a dozen places and not sailing north until the tenth of April, when it "disemboged out of the West Indies." It is probable that there was sickness in the West Indies, but there is little mention of any. In Porto Rico many of the men fainted on a march, but none was lost except Edward Brooks, gentleman, whose "fat melted within him, by the great heat and drought." The Virginia shore was reached on April 26, 1607, and the building of a fort and of Jamestown was begun on May 14. By June 15 the fort was finished and six days later their ship departed, leaving 104 persons "very bare and scanty of victualls."

On August 6 J. Asby died of a bloody flux; on August 9 G. Flower, of the swelling; then two men of wounds; then two suddenly; then almost daily one or more of causes not stated, until by the end of the first week of September forty-six had died. The Honorable George Percy wrote of these deaths: "Our men were destroyed with cruell diseases, as swellings, Flixes, Burning Fevers, and by Warres; and some departed suddenly; but for the most part they died of meere famine. . . . Our food was but a small can of barlie sod in water, to five men a day, our drink cold water taken from the River; which was at flood verie salt; at low tide full of slime and filth, which was the destruction of many of our men. Thus we lived for the space of five months, not having five able men upon any occasion. Except for help from the Indians, all would have died." Captain Wingfield's account of this period agrees with Master Percy's, but is less complete.

Captain Smith wrote: "At this time most of our chiefest men either sicke or discontented, the rest being in such despair as they would rather starve or rot with idleness than be persuaded to do anything for their owne relief without constraint."

Thomas Sudley wrote: "Being thus left to our fortunes, it fortuned that within tenne days, scarce ten amongst us could either go, or well stand; such extreme weakness and sickness oppressed us. . . . Half a pint of wheat and as much barley, boiled with water for a man a day . . . From May to September those that escaped lived on Sturgeon and Seacrabs. Fifty in this time we buried."

Anthony Bagnall, Nathaniel Powell, and Amos Todkill wrote of the party with Captain Smith on a voyage of discovery in the summer of 1608, "The rest (being all of the last supply) were sick almost unto death, until they were seasoned to the Country." One of them died; all others recovered, "notwithstanding their ill diet, and bad lodging and crowded in so small a barge . . ." This trip lasted from July 24 to September 7, the time when men would be contracting malaria had it been present, not a time for recovery from it. These new men apparently suffered from a self-immunizing bacterial disease, such as dysentery, rather than a protozoal disease, such as malaria, which tends to become chronic.

The other descriptions quoted better fit starvation than they do malaria and the incidents are also mentioned in the chapter on famine and scurvy. The descriptions are quoted here rather than in that chapter because writers have attributed the sickness of the colonists to malaria. John Fiske[26] says that "Jamestown had always had a bad reputation for malaria, and after its second burning people were not eager to restore it." A. G. Bradley, editor of Captain John Smith's works, speaks of Jamestown as a malarious peninsula.

The epidemiological evidence is not wholly conclusive, but it makes it almost certain that the causes of death were starvation, scurvy, dysentery, and possibly typhoid. There may have been some malaria among the men, but it is not mentioned. However, Captain Smith wrote of Captain Martin being "so sick and weak" in June, and when Martin returned to England in May 1608, Smith wrote that he had been "sick near a year and not past half a year since his ague left him." If by ague Smith meant malaria, although this is not a certainty, the word then having other meanings, Captain Martin had probably brought his infection from either England or the West Indies, and almost certainly did not contract it between April and June 1607. There are good reasons for this opinion, the first being well stated by Dr. H. R. Carter: "Paludal fevers in that region rarely show to any extent until well in August." The second reason is that in this latitude spring malaria is due to infection acquired in the preceding autumn. This has been shown by a number of writers, but by nobody better than by Colonel W. B. Borden in a statistical study of malaria in the United States Army.* Sydenham observed that the months of greatest incidence of malaria in England were

* This excellent piece of work has not been published at the date of this writing, but Colonel Borden allowed me to read it in manuscript.

August and January. The January cases must have been relapses or delayed infection.

S. P. James has shown[27] that benign tertian malaria inoculated by mosquito bites for the treatment of general paresis has, in England, a mean incubation period of 14.1 days, but that 12 out of 746 instances of infection showed attacks only after periods of from twenty-eight to forty-four weeks. He also observed that spring tertian in England is the result of infections acquired in the preceding summer or fall.

These reasons for not regarding Captain Martin's possible malaria as of Virginian origin also apply to the ague of Lord de la Warre, who went out to the colony as governor in 1610. In his own words, he was "welcomed by a violent ague." He also says that he had flux, gout, and scurvy. John Smith spoke of his disease as scurvy. The trouble clung to him and after eight months he had to leave the colony for his health's sake. He had gone out by way of the West Indies. Any malaria appearing immediately on his arrival in Virginia was necessarily contracted elsewhere, but whether in England or the West Indies is not known.

No clear indication of endemic malaria has been found until long after the introduction of African slaves. Dr. W. B. Blanton stated,[28] as a result of his careful investigations, that he had found but five references to malaria in Virginia before 1700, and he thought that at least some of these cases had come from England. We have just seen that two of them came from there or from the West Indies. Once introduced, malaria would not spread so rapidly as in the tropics, because of the shortness of the season, so we should not expect it to show notable prevalence as soon as in the West Indies and the tropical mainland, and in any event its spread is apt to be slow. James's work with inoculated malaria shows that most anopheles biting malarial patients do not become infected, most of those infected do not survive to infect persons, and most persons bitten by infective mosquitoes do not acquire the disease.

The early settlers did not blame their sickness upon malaria or the climate. John Rolfe wrote: "For the mortality of the people blame not the place, for of the old Planters and the families, scarce one in twenty miscarries, only the want of necessaries are the occasions of those diseases"; and again, "Notwithstanding the ill rumours of the unwholesomeness of Jamestown, the newcomers that were planted at old Paspaheghe, little more than a mile from it, had their health better than any in the country." In the proceedings of 1614 it is recorded: "About fifty miles from there is Jamestowne, upon a fertile peninsula, which although formerly scandaled for an unhealthy aire, we find it as healthfull as any other part of the Countrie." In 1629 Captain Smith wrote of the country, "Few countreyes are less troubled with death, sickness, or any other disease, nor where overgrowne women become more fruitfull."

Reverend Samuel Purchas[29] summed up the matter of the colony's early promise and its trials as well as we can do it today.

Captain John Smith, partly by word of mouth, partly by his Mappe thereof in print, and more fully by a manuscript which he courteously communicated to me, hath acquainted me with that whereof himself with great perill and paine, had been the discoverer. . . . The summe of his observations in that and other discoveries since, concerning the country, is this. . . . The temperature agreeth with English bodies, not by other meenes distempered. . . . . This Captain Smith saith, that he hath beene in many places of Asia and Europe, in some in Africa and America, but of all, holds Virginia by the natural endowments, the fittest place for an earthly Paradise. . . . Yet in all this abundance our men have had small store but of want, and no fire or water could purge that poison which was rooted in some, to the hindrance of the plantation. Idleness in the vulgar, emulation, ambition and covetousness in some of the greater, treacherie in some fugitives, all these ayming more at their own ends then at the common good, have from the beginning (I pray God it be and I hope now is ended) beene the poison to this honorable plantation.

Once introduced, malaria spread slowly but surely, and Dr. Blanton wrote,[30] "There are abundant references to malaria in the eighteenth century. . . . References to malaria become more frequent toward the end of the century, and diaries and letters of the period show that hardly any section of the state escaped the inevitable 'Ague and Fever.'"

CANADA

The Jesuit Relations mention malaria a few times. Some of these relate to disease on the lower Mississippi in the second quarter of the eighteenth century, and they probably related to real malaria, imported by the French or their slaves.

There is mention of fever in a trading post on the Miami but no description or name that serves to identify it. The Relation of 1656–57[31] tells of an epidemic at one of the Canadian missions, when the ration consisted of meal and water. Everybody became sick. Then the Indians brought in game and vegetables in abundance. "Thus we all escaped with a few attacks of tertian fever." The relief of a serious epidemic by fresh food rules out malaria, and the term tertian fever was apparently used without its specific meaning.

In August 1669 Father Bruyas wrote[32] from an Onandaga village that he had been suffering from a tertian but had kept about his work. As he did not describe his symptoms, made no mention of others having tertians, and as there is no contemporary mention of the disease in those parts, it must be assumed that he too used the term in a nonspecific sense, probably to indicate a mild and ephemeral fever due to some cause other than malaria.

THE CENTRAL STATES

A century ago the entire Ohio and upper Mississippi valleys and the shores of the Great Lakes were infested with the disease, and it prevailed in such northern army posts as Forts Brady, Mackinac, and Gratiot in Michigan; Forts Howard, Winnebago, and Crawford in Wisconsin; Fort Snelling in Minnesota; and Madison Barracks in New York. There were great epidemics of the disease in Ohio in 1807 and 1823. Dr. S. P. Hildreth gave an account of his personal observations of these epidemics,[33] from which it appears that the epidemics were a mixture of typhoid and malaria but that the latter disease predominated and attacked persons living on the recently overflowed bottom lands. Of the 1822 epidemic he said:

By the first of August the epidemic was general in this portion of the valley, and especially in Marietta. The largest number of attacks was in September, and at one time there was not less than four hundred cases within the area of one square mile. They were composed of all, from the mild intermittent to the most malignant remittent. . . . The proportion of deaths was about six in every hundred cases, where proper medical attention was given to the sick: but so general was the disease that many lives were lost from lack of nurses. All other disorders were swallowed up by this. It did not sensibly abate until after smart frosts appeared in November. Intermittents were common through the winter months.

Dr. Hildreth states that the early years of Ohio settlement (1788 to 1807) were not marked by malaria, which appeared only after the forests began to be cleared and the swamps to be exposed to the sun. This can be interpreted, in view of our present knowledge, to mean that the white settlers introduced the disease.

The disease has now almost disappeared from the north-central states, probably as a result of improved drainage, preventing the growth of mosquitoes and encouraging further land cultivation and improved living conditions, and it is much less common and less severe in the South, but it is still there a heavy burden in many places, and it has been a factor in delaying the development of that part of our country. As recently as 1929 there were reported in Alabama 10,476 cases with 431 deaths; in Mississippi 9,885 cases with 355 deaths; in South Carolina 3,753 cases with 179 deaths;[34] and it is probable that the actual number of cases much exceeded the number reported.

CONCLUSIONS

The investigation of the early accounts of American settlement and conquest seems to warrant the following conclusions:

(1) There is no real evidence that malaria existed in any part of America before the conquest.

(2) The state of medical knowledge at the time of the conquest was backward and medical practice in America was more backward than in Europe. Nevertheless, intermittent fevers were well known, usually recognizable, and common diseases in England, France, and Spain, and had they been common in America, as they later became, they could not have escaped frequent mention, as they later did not.

(3) There was abundant opportunity for the introduction of the disease by the white conquerors, and this occurred from time to time, but on the whole it was probably infrequent, as the sick man was not apt to emigrate, or, if he did so, to survive the hardships of the voyage and the settlement.

(4) The most certain large introduction of the disease came with African slaves, who, as unwilling emigrants and partly immunized subjects of the disease, were all potential or actual carriers of it. Slavery was introduced early into most or all settlements, but malaria usually spreads slowly and even tropical America was not notoriously malarial for a half century

after its first settlement. Sigaud speaks of the fevers of Angola causing large, hard spleens in the blacks and says that he himself saw a cargo of young slaves, all of whom had greatly enlarged spleens, some of them resembling in size the head of a fetus.[35] Malaria is intimately associated with large spleens, but there are also other conditions in Angola that can cause them.

(5) The geographical distribution of anopheline mosquitoes was possibly always much the same as now, although this is mere surmise. At any rate, if malaria existed in America before the conquest, the anopheles was here. If malaria was introduced after the conquest, the anopheles was either here or was introduced early; otherwise the disease could not have spread, as it certainly did.

(6) Quite probably malaria was an important factor in the degradation of the Indians, in their replacement in lowland tropical and subtropical America by the Negro, in delaying the progress of civilization in all such regions, and in promoting sloth, ignorance, and superstition.

(7) In our own country this disease has been a deterrent to the development of many parts, but particularly of the southern states. Even today it is in many parts of the South a heavy affliction.*

* For further notes on malaria see Appendix A, pp. 228-9.

Chapter VIII

MALARIA was by no means the only intermittent fever to affect American history, although it was so important and its story so instructive that it deserved a chapter to itself. There was another similar disease also deserving careful consideration and that was yellow fever.

Yellow fever, while never attaining the cosmic proportions of malaria, and while differing from it in other important respects, nevertheless in particular parts of the New World and elsewhere was so violent and destructive that its importance seemed to overshadow that of malaria itself.

In America yellow fever has received more publicity and is more known about than malaria; partly because on several occasions (as in the Spanish-American War, in Cuba, and in Panama) it has played a large and spectacular part in our military, colonial, and commercial history; partly because its vanquishment was largely an American achievement—one of our greatest, and the splendid work of Walter Reed, Gorgas, and other Army medical men has been recognized and admired.

There is perhaps no passage in medical history that is more vivid or stirring than that of the defeat of this disease by the doctors of the United States Army. Led by Walter Reed, who with his fellows has become a national symbol of medical heroism, this defeat of yellow fever saved more lives than the conquest of America took, more than Napoleon cost, and made possible the Panama Canal. No better instance of the influence of disease on history could be found.

In respect to the conquest of America, yellow fever falls into the second group of diseases previously mentioned. It does not appear to have been an important factor in the conquest itself, but it was a major by-product of the conquest, with a large influence on subsequent events. Probably brought, like malaria, in the slave ships, it was, as generations passed, the cause of inestimable human suffering, personal and domestic tragedy, economic loss, and diplomatic or political decision.

Like malaria, yellow fever is an illness depending for its survival on stagnant waters and mosquitoes. The villain differs in a number of respects from his malarial rival. His name is *Stegomyia* or *Aedes aegypti*, alias *Culex fasciatus*, and to the lover of mosquitoes he has numerous special claims to interest and recognition. To the layman, who usually regards a mosquito as a mosquito, without further refinement, about the only difference between *Anopheles* and *Aedes* is that one seems to stand on his head in order to secure a better plunging effect as he bites and the other seems to settle more on his heels as though better and more comfortably to savor the sweetness of his bloody drink. Neither breed seems impressive enough to warrant his unquestionable estate of being still man's worst enemy in many portions of the world.

The battle between man and the insects goes on. It is a war lined with human devotion and courage. In few of his wars has man appeared so virtuous and ennobled. Many lives have been given already in the struggle; more will be lost; but one wonders whether ever in any other field self-sacrifice and patient study and quiet willingness to lay down a life for the race were as assured of the validity and mercy of the causes for which men die.

F.D.A.

Yellow Jack

Yellow fever, never having more than a limited geographical distribution, and even where it occurred often showing only seasonal incidence, never excited such general interest or such wide discussion as did syphilis with its world-wide distribution, its year-round prevalence, its usual relation to sexual immorality, and its so-called hereditary manifestations, the last being really examples of intrauterine or congenital infection, not a true hereditary transmission of disease. Nevertheless, because of its high morbidity and mortality among non-immunes, its consequent great influence upon the commercial and social development of Latin America and the southern United States, its long unknown etiology, and its mysterious epidemiology, yellow fever excited much attention and interest and its history was more carefully investigated and discussed in print than was that of most other diseases. Much of the discussion was speculation pure and simple, with the simplicity usually much in excess, but in some instances, notably those of Josiah Clark Nott (1804-73) of New Orleans and Carlos J. Finlay (1833-1915) of Havana, the speculations were so solidly founded upon observation and were in themselves so logical and sound as to constitute brilliant examples of scientific imagination and of clear thought. Both of these men had reached a belief that the disease was transmitted by mosquitoes many years before Walter Reed and his fellow workers, composing a board of medical officers of the United States Army, proved that to be the fact, and so made it possible to bring the disease under control.

None of the investigations of the history of this disease has resulted in incontrovertible proof as to the place of its origin.

The late Henry R. Carter, whose posthumous book[1] contains the most thorough presentation and the most judicious and scientific weighing of all the evidence on the subject, believed that the disease was of African origin and that it was imported to America by slave ships. The evidence seems to me to justify this opinion, but some able investigators have thought otherwise. Carlos Finlay held [2] that the disease was of American origin. George Augustin [3] considered it of Asiatic origin and thought that he could identify it in the writings of Hippocrates and possibly in the plague of Athens described by Thucydides.

The French military surgeon Audouard argued acutely [4] that the disease arose from an infection that was established in slave ships, and that it was in these, and not in vessels used exclusively for freight, that the infection reached a very high degree.

The supposed occurrence of yellow fever at Isabela, Santo Domingo, at the time of Columbus's second voyage, is based upon Oviedo's description, especially the following:

The Indians had a cunning thought, as a result of which more than half of the Spaniards died, and more of the Indians themselves than could be counted. And this was done in a manner which could neither be understood nor avoided, because the Christians were so new in the land that they did not know how to work. All of the Indians of that province agreed not to plant at the time when it should have been done, and as they had no maize, they ate yuca. These are the two bread stuffs and the principal food there. The Christians ate their rations, and when these were finished, they wished to eat the food of the country the Indians used, but the Indians had none for themselves or for them. And in this way men fell dead of hunger, the Christians in the city and in the fort of Santo Thomas. . . . So they did not lack appetite to eat things very harmful to their health and fearful to see. From which and from the great humidity of the land many grave and incurable diseases followed in those who lived. And for this reason, those first Spaniards who came here, when they returned to

Spain, some of them who had come here seeking gold were of the same color as it; but not of the same lustre; for they became jaundiced and of the color of saffron and so sick that when or shortly after they were taken there, they died because of what they had suffered, and because the food and bread of Spain are of stronger digestion that those herbs and poor food which they ate in the Indies, and the airs are thinner and colder than the airs of this land. So that although they returned to Spain, they soon thereafter reached the end of their lives.

It is to be noted that in this description Oviedo attributes the suffering of the Spanish to insufficient and bad food, and that, while he does speak of jaundice, he speaks of it as occurring in men who had returned to Spain. This in itself is sufficient to indicate that the jaundice was not due to yellow fever, as that is a self-limited disease of short duration, and causes a jaundice that is likewise of short duration. Furthermore, it is a disease that usually kills within a few days, if at all, and men surviving it long enough to make the passage to Spain in those days of slow sailing ships would have recovered from it and would have lost all traces of jaundice long before their arrival there, probably before starting the trip.*

Fortunately we have medical testimony as to this sickness at Isabela. Dr. Chanca was physician to the fleet on Columbus's second voyage, and he wrote an excellent account of the voyage and later asked for special compensation or reward, because he had acted as chronicler of the expedition. He wrote about January 1494[5] that a third of the people had become sick

* As one searches the history of yellow fever he is astonished at the frequency with which he meets the statement that there was yellow fever at Isabela in 1493, 1494, or 1495. The proof commonly cited is the statement that the men became yellow, but no thought is given as to when they became yellow. In some accounts there are descriptions of other symptoms, such as vomiting of blood and black diarrhea, which must have come by way of inspiration, as the writers do not give references that may be checked and I have been unable to find such descriptions in the writings of the early historians.

in four or five days and that he believed the principal cause of it was the work and the hard passage across the sea and the difference in the lands, but that he trusted in the Lord that all would soon be well again. He makes no mention of fever, jaundice, black vomit, or other symptoms suggestive of yellow fever. Columbus himself said,[6] "It is certain that if they had fresh meat, they would very soon all be about with the aid of God, and most of them would be convalescent by this time . . . the cause of the sickness so general among all is change of waters and airs; and consequently for the preservation of the health it is necessary under God that this people be provided with the maintenance to which they are accustomed in Spain, and provision should be made for this from the time of the arrival here, till after they have had time to sow wheat and barley and to plant vineyards. . . ." It is to be noted that Columbus made no more mention of jaundice than did Dr. Chanca. Oviedo wrote his description much later and from hearsay, so it is naturally less valuable as evidence. These quotations show little or no reason for thinking the sickness of Isabela was due to yellow fever, and much for thinking that it was due to lack of proper food, or to intestinal infection.

Dr. Carter[7] discusses at some length the high mortality at Darien in the early days, quoting Las Casas, Oviedo, and Herrera, and expressing the opinion that the great epidemic of disease that accompanied the starvation of Pedrarias' force in 1514, and which the writers called modorra, was neither yellow fever nor typhus. In this opinion I concur. However, there is additional testimony by eyewitnesses which is not mentioned by Dr. Carter, and it supports his conclusion.

Andagoya[8] was a member of Pedrarias' expedition. He tells us:

Pedrarius arrived at Darien at the end of July of the year 1514, where he was received by the people who were there, and where he landed all his troops. The settlement was small and there were few resources in the land. The provisions which were on board the ships were disembarked and divided amongst all the people. The flour and other stores were injured by the sea, and this, added to the evil nature of the land, which is woody and covered with swamps, and very thinly inhabited, brought on so much sickness amongst the people that they could not be cured, and in one month seven hundred men died of sickness and hunger.

No single word of this description suggests yellow fever.

In the introduction to this volume, Markham quotes a letter from Balboa to the king, from which quotation has already been made in an earlier chapter. This letter relates to times earlier than Pedrarias' arrival, the times of the great mortality in the parties of Alonzo de Ojeda and Diego de Nicuesa, which mortality Balboa very definitely ascribes to warfare and to starvation.

Another instance that has been cited as possible yellow fever in the early days was the settlement made in Honduras by Gil Gonzales de Avila, which was found and relieved by Cortes at the time of his march into that country in 1524. Bernal Díaz del Castillo tells us:[9]

We found this colony to consist of forty men and six women, all yellow and sickly. . . . We sent a plentiful supply of maize to the wretched colonists, who having been so long starving, ate to such excess that seven of them died immediately. At this time also a vessel arrived there, with seven horses, forty hogs, eight pipes of salted meat, biscuit, and fifteen passengers, adventurers from the island Cuba. All the provisions Cortes bought immediately and distributed them among the colonists, with equally fatal results. They ate of the salted meat to such excess that it gave them diarrhea, which in a very few days carried off fourteen.

This is a clear tale of starvation with the possible addition of dysentery.

Dr. Carter says, and I have found nothing to the contrary, that the first clear description of yellow fever, the first concerning which there can be no doubt, was given by Cogolludo.[10]

As an eyewitness he describes an epidemic in Yucatan in 1648 so vividly and accurately as to symptoms and epidemiology that he leaves no doubt that he went through a very severe visitation of yellow fever, and that it was a disease new and very fatal to both Spanish and Indians. The fact that he does not mention jaundice as a symptom cannot change the verdict as to the diagnosis, in view of the accuracy and completeness of his description of the other features of the disease. Sebastião da Rocha Pitta in 1729 described [11] an epidemic beginning in Pernambuco in 1686, which appears to have been yellow fever. It was a new disease of terrible mortality. The doctors did not know it and it went by the name of *bicha* (leech). (The term *bicho*, worm, is also applied to a contagious endemic disease presenting symptoms that suggest schistosomal dysentery.) The features of Rocha Pitta's description that suggest yellow fever are the rapid spread of the disease, its sudden onset, short duration, and high mortality, the vomiting of blood before death, and the immunity of the Negroes. Since that time the history is reasonably clear and continuous, although presenting many surprising and anomalous features, such as the disappearance of the disease from Cuba for more than a century after having been epidemic there for six years, 1649–55. The irregular and anomalous behavior of this disease always puzzled medical men until the United States Army Medical Board showed in 1901 that the disease was mosquito-borne.

Of the Board's findings, quoted in Appendix A,* and the experiments upon which they were based, Sir Patrick Manson, then the greatest living authority on tropical diseases, said:

> These experiments fully explain: 1st, the impunity with which a yellow fever patient can be visited by a non-immune if outside the endemic area; the mosquitoes in the vicinity are not infective;

---

* See pp. 229–36.

2d, the danger of visiting the endemic area, especially at night; the mosquitoes there are infective and active; 3d, the discrepancy between the incubation period, three to five days, of the disease, and the incubation period, fourteen days and over, of an epidemic; the necessary evolution of the germ in the mosquitoes infected by the original introducing patient demanding the space of time indicated by the difference between these two periods; 4th, the clinging of yellow fever infection to ships, buildings, and localities; the persistence of the germ in infected mosquitoes which are known to be capable of surviving for five months, and probably longer, after feeding on blood; 5th, the high atmospheric temperature required for epidemic extension of yellow fever; such temperature favors the activities and propagation of the mosquito, and is probably necessary for the evolution of the germ in the mosquito.

All of the former peculiarities of the disease thus became understandable. We can know, for instance, that when the disease disappeared from Cuba in 1655, it was because the continuing supply of the germ or virus ceased; because the *Aedes* mosquitoes disappeared; or the temperature became too cold to permit of the development of mosquitoes or of virus in mosquitoes; or the supply of nonimmune persons in whom the virus might be kept going became exhausted.

As there is no reason to think that there was any such climatic change as to destroy the mosquitoes or hinder their development in Cuba, it is virtually certain that the nonimmune material in the infected localities was exhausted by 1655 and that the virus died out. The country was probably sparsely settled. The Indians had by this time been replaced in Cuba by African Negroes and the only nonimmunes in the island were the relatively few Spaniards. Blaev's atlas (1658) described Cuba as very sparsely populated at the time of its publication. ("*De naturalen zijn voor vele jaaren door de Spanjaerden omgebracht, soo dat er wegnigh volcks in dit groote eylandt is.*") No fresh strain happened to be introduced until 1761, when prisoners sent from Vera Cruz as workmen introduced it. That year it ravaged not only the Cuban inhabitants, but also the English that besieged and captured Havana. Thereafter the disease was endemic in Cuba.

It is not necessary to discuss here at length the later history of yellow fever in America.* The striking fact is that the disease was well known in tropical America for well over a century before it was recognizably described in Africa. The first good description of it there was given by Schotte in a communication sent to the Royal Society in 1780, and published by him in 1782.[12] Although his was the first good description of the disease in Africa, Schotte did not regard it as a new disease there. On the contrary, he discussed earlier epidemics. He noted that "Europeans suffered much more by it, in proportion, than the mulattoes, and those much more than the blacks." Schotte undoubtedly included in his description certain symptoms that were not a part of the disease, but were co-existing diseases, especially dysentery and liver abscess, and it is probable that the relapses of which he speaks were recurrences of these other diseases.

Despite the fact that yellow fever was definitely and well described in America almost a century and a quarter sooner than in Africa, it is believed that it originated in the latter continent and was imported to America with slaves. There are sound reasons for this belief.

(1) In the early days of the history of yellow fever, there were no large settlements of whites on the west coast of Africa. Even in Schotte's time, 1780, he wrote of the unwisdom of sending only convicts there as soldiers. The west coast was the "white man's grave" because of its deadly malaria, its dysentery and liver abscesses, and possibly its yellow fever. This last, however, could easily be overlooked, as there were not usually enough whites in one place to provide material for a real epidemic, and the blacks, as now, were either rela-

* Those interested can find full discussions in the works of H. R. Carter, Carlos Juan Finlay, and George Augustin, already cited.

tively immune to the disease or absolutely immune because of attacks in childhood. Malaria and liver abscess were common among the whites and both caused jaundice.

(2) Black slaves from the high interior, who probably were nonimmunes, may have had yellow fever. If so it was possibly mistaken for scurvy. Schotte says that they were very liable to this disease, which so much resembled yellow fever that he thought they had a common origin. "The same cause which produces the scurvy at one time of the year, may greatly contribute towards the generation of our disease at another time of the year, when other concurring causes aggravate and accelerate its effects." It may be that this resemblance so confused Schotte that he really mistook yellow fever for scurvy. This supposition is supported by two of his observations, (a) that those siezed with the disease seldom or never recover, and (b) that "those slaves who are bought nearer to Senegal are seldom affected by it." This last fact he credited to their customary use of salt. It was more probably due to their residence in a region in which the disease yellow fever was endemic and to their having acquired immunity in childhood.

It is noteworthy that several firsthand observers of both diseases have written of the resemblance of yellow fever and scurvy. James Lind, pioneer writer on tropical diseases and on scurvy, mentions it. In his *Treatise on the Scurvy* (London, 1757) he says, "Scorbutic people for the most part appear at first of a pale or yellowish hue, which becomes afterward more darkish or livid," and also, "The disease by occasioning obstructions and putrefaction of the abdominal *viscera*, gives rise to jaundice, dropsy and the *affectio hypochondriaca*."

Dr. H. R. Carter says,[13] "The *course* of *sickness* in yellow fever and scurvy is absolutely different, yet the *appearance of those dead or near dying* of these diseases is not dissimilar, so that one who knew scurvy only from description (or even from having seen the dead bodies) might well mistake between them. Indeed . . . many eminent writers (Bruce, 1759:

Pringle, 1810: Arejula, 1806: and others) . . . believed that yellow fever and scurvy were at least kindred diseases."

(3) Men's minds being prone to see only so far as they are trained to see, yellow fever could and probably did exist and escape recognition in Africa for years, decades, and centuries.

(4) Another suggestive fact is that the occurrence of yellow fever in Africa was long disputed and was in doubt until a very few years ago. At the time of his death, 1920, General Gorgas was on his way to Africa to investigate this very question. Later the International Health Board found the disease there after failing to find it in America.

(5) The African Negro's relative and racial immunity to yellow fever is a powerful argument for agelong exposure to the disease. The International Health Board's commission, working in Sierra Leone, has recently been finding that the Negroes of West Africa easily become infected with yellow fever if there has been no previous immunizing infection, but their power to resist the effects of the virus and to survive is much greater than that of whites.[14] The American Indians, on the contrary, died from the disease as did the whites. Racial immunity such as the Negro shows to yellow fever is known in regard to other diseases. In other chapters it is shown to have existed among the white conquerors in regard to smallpox, measles, and typhus. Similarly, races longest exposed to tuberculosis are less susceptible to it than are those to which it is a new disease. Yellow fever, if always endemic among the Negroes of West Africa, would become a disease of children, all persons being infected before reaching adult life and being thereafter immune. Thus the race would be kept up by persons whose resistance to the disease was sufficient to enable them to survive it. All without such resistance would be eliminated. The survivors would transmit their own qualities, offspring showing atavistic susceptibility would be killed off, and gradually a race of disease-resisting individuals only would be left.

(6) None of the animals thus far found susceptible to the disease is native to Africa. Both Asiatic and South American monkeys can harbor the virus. The chimpanzee and the African green monkey, *Cercopithecus callitrichus*, apparently do not.[15]

In view of the existence of the slave trade from almost the earliest years of Spanish settlement, it would be somewhat surprising if yellow fever were not brought to America long before 1648. Possibly it was, but if so, it apparently did not spread. In view of the requirements for its spread—the virus, the proper mosquito, a high temperature, and nonimmune persons—the only thing that could keep yellow fever from spreading when introduced to the tropical coasts of America was the absence of the proper mosquito. The temperature was always suitable, and whites and Indians were alike susceptible, as shown by later experience. It therefore seems likely that the *Aedes* mosquito was introduced from Africa and that the fever could not spread until the mosquito had first done so. The introduction of *Aedes* by ship was easy, as that mosquito is pre-eminently a close associate of man, pre-eminently a sailor. No infectious disease was so apt as yellow fever to occur in epidemic form in ships on the high seas, with the exception of louse-borne typhus and the occasional exception of dysentery due to a badly polluted water supply, or to such intimate and filthy contact as slave ships afforded.

Dr. Carter cites as suggestive of the African origin of *Aedes aegypti* (formerly called *Stegomyia fasciata*) the fact that there are many species of *Stegomyia* in West Africa, none other in America. "It would seem that this species, so definitely differentiated in its biology as a commensal of man, and not regarded by entomologists as one of the older forms, developed from some similar one with less sharply marked characteristics, and that in the region where this took place, one would be apt to find a number of forms allied to it, but less completely differentiated: that is, different species of the sub-genus and with similar but not quite the same life history."

However, recent experimental work in Brazil [16] has shown that there are at least seven varieties of South American mosquitoes other than *Aedes aegypti* that are able to transmit the virus of yellow fever, so we must not attach too much importance to Dr. Carter's biological argument. The evidence as to the African origin of the disease appears sufficient without it. Its introduction to America, while not an event of the early years of the conquest, was a result of that conquest, but more immediately a result of the slave trade. It is an important item in the economic evaluation of African slavery.

DENGUE

Dengue is a disease of both the old and new worlds that resembles yellow fever in many respects, for which reason it will be discussed here. It is a very painful and distressing affection in many instances, but it causes almost no mortality. It resembles yellow fever so closely in its clinical manifestations as to have been many times mistaken for it in places where both diseases occurred. It is transmitted by the same mosquito that transmits yellow fever, and its epidemiology is the same. Dengue was not recognized as a separate disease until long after the early settlements were made, and if it occurred before the late eighteenth century it was confused with yellow fever, bilious remittent fever, and perhaps scarlatina, as one of its names in later times was *scarlatina rheumatica*. However, I have found nothing to suggest it, and in the absence of those diseases with which it might have been confused, and the probable absence of the mosquito that conveys it, I think it did not exist in America at that time. As it is as much a tropical disease as yellow fever, and has the same epidemiology, it probably came from the same place, Africa.

Chapter IX

Wherever a campaign is waged, it may be assumed that paths of activity that are necessary to the survival of the combatants will be involved. There will occur much of the heaviest fighting. A nation may be conquered by the defeat of its armed forces. It may also be defeated by the impairment or destruction of the channels on which it depends for life and sustenance.

In the human body there are four such great trade routes. One is the circulatory system. Infection or destruction here is apt to be fatal. Another is the nervous system. The third is the respiratory system, without which no human can live. The fourth is the alimentary system, the lifeline of the human being.

It would be strange, then, if we did not find diseases that take one or another of these four essential systems as their hunting ground. As a matter of fact, we find examples affecting them all, and in modern society diseases of the circulatory system have claim to being the commonest killers of all. These diseases are, however, not commonly contagious; they deal with individuals, not masses; and they are usually associated with older age groups rather than with soldiers and settlers. A partial exception could be made, so far as the latter statement goes, with the blood-stream infections, which are of great consequential importance following wounds, but even these are individual sicknesses and not group maladies.

Nor are the diseases of the nervous system necessarily infectious or contagious. Man is only beginning to understand how widespread and how serious they are. Because of their nature, because of their psychic quality, because they are so intangible, and because, in respect to human comprehension, they are so new, they are probably the most mysterious and least understood of all. They were not at all understood at the time of the conquest of America or even recognized, and their effect upon it or its effect upon them was probably extremely slight.

We have already had, however, many instances in which both intestinal and respiratory diseases played an important part. It is characteristic of both these groups that they may appear as either primary or secondary infections. For example, a person's whole alimentary tract could be fatally affected by typhoid; but it could also be fatally affected by yellow fever. In regard to the respiratory tract, a person could die of tuberculosis, but could also die of pneumonia following measles. There can be no doubt that both these systems suffered sorely from many causes all during the conquest.

Among the ranks of the respiratory diseases we find great killers worthy of placement beside even smallpox and malaria, if not exceeding all others. In human history "consumption" probably need acknowledge no superior and few peers; pneumonia today, or possibly until just yesterday when the sulfa drugs came, was an ever present scourge in the earth, and may, even with sulfa, continue to rank with heart disease and cancer as present-day captain of the men of death, whether in peace or war. Diphtheria and meningitis, if lesser potentates in the extent of their realm, have also been great slayers, and perhaps no disease has ever approached the epicure meningitis in its terrifying, lightning-like, and final fatal boldness of attack. Any summary of the medical history of the conquest of America would be faulty if it did not consider this group of diseases.

Yet so far as the conquest of America is concerned, all these must be relegated to a lower place. Their day was still to come when the conquest was on. Tuberculosis came into its own when the crowded cities rose in America. It is not primarily a disease of strong, active men and women. Although in time to come it was to be the Indians' worst enemy, it seems to have had little effect on the conquest itself, and since there is at least a possibility that it may have existed in America before the conquest, we cannot even list it with certainty in the second group previously mentioned of those diseases introduced with the conquest and having large subsequent effects.

In the case of pneumonia, diphtheria, and meningitis the evidence is perplexing as to whether any or all of them existed in America prior to the conquest. Whether or not, there is no reason to believe that any of them exerted a decisive effect on the contemporaneous course of events.

F.D.A.

Pale Killers: The Respiratory Diseases

The knowledge of diseases of the chest in the sixteenth and seventeenth centuries was limited to knowledge of the symptoms and prognosis of advanced disease. Cause, method of epidemic extension, the character of the damage done the tissues, and all physical signs except those visible on inspection were unknown. The chest was examined by looking at it and feeling it. Percussion, auscultation, and other procedures now regarded as routine in its examination were unknown. Symptoms, such as cough or pain in the side, were spoken of as though they were diseases in themselves.

The passions, or diseases, of the lungs and chest described by Francisco Lopez de Villalobos were asthma, hoarseness, cough, emoptoica or blood-spitting, pleurisy, peripneumonia (pneumonia), ulcers of the lung, from which arises "ptisic" (consumption), and empyema, which last was defined as a putrid sputum coming from ulcerated lungs, as an abscess that has broken or as putrid humors that have descended to the chest from a sore throat.

A century and a half later, Sydenham's descriptions of respiratory diseases show no great advance over those of Lopez de Villalobos. Even so great a mind as Sydenham's had to keep step more or less with its time. However, he did not appeal to astrology, and was not afraid to admit inability to explain all things.

TUBERCULOSIS

This disease "transcends all maladies in the total number of its victims and the cost to society. . . . Tuberculosis was familiar to the most ancient civilizations, judging from the inscriptions on Babylonian tablets which represent the earliest human records." [1] Hippocrates and Galen recognized phthisis, the advanced pulmonary consumption, and hunchbacks and other cripplings by tuberculosis of bone were familiar, although not known to be related to phthisis.

Remy[2] states that the ancient Hindus were familiar with tuberculosis and that it was described in the Vedas. Rey Miqueu[3] shows that it was recognized and treated by Susruta in India about as well as in Europe centuries later, at the time of the settlement of America.

Even prehistoric man in Europe suffered from tuberculosis, as shown by neolithic skeletal remains. Raymond states[4] that "one of the most frequent diseases of bone at that time was tuberculosis. Osteitis, peri-osteitis, fistulous tracts of osteomyelitis are common things. And there was Pott's disease." Bartels studied a vertebral kyphosis found in a neolithic burial at Heidelberg, and found the lesions of spinal tuberculosis. As the sick person had recovered, it must be admitted that he was cared for over a long period, "which invites reflection upon the family devotion of those distant ancestors." Egyptian monuments picture the characteristic hunchback from spinal tuberculosis,[5] and Elliot Smith and Ruffer describe the condition as found in a mummy of the twenty-first dynasty.

The bacterial causes of disease were of course unknown at the time of the conquest of America, and Galen's humoral theory accounted for everything. Naturally, therefore, tuberculosis was unknown as a general disease and the phthisis or ptisic, accompanied by hectic fever, constant cough, putrid expectoration, all increased by food, and marked also by sunken eyes, sharp nose, and wasted cheeks, which we can recognize as advanced consumption, was considered a solitary disease arising from cough and catarrh. When recognized it was hopeless, because Galen had said so, if for no other reason.*

I have found no mention by the writers of the conquest of phthisis, hectics, hunchbacks, or other recognizable tuberculosis in Indians, nothing to suggest that this disease existed in America. For many years Dr. Ales Hrdlicka has been engaged in the Bureau of American Ethnology in investigating the diseases of the Indians in historic and prehistoric times, and recently† he informed me in person that he had seen no evidence of tuberculosis in many thousands of pre-Columbian skeletons examined,‡ and he thinks that the disease did not exist in America before the coming of the whites.

* Thomas Sydenham did not recognize consumption at a much earlier stage than did Galen and Lopez de Villalobos, but he insisted that it was curable in some cases. "The principal assistant in the cure of this disease is riding on horseback every day, insomuch that whoever has recourse to this exercise in order to his cure, need not be tied down to observe any rules in point of diet, nor be debarred any kind of solid or liquid aliment, as the cure depends wholly upon exercise."

† February, 1932.

‡ The Smithsonian Institution has some fifteen thousand crania and forty thousand other bones of pre-Columbian Indians.

In view of what has been said, I was of the opinion before I visited Mexico that tuberculosis did not exist in America before the whites came. There I found evidence that forced me to doubt it. A little positive evidence outweighs much negative, so, despite my failure to find tuberculosis in the early writings and despite the most valued and weighty opinion of Dr. Hrdlicka to the contrary, I think it possible that the disease existed before the conquest. The evidence referred to is:

(1) The *Codice florentina* of Sahagun's history depicts clearly (Lamina XXV, No. 36) a hunchback with the most striking characteristic deformity resulting from tuberculosis of the dorsal spine. The date indicated in Aztec picture writing on the same page is clearly pre-Columbian, as I was informed by Sr. P. Aguirre of the Museo Nacional.

(2) In the Museo Nacional I saw two pottery jars in the form of hunchbacks, wrought with such skill that the facial expression as well as the characteristic deformity of spinal tuberculosis was shown. Sr. Aguirre assured me that these jars long antedated the conquest.

(3) Dr. H. A. Monday, for thirty years a resident of Mexico, an explorer and student, presented to me a small terracotta figure showing kyphosis, and assured me that he had excavated it from below the lava on the south side of Popocatepetl. This lava was laid down long before the conquest.

Although uncertain concerning the existence of pre-Columbian tuberculosis in America, I believe that Dr. Hrdlicka's statement that "It is to be assumed on purely logical grounds that the disease must have been less frequent among the Indians in former times, when they lived a more natural and active life, were better inured to hardships, and with exception of particular localities and periods, were better provided with suitable food," may be correct. In this case the prevalence and mortality of tuberculosis among the Indians in recent times is due to the social and economic changes consequent upon their contact with and partial conversion to modern civilization.*

PLEURISY AND PNEUMONIA

Pleurisy and pneumonia were not clearly differentiated by the physicians of the sixteenth and seventeenth centuries, except as this could be done, as it sometimes can, by the severity of the symptoms. Lopez de Villalobos knew the symptomatic differentiation well and he distinguished between the pathology of the two diseases by calling pleurisy an inflammation (*apostema*) over the ribs and pneumonia as the same condition inside the lung. But to the ordinary soldier or priest, writers of the history of the conquest, pneumonia, like pleurisy, was *mal* or *dolor de costado*, "pain in the side." This is mentioned by several writers of the conquest, but they all, like Bernal Díaz del Castillo, were writing of the trouble in Spaniards. Bernal Díaz noted that *mal de costado* was very quickly fatal in Mexico, a condition that still holds true and is supposed to be related to the altitude. He wrote, "This we observed to belong peculiarly to the climate of these countries: that in four days the mal de costado proves fatal, of which we had many instances among our soldiers, both in Tezcuco and in Cuyuacan." Writing of the period about November 1520, he said, "Though we did not suffer much in the field, continual fatigue had made us very unhealthy, five of our soldiers having died of mal de costado within two weeks."

Dazille found pneumonia and pleurisy very serious diseases of Negro slaves in Cayenne and Ile de France in the eighteenth century. I have found nothing to indicate whether or not the Indians knew either disease before the conquest. They are now very susceptible to both.

* See Appendix A, pp. 236–7.

DIPHTHERIA

Victor Reko[6] appears to regard *cocoliztli* as diphtheria. I know of no evidence supporting such a view, or of any throwing any light upon the existence of diphtheria in America at the time of the conquest. This is not very surprising, in view of the fact that diphtheria was not generally recognized as a specific disease until the nineteenth century, and that there is by no means unanimity of opinion as to the cause of the death of George Washington, who was attended by eminent physicians who diagnosed his case as *angina membranosa* or *cynanche trachealis*, both names descriptive of the disease that we now call diphtheria.[7] A fatal form of sore throat was reported as a new disease in Panama in 1600 (see Chapter II) and Farfan gave a description of sore throat in Mexico a few years earlier (1579) which must have included laryngeal diphtheria, as it began as follows: "If the sore throat begin with smothering, great pain and fever, and the inflammation and swelling are not seen either inside or outside the throat, it is a sign that it will kill the patient on the first or the second day."[8] However, I have found no evidence of great epidemics of the disease and no earlier description of it in America than that given by Farfan.

INFLUENZA AND COMMON COLDS

These affections, if they existed among either whites or Indians at the time of the conquest, have escaped mention or have been mentioned under such unidentifying terms as pestilence or rheuma. For example, Father Garnier wrote[9] that he had baptized sixty little children who had died of *un Rheume general*. The tranlator has rendered *rheume general* as influenza, but it was not necessarily such. As *rheuma* was then used it might have been almost any epidemic, and in view of the death of so many little children, it might well have been measles.

MODORRA AND MENINGITIS

A disease that wrought havoc among the Spaniards, who imported it to America early in the sixteenth century, was known as *modorra*. I am unable to identify it definitely, although there are some brief descriptions of it, the best being Díaz del Castillo's and Gómara's descriptions of the fatal illness of Luis Ponce de León, who was sent out to succeed Cortes.

Georg Sticker[10] expresses the opinion that the disease was epidemic cerebro-spinal meningitis, and the available information more nearly justifies that diagnosis than most others. He says:

> Epidemic cerebrospinal meningitis, according to my report in *Janus*, 1921, appeared on the Mexican coast at Vera Cruz and in Yucatan in 1526, and was an offshoot from the western European epidemic which occurred at the beginning of the 15th century. This epidemic had a predecessor in 1409 on the wharves of Biscay, according to the reports of Master Juan de Aviznon, the body surgeon of King Pedro I, who wrote Sevillan medicine in 1419. The great epidemic two generations later started as a military and naval disease in upper Italy in 1478 and was called *mal de zucch, mal zucho*, head blow, neck grab. It existed from 1494 in the Canary Islands and in Spain under the name of *modorra* or *modorilla* and was carried to Flanders by ships in 1501.

Whatever its nature, modorra is mentioned in America, at Darien in Panama, several years before the date given by Sticker, which is correct for its introduction to Mexico. The outbreak at Darien in 1514 is described by both Herrera and Andagoya and has been mentioned before. It accompanied a famine and we cannot know surely that in this instance the term modorra was not used to signify a state of extreme dullness, apathy, and coma marking the terminal stages of starvation; nor, on the other hand, that it was not an infection, such as meningitis, that had started on shipboard and spread widely and resulted fatally because of the lowered state of vitality of the starving men (see description of starvation in Chapter V). Herrera does not describe the disease or its symptoms, but he tells of the event as follows:[11] In 1514 Pedrarias returned from Spain, bringing enough people to found three towns. They wasted their rations, which were already beginning to spoil.

And when all of the King's rations were gone, the calamity of hunger grew to such an extent that many caballeros who had mortgaged great estates in Castile died begging bread; and others traded a shirt of scarlet silk and other rich clothing for a pound of corn bread, cassava or Spanish biscuit. One of the principal caballeros who had accompanied Pedrarias went into the street crying that he was dying of hunger, and falling on the ground before the whole town his soul left him. The like was never seen, that persons so adorned with silk and brocades worth great sums of money, should fall dead everywhere of hunger. . . . In one month seven hundred persons died of hunger and modorra.

Bernal Díaz del Castillo[12] thus describes the death of Luis Ponce de León:

He fell sick with modorra, and it was in this manner. Coming from the Franciscan monastery from hearing mass, he was taken with a high fever, and was for four days heavy with sleep and without his usual senses, and he slept most of the day and night, and his doctors [who are named] agreed that he should make confession and receive the holy Sacraments, and he did it willingly; and after having received them with humility and contrition, he made his will and designated the licenciate Marcos de Aguilar as acting governor. On the ninth day from his falling ill he yielded his soul to our Lord Jesus Christ.

Díaz also tells us that a hundred men of the ship that brought Ponce de León to Mexico died of this disease, and four of twelve Dominican friars also died of it.*

Gómara, who was Cortes's chaplain, tells us[13] of Ponce de León's death as follows:

One day the Licentiate Ponce went to hear mass at San Francisco [convent] and returned to his inn with a high fever, which was really modorra. He went to bed and was three days without consciousness, and his fever and stupor always increasing. He died on the seventh; he received the sacraments, made his will and left for his substitute the bachelor Marcos de Aguilar. Cortes wept for him as though it were his father. They buried him at San Francisco with great pomp, mourning and candles. Those who did not like Cortes said that he (Ponce de León) had died of poison, but the Licentiate Pero Lopez and Doctor Ojeda, who attended him, used the terms and the treatment for modorra, and they swore he had died of it, and they told also how the afternoon before he died he ordered a *baja* [a Flemish dance] to be played; and he lying on his bed walked it, as it were, with his feet marking the steps and counter-steps, a thing which many persons saw; and then he lost his speech, and that night he expired before the dawn. Few die dancing like this scholar. Of a hundred persons who embarked with the Licentiate Luis Ponce de León, the most died at sea or on the road within a few days after landing; and of a dozen Dominican friars, two. It was suspected that it must have been a pestilence which spread to others who were there, of which they died.

---

* Georg Sticker says (*Janus*, 1921, XXV, 105) that the lay description of the disease by Bernal Díaz del Castillo is very clear (*deutlich*), meaning that it clearly indicated meningitis. This does not seem to me to be true. I have just quoted what Díaz del Castillo said and his description would not at all justify a definite diagnosis of meningitis, and the agreement among the attendants that Ponce de León should make confession and receive the sacraments and make his will indicates that he could be roused from his stupor, which would not be probable if this were due to cerebral inflammation or to pressure from meningeal exudate.

Gómara's description of the death casts still more doubt on the diagnosis of meningitis.

The disease did not spread widely, which would accord with the diagnosis of meningitis, as this is not highly contagious in the absence of overcrowding, such as the passengers had been subjected to on board ship. Cortes wrote to the king that it had spread to some persons in the city and that two of them had died.

There is another and more plausible explanation of these deaths from modorra. I learned from various medical men in Mexico that the word is still in use there among the common people, but that it indicates a symptom rather than a specific disease, the condition that in English would be called lethargy, heavy somnolence, or light coma. Quite possibly it had the same or a similar meaning at the time of the conquest, but then, like cough, dropsy, jaundice, headache, fever, and many other symptoms, as we now regard them, it was considered a disease in itself. The causes of this condition are numerous and among them may be mentioned, as most familiar, poisoning by alcohol, opium, and other drugs. In addition, many diseases cause it, among them inflammation of the kidneys, obstruction of urine, diseases of the brain or its coverings such as encephalitis lethargica and meningitis, acidosis as seen in diabetes and in various diseases of the liver, and in starvation. Starvation is always a cause of acidosis[14] and it does not require a great effort of imagination to believe that the great famine that killed seven hundred men at Darien caused a lethargy or light coma before death, to which the term modorra, as used at present in Mexico, would be quite applicable.

It is not probable that Luis Ponce de León, a very high official, died of starvation, as he had left his ship and entered upon his duties in Mexico, but he was a man with great responsibilities and far enough along in years that he was a fit subject for one of the degenerative diseases that still kill many big men in middle life: arteriosclerosis, nephritis, enlarged prostate gland, degeneration of the heart muscle, cirrhosis of the liver, or even diabetes mellitus. Any one of these could as well cause lethargy, heavy somnolence, or coma as could meningitis.

There are a few other references by early historians to what may have been meningitis. Pedro de Cieza de León[15] tells us that "in the past year of 1546, when the Viceroy Blasco Nuñez Vela was involved in troubles with Gonzalo Pizarro and his consorts, there came a great pestilence throughout the kingdom of Peru, which began beyond Cuzco and spread through all the land: where innumerable people died. The disease was one which caused a pain in the head and very high fever and then the pain passed to the left ear and the disease got worse, so that the sick survived but two or three days." The passage of the pain to the left ear was probably either an artistic touch or a generalization based upon a special experience or observation.

Father Bruyas[16] tells of an epidemic at the Mission of Ste Marie, among the lower Iroquois, which he describes thus: "This country has been greatly afflicted this year [1672–73] by a kind of pestilence which began in June and ceased only in September. It was a fever of so malignant a character that in less than five days one would either recover or succumb to its violence. It was a sad spectacle for us to see brought into the village on all sides the dead and dying, whom two or three days of illness had either carried off or reduced to the last extremity. Most of those who were attacked by the disease felt such violent pains in the head that they lost their reason."

The Relations for 1661,[17] telling of a journey to the North Sea, state, "We were detained at Tadoussac by a kind of contagious disease, hitherto unknown, which swept away the greater number of those whom it attacked. Their deaths, however, were due only to the violence of the convulsions, by which they were shaken in the strangest manner, yielding up their lives as if desperate, or at least with contortions of the limbs which rendered a patient stronger than three or even four men together."

It cannot be stated positively that all of the epidemics described here were meningitis, or in fact that any of them was, but that seems a more probable diagnosis than most others.

At any rate, meningitis was never a major plague of the Indians in the sense that tuberculosis, malaria, smallpox, and measles were, and it did not greatly influence their fate or hasten their subjugation.

Chapter X

MAN, the greatest devourer of all living things, who takes his food and drink, both for life and pleasure, from the land, sea, and air and from the animal, vegetable, and mineral kingdoms, must appear to all living things to be saturated with blood and to smell of killing. He is himself, however, a prime form of food to countless organisms that munch, bite, and suck him as a tasty dish or an intoxicating liquor. These feeders upon him vary from submicroscopic life forms to such prosperous and unparticular gourmets as that model of evolution, that perfect example of adaptation to environment, the tapeworm.

We have seen already man's alliance with the insects, notably in these pages the mosquito and the louse, and it is well known that his relationship with the fly is commonly productive of results. It is a painful thought that rodents in contact with man almost invariably become dangerous. The importance of micro-organisms, tiny parasites, has been implicit in many parts of the book. But there is another large family of living things that finds man a most attractive host and that offers him in exchange a dreadful commerce in sickness and death: the family of worms. These may properly be considered in connection with a great group of diseases included under the heading "Intestinal Infections and Parasitic Worms."

Some of the intestinal infections played important parts in the story of the conquest. The dysenteries, bacillary and amoebic, are old woes in the story of mankind; they undoubtedly were responsible for local successes and failures of many endeavors. It is not clear whether either was indigenous to America; the best guess is that one was and the other was not. They fought equally against reds and whites, but took appalling toll of the blacks, who were the main importers, if they were imported at all. For all that they were so formidable, neither bacillary nor amoebic dysentery played a determining part in the invasion.

Another disease of extreme economic importance, although it is not one of the great killers, is hookworm. This is again a disease that was almost surely brought to America by the Negro. If so, it is the outstanding example of those diseases introduced as part of the conquest, having no great effect on the conquest, but being of tremendous import for later generations. Its cost has in all probability exceeded all the wealth ever produced by the institution of slavery. Man's war against hookworm has been waged more by Americans than by any other nationality, and its story marks another of the splendid pages of the United States Army Medical Corps and the United States Public Health Service.

With the Second World War and the launching of white troops once more into tropical jungles, the importance of many diseases whose very names were unknown to us has become more clear. With all our modern drugs, sanitation, and preventive medicine, we have had to learn all over again how dangerous a place the jungle is to the man who has not acquired an immunity to it. In Guadalcanal and New Guinea, as at Vera Cruz, Panama, and all along the line of the conquest, disease went to war again. If it has been so serious with us, we may well pause at thinking what it must have been three and four hundred years ago!

F.D.A.

Sickness in the Noonday: Intestinal Infections and Parasitic Worms

The most serious and most widespread and destructive infections of the intestine are typhoid fever and dysentery. Until the twentieth century they were the most destructive diseases of armies. Typhoid was always confused with typhus fever until well into the nineteenth century. It had no specific name and was not known as a distinct and separate disease. There are no descriptions of early American epidemics sufficiently clear-cut and definite to let us separate this disease from typhus and malaria on the one hand and from dysentery on the other, and it is impossible to say with any feeling of certainty whether or not it existed in the New World before the arrival of the Spaniards. I am of the opinion that it did not, mainly because I think that the evidence excludes typhus and malaria as pre-Hispanic diseases in America, and typhoid was most apt to pass as one of these.

DYSENTERY

Dysentery is the name for a group of symptoms that may be caused by infection with any one of several micro-organisms; but there are two important and widespread groups or types, the bacillary and the amoebic, due respectively to infection with any one of a certain group of bacteria (the bacilli of dysentery), or with a protozoal parasite, a pathogenic amoeba, *Entamoeba histolytica*. These are quite distinct diseases, resembling one another only in that, like typhoid, they are due to the ingestion of food or water contaminated by the intestinal discharges of another person who carries the infectious agent, and that they are both inflammations of the large intestine producing the usual symptoms of that condition: diarrhea, cramps, tenesmus, and frequent bloody stools. Bacillary dysentery and amoebic dysentery may exist together in the same patient, but they are as unrelated as are typhus and typhoid fevers. It is quite evident, therefore, that one of them might exist in a country that has no cases of the other. However, it was not until 1873 that the amoeba of dysentery was discovered, and it was much later that the bacilli of dysentery were identified. Before 1873 dysentery was dysentery, and it was nothing more.

That dysentery of this indefinite sort was a well-known disease of the Old World is demonstrable by many references, but two will suffice here. Herodotus[1] tells us that it wrought great destruction in Xerxes' retreating army as that monarch fled from Greece after the battle of Salamis, and in Acts 28:8 we are told that Paul healed the father of Publius of a fever and of a bloody flux, the latter being English for dysentery.

There is also evidence that dysentery existed in America at a very early date and probably before the conquest, as there are numerous references to epidemics of disease characterized by bloody stools. Typhoid fever at times shows this symptom but with no such constancy as does dysentery, nor is it usually the most marked feature of the disease, and a description of an epidemic or a case of sickness by mention of this one symptom justifies the assumption that it is dysentery. The disease was always common among Negro slaves, and it is quite probable that they brought one variety or another from Africa with them. The Professional Planter[2] said that it caused one half of all deaths among Negroes.

Benjamin Rush stated that it existed among the North American Indians before the coming of the whites, and the Jesuit Relations[3] tell of its epidemic prevalence among the Canadian Indians in 1610. One of the earliest of the Jesuits' converts to

INTESTINAL INFECTIONS, PARASITIC WORMS

Christianity, a Sagamore, died of it in that year. It is stated also[4] that the Indians always had dysentery in the autumn. It is again spoken of as very prevalent in 1660,[5] and in 1695 Father Lamberville wrote of a French and Indian army "reduced to such a bad condition through fevers and dysentery that the place to which it had proceeded was more like a hospital than a camp." That was an incident of military history frequently repeated in the United States until after the Spanish-American War,[6] and even in World War I there were extensive outbreaks of dysentery in the armies of all belligerents.[7]

The descriptions of the diseases at Jamestown are very imperfect and mostly lacking entirely, the record merely showing that such and such a man was sick or died. However, the Honorable George Percy, in his account of the epidemic that destroyed almost half of the colony in the late summer and early fall of 1607, begins thus: "The sixt of August, there died John Asbie, of the bloudie Flixe"; so there is no doubt of the existence of the disease there. However, there is room for doubt as to whether it had originated there, as the expedition had been five months at sea and had stopped at several places in the West Indies on the way out.

Another entry suggestive of endemic dysentery is found in the early history of Jamestown. In July 1608 John Smith with a party of twelve others set out to explore the Potomac and the country bordering it. Seven of these men were newly arrived in the country, "being all of the last supply," and within two days after leaving Jamestown they were taken "sicke almost to death, until they were seasoned to the country." One of them died but the others recovered, "notwithstanding their ill dyet, and bad lodging," and returned safely to Jamestown on September 7.

This account, with its reference to "seasoning," strongly suggests a self-immunizing, severe disease of relatively short duration, which all newcomers acquired. Its summer incidence, great prostration "almost to death," followed by improvement and recovery while continuing a hard voyage, suggest a bacillary dysentery. No other disease so well meets the specifications, especially in view of our knowledge of the existence of "bloudie Flixe" the previous summer.

We also know that dysentery was present at the settlement of Louisiana. La Salle had dysentery before he started on the expedition on which he lost his life, but he had come by way of the West Indies, had landed and rested and taken sick there, although it is not known whether he acquired his dysentery there or in Louisiana later.

At a still earlier period the unfortunate expedition of Pánfilo de Narváez for the conquest of Florida had apparently suffered from the same disease, as Núñez Cabeza de Vaca, who survived, tells us that of eighty men who reached Malhado Island, all but fifteen were soon dead, some of them certainly from hunger, others possibly from disease. "After this, the natives were visited by a disease of the bowels, from which half of their number died. They conceived that we had destroyed them, and believing it firmly, they concerted to despatch those of us who survived." *

However, one of them argued that the Spaniards themselves had died in just as great relative numbers, so it was not likely that they had sent the disease, and their lives were thus saved.†

---

* The diagnosis of dysentery is based upon the fact that it is the only disease of the bowels—except typhoid, which would probably have been described as a fever—apt to occur as a hightly fatal epidemic.

† *Naufragios de Alvar Núñez Cabeza de Vaca, y Relacion de la Jornada que hizo a la Florida con el Adelantado Pánfilo de Narváez*, in Vedia's *Historiadores primitivos*, Vol. I. This amazing story of ten years' wandering and suffering by the few survivors may be summarized as follows:

Set our from Bahia de la Cruz (Florida)	300	men,	40	horses
Drowned or killed on march	3	"	3	"
Killed by Indians at Bahia de Cavallos	10	"	0	"
Died from disease & hunger	40	"	0	"
Killed for food	0	"	37	"
Embarked in boats to seek Mexico	247	"		
Eventually reached Mexico	4	"		

There is a good English translation of this account by Buckingham Smith, published in New York in 1871.

A very great epidemic of what appears to have been dysentery was an incident of Nuño de Guzman's conquest of Nueva Galicia.* García del Pilar, Guzman's interpreter and apparently a rogue fitted for treasons, stratagems, and spoils, certainly for spoils, says that at Astatlan, near the South Sea, there was a great flood about September 20, 1529, after which, as the Indians accompanying Guzman were fatigued and long without necessary food, of more than eight thousand of them, all fell sick except about two hundred, who fled, for which act fifty of them who ventured to return were hanged. Nearly all of the Indians and some Spaniards died. Other Indians were obtained at Xalisco and of these two thousand died, while so many children died along the way as to make this the greatest tragedy in the world (*"que es la mayor pasion del mundo los niños que por este camino quedan muertos"*). This account would not justify a diagnosis of dysentery, but two others are more definite. Padre Fray Antonio Tello tells of a great flood in the valley of Acaporeta that would seem to be the same, although he puts it a year later. He says, "This flood lasted six days, after which the land was so swampy that the army had great difficulty in retiring to some hills to dry itself: but being there it was overwhelmed with plagues of toads and other unclean things: and the worst was that, as there was such hunger, many began to eat them and they caused bloody stools, from which died so many Indians of the army that out of twenty thousand of them, what with the flood, the famine and the pestilence, very few remained." An anonymous reporter ascribes a different cause to the disease. He says that the Indians of Culiacan had no food left except conserve of maguey made with honey, which gave them all bloody stools and they all died. Another anonymous reporter tells of the great flood, the famine, and the dysentery, from which most of the Indians

* There are several reports of this in Icazbalceta's *Colección de documentos para la historia de México*. The quotations relating to it are from some of these documents.

died. Still another says that the whole province was depopulated. ("*Por manera que esta provincia se vino a destruir e despoblar, que no hay agora casa ni señal della.*")

The acute outbreaks of epidemic dysentery described above suggest the bacillary type of the disease, as the amoebic is not so apt to occur in acute and large epidemics. Rather it is endemic and chronic; that is, it is constantly present in a region, affects many people but not all at once; its onset is usually insidious and it may have established chronicity before it attracts much attention. Furthermore, its incubation period is much longer and much more variable, so that it would not be so apt to seem related to a single definite event, such as a flood or the arrival of strangers.

Other signs differentiating a prevalent amoebic dysentery from the bacillary are the relatively frequent complication of the former by abscess of the liver and the results of treatment with ipecac or its derivatives. These last have no influence upon bacillary dysentery, while they constitute the best and a practically specific treatment for the amoebic variety. By these signs we may know that amoebic dysentery was common in the West Indies and Brazil in the seventeenth century.

Dysentery was the chief cause of the terrible mortality among slaves on the slave ships, a mortality often reaching from 25 to 65 per cent in the trip of two or three months. It is much more frequently mentioned by the old slavers than any other disease, and we frequently find such statements as the following: "White flux, which is the inveterate distemper that most affects them, and ruins our voyages by their mortality"; "very great mortality from flux"; "slaves in very bad condition, flux and Small Pox having made great destruction amongst them"; "lost 14 whites and 320 blacks from white flux."

There were few if any cargoes that were free from this disease. What its type was is unknown. Its epidemic prevalence in ships suggests the bacillary type, but the hardships and dep-

INTESTINAL INFECTIONS, PARASITIC WORMS

rivations to which slaves were subjected on the march, at the trading post, and on ships might have so reduced vitality as to cause latent amoebiasis to become active and epidemic.

Colonel William Byrd wrote of an epidemic of "Blood Flux, that was brought us in the negro-ship consigned to Colo. Braxton."

Jean Baptiste Labat tells us (*Nouveau voyage aux isles de l'Amérique*) that in 1699 at Martinique he was sick with double tertian fever and with dysentery, but that the latter was cured by the use of ipecac, which was regarded as a specific treatment. Cabanés[8] says that ipecac was first made known in France in 1672, but that Pison and Maregraf had found it used by natives of Brazil as a cure for dysentery in 1648, and a Portuguese monk had written of its use during his residence in Brazil from 1570 to 1600, or at least of the use of *igpecaya* or *pegaya*, which was probably the same.

This drug has a romantic early history that may interest those who have not read it. In 1686 a young Dutch doctor in Paris, named Helvetius, heard of it from a druggist who had received some from a friend in the West Indies. Helvetius got some of it and tried it on dysenteric cases with such success that he arranged for a regular supply from the druggist, advertised it widely, treated great numbers and finally the Dauphin, whom he cured. He interested Madame de Sévigné and many of the nobility, became a royal physician, and rose to wealth and high office. Ipecac was known as Helvetius' powder. The name Helvetius was made more lastingly famous by the grandson of our Dutch doctor who was the philosopher Helvetius. Dr. Helvetius was sued by his druggist friend for a share in his profits, but unto every one that hath shall be given, and from him that hath not shall be taken away, so the doctor won the suit. Helvetius' great success with ipecac strongly suggests that the common dysentery of France in the late seventeenth century was amoebic.

Later, Dr. Thomas Dover (1660–1742), English buccaneer

of the Spanish Main, having retired from the piracy in which he had made a fortune, and in the course of which he had rescued Alexander Selkirk, the original of Defoe's Robinson Crusoe, added opium, saltpeter, and sulphate of potash to Helvetius' powder, thus making the still famous Dover's powder, a diaphoretic and anodyne medicine useful in many conditions other than dysentery. Dover's powders have eased more pain than Dover's piracy caused and possibly saved more lives than it sacrificed. Dr. Dover's works still bless him; Pirate Dover has been forgotten, thus completely reversing the poet's statement that

> The evil men do lives after them:
> The good is oft interred with their bones.

Similarly, in our own day, former pirates in the business world turn to good works after "getting theirs" and become philanthropists and public benefactors.

Unlike most of the marvelous drugs found in America in the fifteenth and sixteenth centuries, such as sassafras, sarsaparilla, and guiac, ipecac is still regarded as of great value, and its alkaloid and active principle, emetine, enters into the most modern treatment of amoebic infections.

Another form of dysentery is caused by a large protozoal parasite, *Balantidium coli*. This is normally a parasite of the pig, which was not indigenous to America. Its occurrence in America must have followed the whites. Schistosomal infection may also manifest itself as dysentery, but that disease is discussed elsewhere.

In conclusion it may be stated that dysentery existed very early in the history of the conquest; but that it is impossible to say definitely whether both bacillary and amoebic dysentery existed before the arrival of the whites. There is reason to believe that both varieties existed in the Old World and both are now common in America. I think it possible, even probable, that bacillary dysentery was indigenous and that the amoebic

INTESTINAL INFECTIONS, PARASITIC WORMS 165

was introduced to America. The arguments for this are the occurrence of the "white" dysentery of slave ships, previously mentioned, and the frequent occurrence of liver abscess, a common complication of amoebic dysentery, in slaves, together with the fact that the dysentery among Indians of which we read in the early histories was always in the form of acute epidemics, and therefore probably bacillary in type. Shattuck[9] states that at the present time the mortality in Yucatan is enormous and that 39 per cent of it is due to intestinal disorders. "A large proportion of diarrhoeas, and probably most of those in young children, are attributable to bacillary infection or to indigestion and the same is true of a considerable remaining portion of diarrhoea in older children and adults. . . . There is reason to believe that, in Yucatan, a very large proportion of cases of clinical dysentery showing blood and mucus in the stools is caused by Entamoeba histolytica."

HOOKWORM

Since 1899, when Bailey K. Ashford, an assistant surgeon in the U.S. Army, determined that the tropical anemia prevailing everywhere in Porto Rico was due to infestation with hookworm, and especially since Charles Wardell Stiles determined in 1902 that the common hookworm in most parts of North and South America and the adjacent islands is a species first differentiated and named by him *Necator americanus*, that parasite has received an amount of notoriety and advertisement so great as to be enjoyed by no other parasite and by few soaps, mouthwashes, cigarettes, or other publicity pests. In 1909 the Rockefeller Sanitary Commission for the Eradication of Hookworm was organized and was authorized by Mr. John D. Rockefeller to call upon him for sums up to a total of one million dollars for carrying on an aggressive campaign against the disease. Five years later the work was taken over by the International Health Board of the Rockefeller Foundation, which enlarged its scope to include many warm countries. Working in conjunction with various state and national governments, the Rockefeller Foundation spent millions of dollars in initiating campaigns for the respective states and countries to carry forward. That institution and those states and countries were and are all convinced that hookworm infestation is one of the major problems of tropical pathology and tropical sanitation. There is no doubt that this problem existed long before, but its nature was not recognized, nor was the ease and simplicity of its solution known. Most reading persons and the inhabitants of many warm countries now know that the hookworm is a small parasitic worm, which attaches itself to the wall of the small intestine of man or other animals, lives on its host's blood, the loss of which causes severe anemia that can be readily corrected by appropriate use of iron. Meanwhile the parasites produce enormous numbers of eggs, which are passed from the host's bowel, hatch, and undergo part of their life cycle in moist soil and thereafter penetrate the skin of the feet of a new host, pass thence to the right heart, thence to the lungs, up the trachea to the throat, and thence by way of the stomach to the intestine, where the cycle begins again. The curative treatment lies in the administration of certain drugs that kill or expel the worms; the preventive is found in such disposal of intestinal discharges as to prevent the pollution of surface soil, and the use of shoes to protect the feet from contact with polluted soil. The good resulting from the application of these simple measures has been such as to constitute one of the major triumphs of tropical and subtropical medicine.

In 1920 the Rockefeller Foundation published a bibliography of hookworm embracing 5,680 titles. It is possible that the list has since doubled. No attempt will be made to analyze or discuss this enormous amount of writing, but a few quotations will serve to show the seriousness of the disease. Sir Patrick Manson said "that in many tropical countries, because

INTESTINAL INFECTIONS, PARASITIC WORMS 167

of the dangerous cachexia to which it gives rise, it amounts to a positive curse."

Mr. Rockefeller, before pouring millions into hookworm eradication, had a thorough investigation made as to the importance of the disease, and wrote of the result as follows: "The wide distribution and serious effects of this malady, particularly in the rural districts of our Southern States, first pointed out by Dr. Charles Wardell Stiles . . . have now been confirmed by independent observations of other distinguished investigators as well as educators and public men of the South." In consequence he endowed the Hookworm Commission.

Bailey K. Ashford states[10] that in 1902, 90 per cent of the rural inhabitants of Porto Rico were infested with hookworm, and that 70 per cent of them were actually sick as a consequence. Treatment had resulted in an improvement of 60 per cent in the efficiency of laborers treated. Stiles[11] considered the number of infected persons in the United States to be at least two million, and that the economic loss due to infection was at least fifty million dollars annually, possibly twice as much. Among the evils resulting from the infection, in addition to the anemia, stunted growth, physical debility, and increased susceptibility to other diseases, he enumerated scarcity and inefficiency of labor, lowered standards of home, inhibited mental development, increased illiteracy, and a tendency to wear out early, especially noticeable in child-bearing women. Victor G. Heiser, director of the Bureau of Health of the Philippine Islands, wrote[12] that the annual death rate in Bilibid prison was 200 per 1,000 prisoners in 1905. General sanitary and dietetic measures reduced this to 75 per 1,000, and there it remained. "A study of the hospital patients showed that they were dying with ailments which should not have killed them. Their powers of resistance were evidently impaired." Eighty-four per cent of the prisoners were found to harbor intestinal worms; 52 per cent had hookworms. Treatment for this condition was instituted and the death rate fell to less than 20 per 1,000. "The records of the prison show that there was a most marked reduction in the incidence of all diseases, which demonstrates in a most conclusive manner that parasitic intestinal infections are not only of direct harm to the human organism, but their indirect effect in lowering the resistance of an individual to disease is also of the utmost importance."

The annual report of the Rockefeller Foundation for 1920 says that "hookworm is one of the most serious of the disabling diseases of man."

Although hookworm infestation as a cause of serious, widespread, and sometimes mortal disease is of recent discovery, especially as related to rural life, less recent as relating to miners and tunnel workers, certain symptoms and results of such infestation were long recognized as economically important to the slave traffic. In 1670 Du Tertre[13] spoke of *mal d'estomac* among the Negroes. Jean Baptiste Labat[14] spoke of *mal d'estomac* as very severe among Negroes, especially in Brazil, giving them a very bad color and often degenerating into dropsy. Pouppé Desportes[15] described the disease as *cachexie* or *mal d'estomac* with earth eating as a prominent symptom.

The Professional Planter[16] described *mal d'estomac* and dirt eating as synonymous terms for the designation of a severe disease among slaves. James Thomson[17] described under the head of dirt eating the very severe anemia of Negroes. He regarded the earth eating as a vice deliberately indulged in through melancholy, revenge, dissatisfaction, etc., and his treatment was mainly punishment. He also said, "Formerly whole gangs of newly-imported negroes resorted to this custom with the most fatal consequences, particularly those from the Angola country." This shows that the poor creatures were badly infested when imported.

David Mason[18] gave a good description of severe hookworm

disease in Jamaican Negroes under the title "*Atrophia ventriculi, mal d'estomac* or Dirt-eating." F. W. Cragin[19] wrote of the same disease in Negroes of the West Indies and of Guiana as *cachexia Africana*, dirt-eating, and *mal d'estomac*. He said that "no age beyond three or four years at the farthest enjoys an immunity from its ravages." John Imray[20] wrote of "*cachexia africana*, dirt-eating of the English, *mal d'estomac* of the French," as a disease peculiar to the Negro race and very destructive among the black people of the West Indies. Ulrich Bonnell Phillips[21] says that dirt eating was recognized as a factor in the high mortality among slaves newly imported from Africa. But none of the early writers and none of their contemporaries knew that the severe disease they described was due to an infestation with a small worm, so they had no rational idea as to its treatment and were practically helpless before it. This continued even for many years after the discovery of the worm in 1838. It was not known to cause disease until 1853, when it was recognized as a widespread danger and a successful treatment was found. H. Rey wrote in that same year[22] that hookworm was the cause of much severe disease in Brazil, West Africa, the West Indies, French Guiana, and other tropical places, but it was only after Stiles's discovery of *Necator americanus*, Ashford's finding that it was a main cause of disease in Porto Rico, and Stiles's studies on its prevalence in our southern states that the disease was recognized as having a world-wide rural distribution in warm countries.

The name *Necator americanus* was given to the variety of worm found almost alone in America, from Paraguay and the Argentine to the Ohio River, because it was not then known elsewhere and was supposed to be the New World hookworm. Later investigations have shown that it is also the common hookworm of all Africa south of Egypt and the Sahara, and also of southern India, Ceylon, and many Pacific islands. Samuel T. Darling[23] thought that "the primitive distribution of *Ancylostoma duodenale* seems to have been limited to regions north of 20° north latitude, while *Necator americanus* was distributed south of this line," that migration from the one area to the other would result in a mingling of species, and that important light might be shed upon prehistoric migrations by a study of the hookworms found among peoples. He shared in the opinion, first advanced by R. T. Leiper, but now accepted by practically all investigators, that Africa was the source of America's hookworm, which was introduced by slaves. This opinion is much strengthened by the finding that *Necator americanus* is not only widespread in those parts of Africa from which slaves were sent to America, but that it is also a parasite of the long inaccessible Pygmies[24] and of the chimpanzee.[25] Stiles and Hassell[26] say that it has also been reported in the gorilla and the rhinoceros.

These facts, plus the additional one that *Necator* is practically the only hookworm in the southern states, although the white population of those states came almost entirely from countries where it is not found, and the other fact, already cited, that for a long time the disease that we now recognize as due to hookworm was looked upon in Brazil, the West Indies, and our South as a disease peculiar to Negro slaves, force us to the conviction that Leiper's suggestion was correct and that *Necator americanus* came to America with Negro slaves, thereby assisting in raising the price upon slavery to a degree far exceeding its worth, to such an extent that we are still paying heavily.*

OTHER INTESTINAL WORMS

I have nowhere come across any contemporary discussions of intestinal worms as afflicting the fifteenth- or sixteenth-century Spanish settlements or the seventeenth-century English or French settlements. They were recognized by the

* For further notes on hookworm see Appendix A, pp. 237-8.

eighteenth-century writers as common in slaves and in armies. They were regarded as rather a normal part of life for such low creatures as slaves and soldiers, much as were lice, although it was recognized that they occasionally caused serious troubles by balling in great masses in the bowels, by crawling into the bile ducts or the nasal sinuses or by perforating the bowel.

James Thomson in his *Diseases of Negroes* says that "of all complaints this [worms] is the one the planter should make himself most completely master of, from its varied appearance, fatality, and being so much under his power of judicious management."

Sir John Pringle[27] said that "both fevers and fluxes are often accompanied with worms, which are not to be considered as the cause of either, but as a sign of the bad state of the bowels, of the corruption of the aliment, and of the weakness of the intestines, owing to the heat, the moisture, and the putrid state of the air." Van Swieten also attributed them to bad or corrupted food. Strangely enough, the belief in their spontaneous generation was nearly, if not quite, universal.

In the early nineteenth century they are reported as common in Canadian Indians, but I find no mention of them in the Indians at the time of the first settlements.

Being such commonplace things among the whites, they might well have escaped mention had they been common among Indians, but Benjamin Rush stated that they were rare among them late in the eighteenth century. This negative sort of evidence, if it have any value at all, points to the absence of such parasites before the whites came.

However, in Mexico I was convinced that the ascarids or common roundworms were present prior to the conquest. The facsimile reproduction of Sahagun's work published by the Mexican government shows[28] an Aztec painting depicting the passage of lumbricoids by both man and dog, and Sr. P.

Aguirre of the National Museum informed me that there could be no doubt that the picture related to a pre-Columbian date.

TAPEWORMS. The common tapeworms of men are *Taenia solium*, which passes one phase of its life in the hog; *Taenia saginata*, which passes its encysted state in the beef animal; *Hymenolepsis nana*, a parasite of the rat; and *Dibothryocephalus latum*, which man gets from fish, formerly only the European sturgeon. This last worm has been introduced into America in recent years by immigrants from Russia and Finland. The others were certainly introduced, as their necessary animal hosts, ox, pig,* and rat, were all importations. The Indians had dogs. Whether or not these carried the dog tapeworm, or *Echinococcus*, now common in Argentina and Uruguay, is not known.

Another type of parasitic worm, trichina, which infests human muscle and soft tissues, sometimes with very serious or fatal results, is obtained by man from pork. It also is an importation, but as its existence was not known until within a century, there is no means of telling when it came to America.

SCHISTOSOMIASIS. Still another parasitic worm found in the West Indies and South America is the blood fluke, *Schistosoma mansoni*, a worm that resides in the portal vein or its branches, whence its sharp-spined eggs are discharged to be eliminated through the rectum, bowel, or bladder, principally the rectum, where they set up severe inflammation with dysenteric symptoms or formation of irritable, bleeding, tumor-like masses. The liver often shows cirrhosis and the spleen enlargement. Schistosomal infection is incapacitating, often completely and painfully so, and occasionally fatal.

* The peccary is indigenous to South and Central America and some of our own southwestern states, and it is mentioned by the early Spanish writers as a pig with its navel in the middle of the back, the supposed navel being a large sebaceous gland. However, the peccary was never domesticated, and because of its strong flavor rarely eaten, and it is not probable that it was the host of either the pork tapeworm or of trichina.

INTESTINAL INFECTIONS, PARASITIC WORMS

Schistosoma mansoni is found only in hot countries, its distribution probably being limited by that of the water snails of the genus *Planorbis*, in which it undergoes a part of its life cycle. There has long been known in Brazil, under the name of *bicho*, an endemic, contagious disease of unknown causation and characterized by dysenteric symptoms leading to prolapse and gangrene of the rectum, or to chronic disease of the colon. The accounts of it correspond sufficiently to Manson's description of intestinal schistosomiasis to suggest that they are the same disease.

Schistosoma mansoni is almost certainly an importation to America through slaves. This opinion is based upon the facts that the worm is not a common parasite in America, that it occurs mainly in that part of South America that includes coastal Venezuela and Brazil and the Amazon Valley, and in some West Indian islands, and that it is found nowhere else in the world except in Africa. Schistosomiasis has been found in Egyptian mummies.

FILARIAL WORMS. The most common filarial parasite of man is *Filaria bancrofti*, a hairlike worm three to four inches in length, which lives in the lymphatic vessels and obstructs them, causing elephantiasis, chylous urine, and other symptoms. The embryos or microfilariae circulate in the blood, especially at night, and may be imbibed by mosquitoes, in the tissues of which they undergo a phase of development culminating in the salivary glands and the proboscis of the insect, whence they enter the skin of another host that the insect bites. Two or more species of mosquito may play the insect host.

The deformities caused by elephantiasis are so striking, at times so monstrous, that no one seeing them can fail to be impressed, and no curious writer, such as were most or all of the old Spanish chroniclers of the New World, would have failed to mention the condition had he seen it. As none of them, so far as I have seen, does mention it, I am inclined to believe that it did not exist in America in their day. At the present time it occurs in all tropical America, as it does in all tropical Africa, Asia, and Australia. It was probably introduced to America with slaves, as the Europeans were not apt to have had the parasite in their home countries.

ONCHOCERCA. A parasite that has excited much interest recently because of the large amount of blindness that it produces in Honduras and southern Mexico is the *Onchocerca volvulus*, a filarial worm that lives in lymph spaces in or beneath the skin, where it causes small tumor-like swellings varying in size from a pea to a pigeon's egg. It is transmitted by a small blood-sucking fly (*Simulium damnosum*), as *F. bancrofti* is transmitted by mosquitoes. The eye lesions that it causes are associated with fever and inflammation, and frequently result in blindness.

This worm has been recognized in America only since 1915, although it was known on the west coast of Africa and in the Congo basin for a quarter of a century before that. It was probably brought to America by Negro slaves.

THE GUINEA WORM. *Dracunculus medinensis*, the Guinea worm, much larger than the filaria, lives in the connective tissue until ready to produce young, when it pierces the skin, usually of the feet or legs, and discharges the embryos into water. There they undergo a phase of development in a *Cyclops*, with which they may be swallowed in water to infect a new host. Widely spread in Africa and in some parts of Asia, it is known in America only in a small part of Brazil, where it was probably introduced with slaves.

It was described in 1599 by Diego Rodriguez de Valdes y de la Vanda, governor of the Plata provinces, as "worms that occur on the coast of Minas, which are maggots that breed in the legs and other parts, keep growing and become two or three varas long, and I here saw two withdrawn from prisoners whom we had captured." [29]

Chapter XI

> What dire offence from am'rous causes springs,
> What mighty contests rise from trivial things . . .
> Pope: *Rape of the Lock*

To the ordinary reader it is probable that no investigation of the origin of disease would be more intriguing than that of syphilis. This horrible plague, visiting the sins of the fathers on the children unto the third and fourth generation, all the more hideous because it makes no distinction between pure love and the grossest passion, is perhaps the most frightening and spectacular of all in our long catalogue of woes. More coarse and loathsome than smallpox itself, it arises out of exaltation or loneliness; it is the by-product of intense emotion, with which smallpox has nothing to do. As deliberate as tuberculosis, it exhibits a maiming cruelty that tuberculosis does not. More widespread geographically than malaria, it does more than debilitate the mind as malaria does; it destroys it. And, unlike malaria, it may lie long in wait and pass from parents to innocent children.

It exists in both hemispheres and there is no important disease whose origin is more in dispute. The doubtful honor of infecting half a world is claimed for both sides of the Atlantic. The sad fact is that in a sense it does not matter in the least, so far as the result is concerned. For a result of the conquest of America was that the venereal diseases, including syphilis and gonorrhea, spread all over the world. Some hold the whites brought it to the Indians. If so, they brought the red men "curses greater than were inflicted by the bloodthirsty gods of the Aztecs or the Incas." Others say the giving was the other way. If so, "the Indian thereby inflicted a more potent revenge upon his conquerors than he was ever able to obtain by warfare, cultivated hatred and studied cruelty, and the end is not yet."

F.D.A.

The Kiss of Death: Syphilis

Soon after the discovery of America, Europe suffered from a widespread epidemic of the French pox, *morbus gallicus, mal franzoso, bösen Blattern, grosse vérole,* bubas, English disease, German disease, Polish disease, Turkish disease, Spanish disease, Neapolitan disease, disease of Hispaniola, or new disease, all names applied to the disease now known to us as syphilis. It also spread widely in Spanish America, and practically all of the early historians mention its prevalence there, and many of them (Las Casas, Oviedo, Sahagun, Gómara, Herrera), as well as medical writers (Ruy Díaz de Isla, Lopez de Villalobos, Juan Cárdenas, Francisco Hernandez), state that it originated in America. So common was this belief in the early sixteenth century that its acceptance was practically general. Astruc, the leading French writer on the subject in the eighteenth century, as well as Iwan Bloch and others of our own day, fully accepted this view.

Jeanselme states that the earliest claim for the Old World origin of the disease was advanced by André Alcazar in 1575.[1]

In the past four hundred years there has been much speculation and more than a little controversy as to the place of origin of syphilis, and a very extensive literature has grown up in regard to it, but opinion is yet deeply divided, a very impos-

THE KISS OF DEATH: SYPHILIS 177

ing group of writers, especially of the moderns, arguing that it was of Old World origin.

Those who believe this claim documentary support for their views in various literary, official, and medical writings, but the weak point in their argument is one of nomenclature, the meaning of certain terms such as *grosse vérole*, *gros mal*, and even of *morbus gallicus*, used in them, and the nature of genital lesions described in them as ulcers, inflammation, gangrene, rotting, etc. Some of these terms, *grosse vérole* and *morbus gallicus*, in later times meant syphilis. That they meant it prior to Columbus's voyages is not so certain. This uncertainty as to the meaning of medical terms applies to many diseases other than syphilis. The leprosy of the Bible and of the Middle Ages is scarcely identifiable with the leprosy of today. It was in those old times regarded and feared as a highly contagious disease often transmitted by sexual intercourse. The term almost certainly covered other skin diseases and possibly syphilis, as we now know that the communicability of leprosy is low and that numerous attempts to inoculate it have been uniformly unsuccessful. Some writers believe that much of the leprosy in medieval Europe was syphilis, and we know that as syphilis became generally recognized, leprosy ceased to be common. In Mexico, after the conquest, the term *gran lepra*, great leprosy, was applied to smallpox, to distinguish it from measles or *pequeña lepra*, little leprosy.[2] Pulmonary tuberculosis and pneumonia were in the sixteenth century commonly confused with pleurisy or *mal de costado*, "the pain in the side." Such well-known and common diseases as typhoid fever and diphtheria were not recognized as distinct diseases until the nineteenth century, and until then gonorrhea, chancroid, and syphilis were grouped together as "the venereal disease." Such being the case, it is not surprising that there should be confusion as to those diseases in the fifteenth and earlier centuries. Some writers, notably Astruc, definitely denied that there was any form of venereal disease in Europe prior to Columbus's voyages. However, the proof of the earlier existence of venereal disease, including gonorrhea, sores, ulcers, and "rotting" of the genitals, seems clear. Whether or not there was syphilis is debatable. After 1495, the evidence as to that also is clear. In addition to the uncertainty as to the meaning of terms in the pre-Columbian literature, there is also dispute as to dates of certain documents that were given key positions by those arguing for Old World origin.[3] Hans Haustein[4] cites some of these as proof of his contention that the disease came from America. There is similar dispute as to the pathology of certain pre-Columbian bones that have been adduced as evidence of ancient, Old World syphilis.

The theory of the American origin of syphilis rests upon the undoubtedly rapid spread of the disease after Columbus's first and second voyages, upon the generally accepted belief of the early sixteenth century, and upon the finding of apparently syphilitic bones of supposedly pre-Columbian origin. Some such bones, taken from Indian mounds of the Mississippi Valley, are no longer considered pre-Columbian, and so great a student of Indian bones as Dr. Ales Hrdlicka, who has for many years been studying the American Indian and the great number of pre-Columbian skeletons in the Smithsonian Institution, believes that no syphilitic bone has been found in Indian burials that are clearly pre-Columbian.

On the other hand, Tello[5] pictures bones that he believes both syphilitic and pre-Columbian, and so recently as July 1930 he and W. U. Williams describe[6] new finds of bones that their descriptions and pictures of the site and method of burial seem to prove pre-Columbian. Examination of these bones, their gross and microscopic appearance, Roentgen examination, and cross section point to syphilis. Professor G. Elliot Smith[7] states that he had personally examined about thirty thousand bodies of ancient Egyptians and that there is no evidence of syphilis existing in Egypt before modern times.

Joseph L. Miller[8] concludes that "There is no evidence in

THE KISS OF DEATH: SYPHILIS 179

ancient manuscripts or ancient bones that syphilis had existed in the Eastern continent prior to the discovery of America." It is thus seen that there is complete disagreement as to the meaning of such tangible facts as necrosed or thickened bones of pre-Columbian burial in both the old world and the new. Writers on both sides cite some of the same writings respectively to prove and to disprove the existence of the disease in Europe before 1493.

Jeanselme's scholarly, thorough, and scientific *Traité de la syphilis*[9] has just come to hand. A careful review of all the evidence leaves him a believer in the American origin of syphilis. Astruc's citations to prove the disease of American origin appeal to some minds as stronger proofs to the contrary than some of the writings of Sudhoff and Sticker on the other side, great as is the erudition and extensive as are the investigations of these writers. These have been most powerful and important in leading much of the modern medical world to believe in the Old World origin of syphilis, mainly by citing fifteenth-century writings of pre-Columbian dates in which mention is made of the French disease, *grosse vérole*, *gros mal*, or *bösen Blattern*.

Writers on both sides of the controversy agree that syphilis spread widely soon after the siege of Naples (February to May, 1495) by Charles VIII of France and that it then for the first time received much attention from writers, all of whom regarded it as a new disease. Whether or not Charles's stay at Naples should be called a siege is doubtful, as it is said that he was welcomed by the inhabitants and that his army fraternized with the people, besieging a few fortresses for two or three weeks. His army suffered a frightful morbidity and mortality and as syphilis became widely recognized in 1495 and 1496, it became a widely held belief that the army's mortality was due to syphilis and that the scattering of the disbanded mercenaries, French, Swiss, Spanish, English, Hungarians, Italians, and Slavs, had spread it over Europe. So widespread was the disease that some writers[10] contended that it could not have been spread by venereal contacts but was air-borne. The general belief of that time was that the disease had been brought to Europe from America in 1493 by Columbus's men, that they had introduced it to Spain, that Spanish soldiers in Charles's army had taken it to Naples and there infected the women,* who in turn infected the rest of the army, which in turn infected Europe.

Sudhoff says that the French mortality at Naples was due to typhoid fever. He denies that there was an epidemic of syphilis at the time.[11] "And what of the much heralded epidemic in Naples from March to May, 1495? It is empty 'historical' babble. Careful researches in the Neapolitan archives and in all the old chronicles leave no doubt as to this. . . . For the frightful decimation of the garrison at Naples, under the Duke of Montpensier and the Constable d'Aubigny, during the winter, spring and summer of 1495–1496, typhoid fever, and not syphilis, was demonstrably responsible."

Thom[12] says, "The detailed accounts which have come down to us agree far better with the description of acute and chronic farcy than they do with syphilis," and he thinks it more than a coincidence that there was an epizootic of glanders among the horses of the French army at the time.

There are three very important and early writings supporting the American origin of syphilis. The first is the *Tractado contra el mal serpentino: que vulgarmente en España es llamado bubas que fue ordenado en el ospital de todos los santos de Lisbona: fecho por Ruy Díaz de Ysla*. This book is often referred to but is exceedingly rare, as indicated by the fact that there is no copy in the British Museum, none in the Bibliothèque Nationale of Paris, none in our Library of Congress. The Huntington Library of San Marino, California, has a copy,

---

* Jeanselme (*op. cit.*, I, 78) states that 800 prostitutes accompanied Charles's army. Many may have been infected and infectious before Naples was reached.

and the Army Medical Library* possesses a photostatic reproduction made from it. The book is dedicated to King Juan III of Portugal and was published in 1539, but the writer states in his prologue that it had been his intention to present it to King Manuel, the father of King Juan, but since it had pleased the Lord God to call Manuel to his glory, he asked Juan to accept the book and protect him from copyists. Inasmuch as Manuel died in 1523, the book must have been at least partly written before that time. There was a later and somewhat changed edition in 1542, which I have not seen.

The second very important writer on the subject was Fray Bartolomé de Las Casas, the best and most useful friend the Indian race ever had, and the most severe critic of Spanish treatment of the Indians. He went to the Indies in 1503 and spent the greater part of his life there and he wrote[13] that bubas, which in Italy was called *el mal frances*, was taken from Hispaniola when Columbus returned from his first voyage and that it then infected the air of Seville (or was spread in some other way), where Las Casas was at the time. "I was at times diligent in asking the Indians of this Isle [Hispaniola] if this disease was very ancient here, and they said that it was, before the Christians had come and that there was no memory of its origin, and of this there can be no doubt." (*"Yo hice algunas veces diligencia en preguntar a' los Indios desta Isla si era en ella muy antiquo este mal, y respondian que si, antes que los cristianos a ello viniesen, sin haber de su origen memoria, y desto ninguno debe dudar."*)

Thirdly, Oviedo[14] wrote that he was informed by friends, whom he named, including the pilots Vicente Yanez Pincon and Hernan Perez Matheos, that they saw bubas in the island at the time of Columbus's first and third voyages, and by two others who had gone out with Columbus on his second voyage and were still living in Santo Domingo when Oviedo wrote, in the same city, that they had seen it at that time.

* Now the Surgeon General's Library.

(Columbus's son tells us[15] that on his arrival at Santo Domingo on August 30, 1498, Columbus found "all the families of the island in great tumult and sedition, from which many people were already dead, and there remained only 160 men, full of the French disease.")

The value of the testimony of Las Casas and Oviedo is impaired by the facts that both wrote a full generation after Columbus's first voyage,* that neither was a medical man or was primarily interested in syphilis, and we cannot know just what they included under the term *buas* or *bubas*. Their use of the words was probably even looser than that of the physicians of the day. Possibly they used the term as loosely as did Juan Cárdenas, a writer on medicine and a professor in the University of Mexico, who said that bubas was both hot and cold (in complexion), that everybody had it, and that there were seventy kinds of it, including gout, sciatica, headache, asthma, pain in the stomach, and other diseases of the sort. With such an all-inclusive definition, it would not be very difficult to prove that the disease existed anywhere and had always done so. What the Indians told Las Casas and what his friends told Oviedo may possibly have related to other diseases.

Sahagun is also quoted by Bloch and others to prove the American origin of syphilis, but I value his testimony only lightly, as he was not a medical man and he wrote half a century after the conquest. Furthermore, there are other things discussed by Sahagun in his description of Aztec medicine that the Aztecs could not have known prior to the conquest. We know definitely that smallpox and iron weapons were both of Spanish introduction, yet the treatment of the scars of smallpox and of wounds made by iron weapons constitute a part of Sahagun's chapter on Aztec medicine.

The rapidity and extent of the spread of syphilis in the final

* Las Casas began his history in 1527 and finished it in 1560. Oviedo's first volume appeared in 1526.

THE KISS OF DEATH: SYPHILIS 183

years of the fifteenth century and the early decades of the sixteenth century suggest a state of sexual promiscuity not since equaled. Manners and morals vary with time and place, and it is possible that in that Rabelaisean period and under such leadership and example as were furnished by Pope Alexander VI, Emperor Charles V, King Henry VIII of England, and Francis, all reputed syphilitics, and by that clergy whose incontinence and corruption so many medieval writers scourged and ridiculed, this may have been true. And the sale of indulgences tended only to increase the evil. "From Innocent III in 1215 to Leo X in 1512, nine great world councils were held, with church reform in the fore front of the programme, yet each in turn confessed the failure of its predecessors, and the Council of Trent (1545) testified to the impotence of all."

Then too the land was distressed from wars. The Hundred Years' War between France and England was not so far behind that recovery could have been complete. Constantinople was in the hands of the Turk, who threatened Europe by way of Austria. The rise of the house of Hapsburg was not a wholly peaceful event; the wars of Charles V involved much of Europe. Robber barons and mercenary bands were existing evils. The Moors and the Jews had been expelled from Spain, and elsewhere religious persecutions throve and religious wars were beginning. The Inquisition, become a terrible economic burden, was rejuvenated by a bull of Innocent VIII in 1484, making it a sin to question the reality of witchcraft.

Sticker informs us that about 1495 bad weather and spoiled crops were followed by famine and that great suffering and much disease afflicted Europe. There was much movement of people hunting work. Men left home and traveled in search of employment. Among the migrants were also many beggars, students, and girls. These conditions approached those described for Russia in 1921–23.[16]

Under such circumstances and as a new and strange disease,

poorly treated, highly virulent, and occurring in very unhygienic conditions, syphilis had opportunities for nonvenereal spread that may not have been equaled since until the Russian famine of 1921–23. Of this, Gantt wrote:[17]

> In Russia there was not only social reason why syphilis should increase, but another important one absent in other countries—the lack of means of treatment: there were no arsenicals and few institutes. Overcrowding and filth contributed their share toward the increase. Under such conditions [the augmented chances of infection and the lack of treatment] syphilis mounted until in 1922 Dr. Semashko said that 80 per cent of the population was infected in some sections (L. H. Guest). In 1923 doctors from northwestern Russia reported to me that 95 per cent of the population of their districts were syphilitic and the available supply of arsphenamine was far too small. In the same year the disease was so prevalent that I saw many who had been infected by other than sexual means—primary lesions in the nose, etc., whole families infected by ordinary contact under the extreme conditions of filth.

Many modern medical historians, Sudhoff, Sticker, Garrison, Flores, and others, think that syphilis had long existed in Europe, was well known to prostitutes, barber surgeons, and the disreputable fringe of society, who were able to treat it effectively as soon as it became widely known, although the reputable physicians were not. Possibly, as Sudhoff suggests, "The convenient and effective form of publicity that we call printing played no small part in the new recognition of an ancient evil." Sudhoff has published facsimile reproductions of ten tracts or printed pamphlets on the disease that were published between 1495 and March 1498.

A few writers, among them Thom, believe that syphilis was of ancient standing in both hemispheres, having been taken to America by the East Asiatic stock from which the American Indians were derived. Keizo Dohi,[18] after a careful investigation of ancient Chinese and Japanese writings, thinks that syphilis was taken to the Orient by the Portuguese.

Ferdinand Thugut[19] believes that it was a quite new disease originating from the union of the white and Indian races. He thinks that prior to 1492 syphilis had never existed in the world, but that when the Spaniards reached America either they or, more probably, the Indians were carriers of a harmless, saprophytic, spirochetal parasite, the ancestor of the *Treponema pallidum*, the germ of syphilis. In the new and strange incubator and culture medium of the bodies of the other race, it developed pathogenic properties and caused a new disease. "In the bridal night of the two races was syphilis conceived." The disease so developed, if carried to Europe by even one man, would serve to start the epidemic that followed.

A fifth view is that syphilis is a derivative from the tropical disease yaws, probably African, a view expressed in the seventeenth century by Sydenham, and today held by Admiral Stitt[20] and actively championed by Captain Butler of the Medical Corps of the U.S. Navy.[21] The two diseases have many points of clinical resemblance, they are caused by organisms morphologically indistinguishable (*Treponema pallidum* and *T. pertenue*), and they give cross reactions of immunity.

However, it is to be noted that Schöbl, whose work on immunity is cited by Butler as proof of the unity of the diseases, himself says:[22]

The experimental evidence that has come to light through our researches, which shows that reciprocal immunity exists between yaws and syphilis, does not prove that the two diseases are one and the same, appears at first sight. On the contrary, the difference in immunologic conditions existing in yaws and syphilis, both in animals and humans, as well as the difference in the behavior of the two infections with regard to cross immunity, shows plainly that fundamental immunologic differences exist between yaws and syphilis. The differences, like those of the tissue selectivity of the respective parasites, the pathology, pathogenesis, clinical course, transmission, geographic and age distribution, stand in complete agreement with the fundamental biologic distinction between the parasite that causes yaws and the parasite that causes syphilis.

There is no one of these five views that has not its weak points, that has not been opposed and combated. Possibly the truth may never be known.

I bring no original observations upon the subject, but I incline to believe that some, if not all, venereal diseases were brought to America by the whites. I am influenced to this opinion by the following facts, which I cite without argument or discussion.

(1) The fifteenth chapter of Leviticus suggests that Moses knew gonorrhea.

(2) Herodotus tells of Scythians who were diverted from an invasion of Egypt by gifts from Psammiticus and on their way home pillaged the temple of Celestial Venus in Ascalon, being punished therefor, as were their posterity, by a "female disease" inflicted by the goddess.*

Articles in Russian medical journals[24] discussing the spread of venereal disease in Russian villages in recent years led me to

---

* Herodotus says,[23] "Thence they marched against Egypt: and when they were in the part of Syria called Palestine, Psammiticus King of Egypt met them and persuaded them with gifts and prayers to come no further. So they turned back, and when they came on their way to the city of Ascalon in Syria, most of the Scythians passed by and did no harm, but a few remained behind and plundered the temple of Heavenly Aphrodite. This temple, as I learn from what I hear, is the oldest of all the temples of the goddess. . . . But the Scythians who pillaged the temple and all their descendants after them, were afflicted by the goddess with the 'female' sickness: insomuch that the Scythians say that this is the cause of their disease, and that those who come to Scythia can see there the plight of the men whom they call *enareis*." In a footnote the translator states that the derivation of *enareis* is uncertain but that in another place (Book IV, 67) it is used as equivalent to *androgynos*.

consult Russian friends as to the conditions before the Revolution, and the information obtained seemed to me to bear a relation to Herodotus' statement. Briefly, that information was to the effect that when a peasant in a Russian village in the days of the czars was known or believed to have venereal disease, he was shunned by all his fellows, was regarded as unfit for marriage and as outside the circle of men fit for women, and he was called by the Russian name *porchennyi*, meaning "tainted," signifying these things. The village of his residence was shunned by people of other villages and strangers were warned against it as a place of business. Since the Revolution, which has been a revolution of religion, standards, manners, and morals, as well as of economic and political conditions, the facts as to venereal disease and its spread have changed. It is very interesting to speculate as to the relationship of the ancient *enareis* and the modern *porchennyi*.

(3) Hippocrates[25] speaks of "inflammation of the genitals, ulcerations, swellings inside and out, swellings in the groins . . . the genital parts the sites of many fungosities." One of his aphorisms (Aphorism 4 of Section VI) seems to me to point clearly to syphilis. (This aphorism reads in Greek, "*Ta perimadara helkea kakoethes.*" Francis Adams, in his English translation of *The Genuine Works of Hippocrates*, renders this, "Ulcers attended with falling off of the hair, are *mali moris*." Littre, in his French translation, renders it, "*Les ulcères autour desquels le poil tombe sont de mauvaise nature.*" Either translation is compatible with the belief that Hippocrates was writing of syphilis. That is pre-eminently the disease with which ulceration and falling of the hair are associated. Adams's phrase that the association is *mali moris*, or due to bad manners, bad habits, or bad manner of life, certainly suggests venereal disease. On the other hand, Littre's phrase *mauvaise nature* is still used in French to characterize syphilis, *une maladie de mauvaise nature*, and at a time before

mercurial treatment of that disease was known, it was of as evil a nature as could be imagined. This was true at the end of the fifteenth and the beginning of the sixteenth centuries.)

(4) Josephus Flavius says[26] that Apion had an ulcer on his person that rendered circumcision essential. The operation brought no relief and gangrene set in, causing death.

(5) Aurelius Cornelius Celsus (53 B.C.–A.D. 7) tells us enough of diseases of the *partes obscoenae* to indicate that he may have been familiar with the three common venereal diseases.[27]

(6) Astruc[28] cites and tries to prove of no importance in the controversy as to the origin of the venereal diseases the following writers in regard to them prior to 1492:

Gulielmus de Saliceto, who wrote in 1270 of buboes and of corruption, pustules and similar diseases of the genitals caused by commerce with impure women; Lanfranc, who wrote similarly in 1390; Bernard Gordon, of Montpellier, who wrote of the same in 1200; John of Gaddesden, who wrote of them in his *Rosa Anglica* in 1310; Guy de Chauliac, who wrote of them in 1360; Valescus de Taranta, who wrote of them in 1400; Petrus d'Argelata, who wrote of them before his death in 1423.

(7) Both Astruc and his assailant, Richard le Brun,[29] quote from a statute of 1347 of Jeanne I, Queen of the Two Sicilies and Countess of Provence, concerning the discipline of a public house of debauchery in Avignon, in which it is provided that the abbess or *baillive* in charge and a surgeon visit each courtesan every Saturday, and if any be found to have contracted disease coming from lewdness (*"mal vengut de paillardiso"*), she is to be separated from the others and to remain apart, so as to avoid the evil that youth might acquire.

(8) Aneurysm is now known to be almost always due to syphilis. The fair assumption in a case of aneurysm is that the sufferer has had or has syphilis and a positive Wassermann re-

action is expected. Where the one disease prevails the other exists. There were two well-known operations for the treatment of aneurysm long before the discovery of America, that devised by Antyllus in the second century and that by Aetius in the sixth century of the Christian era.[30] Galen was quite familiar with aneurysm and described it, distinctly differentiating traumatic aneurysm, due to injury and most often to wounds of arteries in the performance of the bloodletting that was very common in his day as for centuries after him, from that due to "aboundance." [31] As aneurysm is not due to abundance, unless it be that "abundance of naughtiness" that St. James advises us to cast away,* it is quite possible that Galen was dealing with persons who had aneurysm because they had had too great abundance of carnal joys, had lived "after the flesh" too abundantly.

(9) Benjamin Rush states[32] that the Indians had no venereal diseases until after the whites came. He was writing toward the end of the eighteenth century, of the Indians of the English colonies.

Conclusion: It seems probable that the three common and widespread venereal diseases, syphilis, gonorrhea, and chancroid, were introduced to America by the white conquerors. If this be true, they thereby placed upon the poor Indians curses greater than were inflicted by the bloodthirsty gods of the Aztecs or the Incas of Peru, agelong afflictions, potent causes of miscarriages, still births, and infant mortality, of sexual sterility, blindness, insanity, and nervous disease, cardiac and vascular disease, much invalidism and many deaths, lasting causes of decadence of individuals and of race.

Possibly, however, the transfer of syphilis (not of gonorrhea and chancroid) was in the opposite direction, from America to Europe. If so, the Indian thereby inflicted a more

* St. James 1: 21, Douay version. The King James version renders this "superfluity of naughtiness."

potent revenge upon his conquerors than he was ever able to obtain by warfare, cultivated hatred, and studied cruelty, and the end is not yet.

In either event, the discovery and conquest of America by the whites resulted in the infection of a world hemisphere with disease of tragic nature, thriving upon a primal instinct and proving the direful spring of woes unnumbered.*

* For further notes on syphilis see Appendix A, pp. 238-40.

Chapter XII

EVEN yet the pitiful story of the slave ships cannot be closed. We have done with the great killers and broad canvases, but in leprosy and trachoma we have two more diseases that probably came to America with the Negroes. The second of these, while not decisive in the conquest itself, has been one of the Indians' worst plagues since, possibly ranking next to tuberculosis. A third group of related diseases known under the general heading of leishmaniasis is discussed because of its possible association with the conquest.

F.D.A.

Skin for Skin: Leprosy, Leishmaniasis, and Trachoma

LEPROSY

True leprosy may be grouped with cancer as practically incurable,* a cause of great suffering, an unsolved problem of

* This statement as written plainly needs amendment. Most skin cancer is curable, and many other types, if properly diagnosed and treated, may be either cured or alleviated.–Ed.

medicine, but so rare even where most prevalent as not to be important in the history of America. However, it has an importance for us as a part of the general subject of the medical history of the conquest, and also because, like the terms pestilence and plague, it for centuries covered a multitude of diseases, one of them possibly syphilis. As mentioned in the chapter on syphilis, leprosy disappeared rapidly as that became known, and before its disappearance was believed by all Europe to be highly contagious and to be transmitted by sexual intercourse. So great and thorough an investigator as Hirsch lays emphasis on these facts and implies that it was more than a coincidence.[1]

As for leprosy in America, most investigators are of opinion that it was brought to the Western Hemisphere by Negro slaves. Its prevalence in Spain, France, and England before the time of the earliest settlements would suggest that it might have come from those countries, but those who have investigated the subject usually agree that the Negro was the main source of this disease. Hirsch, whose encyclopedic work has been the standard reference book on the geography of disease for a half century past, says that leprosy was unknown in the Western Hemisphere until after the arrival of the Negro. Raymond[2] says the same thing, and Munro was convinced of it.

The early historians and writers of the conquest make no mention of the disease. No bones of pre-Columbian Indians show it.

There was but one contributor to the Berlin Lepra-Conferenz in 1897 who believed that the disease was indigenous to America. Domingo Orvañanos said, "There can be no doubt that leprosy existed in this country [Mexico] long before the Conquest as Hernan Cortes established a leper hospital in Mexico and there is no reason to believe that the Spaniards communicated the disease to the Indians, as the latter would not have presented any signs of its existence within the first years of the Conquest, seeing that the incubation of leprosy generally requires several years."

We have already seen that the diagnosis of leprosy at that time was very uncertain, and that in Mexico in the early years of the conquest the term leprosy was used for smallpox (*gran lepra*) and measles (*pequeña lepra*). The foundation of a so-called leper hospital is no proof of the existence of true leprosy.* As for the incubation period and rapidity of spread of that disease, attention is invited to the experience of the island of Narau, to be detailed below,† and to the fact that the period of the conquest of Mexico was a period of terrible epidemics and hardships among the Indians.

Leprosy, although contagious, is so to a low degree; its incubation period is long and its development is slow, and it cannot possibly occur in acute epidemics, like those of smallpox, measles, or even syphilis. But once introduced in numbers to a country, it tends to establish itself and become endemic. For example, it was apparently first introduced to the Hawaiian Islands about 1842 and by 1865 there were 230 known cases.[3] How many of these were imported cases is not known. The disease first reached New Caledonia in 1865; in 1888 the lepers numbered a thousand.[4]

Justin Foley Donovan[5] said that all writers agreed that the

---

* I have not myself seen proof that Cortes did found a leper hospital, although the statement is made by many writers. By his will he left endowment for three philanthropies: (1) a hospital dedicated to the Immaculate Conception; (2) a convent for nuns; (3) a college for missionaries. See J. O'K. Murray, *Catholic Heroes and Heroines of America*. New York, 1896. During a recent trip to Mexico I made inquiry as to whether or not Cortes had founded a leper hospital, and I was assured by eminent specialists in Mexican history, among them Sr. Federico Gomez de Orozco of the Department of History of the National Museum of Mexico, Sr. Licenciado Don Ezequiel Chaves, and Dr. Ignacio Alcocer, that he had not. I have since found (p. 166, *Bibliografía mexicana del siglo XVI*, by Icazbalceta) that the San Lazaro Hospital in Mexico City was founded by Dr. Pedro Lopez in 1572.

† See pp. 240–2.

disease was introduced to Jamaica by slaves from the west coast of Africa. T. Broes van Dort[6] said it was introduced to the Dutch colonies by the Negroes. In my readings of the historians of the conquest I found no mention of the disease.

I think that leprosy, like malaria, yellow fever, smallpox, and several other diseases, should be charged to the account of Negro slavery. Although not of great importance historically and without influence upon the progress of the conquest, it is for the individual that it afflicts one of the heaviest curses, misery long drawn out and frequently death in life.

LEISHMANIASIS

There are three or four diseases found in different parts of the world and presenting different clinical pictures that are grouped under the name leishmaniasis or leishmaniosis, for the reason that all show the presence, as the apparent cause, of a protozoan parasite known as *Leishmania*, which can be grown in test tubes and then shows a flagellate stage.

These diseases are *kala-azar* of India and China, oriental sore, Aleppo boil, or *bouton d'Orient* of the Near East, infantile and canine leishmaniasis of the Mediterranean littoral, and a disease found in tropical America under the names of *uta*, *espundia, bouton de Bahia,* forest yaws, and other local names, and as naso-pharyngeal leishmaniasis. This last name is descriptive of the most common form of the American disease and serves to differentiate it from *kala-azar*, which is a general disease with serious anemia and marked changes in the spleen and liver, but not from oriental sore. This last may affect the mouth and nose, and conversely, American leishmaniasis may and sometimes does appear on the limbs, the trunk, the neck, or the ears. These two forms of cutaneous leishmaniasis bear much resemblance to one another.[7]

The disease may cause extensive destruction of the tissues

involved, and certain clay water bottles or *huacos* found in ancient Peruvian graves and appearing to show loss of the upper lip or deformity of the nose have been cited as proof that it was pre-Columbian in America.

However, these *huacos* have also been cited as proof of pre-Columbian leprosy and syphilis. I have examined published pictures of bottles thus cited and have also examined *huacos* in the Smithsonian National Museum in Washington. Some of these show a loss of the lip but also the presence of tusks, both upper and lower, suggesting those of a boar. My opinion, that of a person without any special knowledge of such pottery, is that the *huacos* are in most instances mere grotesqueries, and that to attempt to diagnose disease from them is scarcely less grotesque than they.

Whether leishmaniasis existed before the conquest is unknown. Although now found from Yucatan to Peru and the Argentine and said to be very common in Paraguay,[8] it is not definitely known to be ancient in any of the countries or to have had any influence upon the course of the history of any of them.

Victor A. Reko's statement[9] that leishmaniasis or anything suggesting it was mentioned by Bernal Díaz del Castillo in his description of Cortes's expedition into Honduras is wholly without foundation, so far as I have been able to determine by a careful reading of this author's account (Chs. CLXXIV to CXCI). The expedition extended over two years and three months and was marked by the greatest hardship and privation. Díaz tells of much sickness, many deaths, and some desertions, but time after time, and apparently with complete justification, he ascribes them to lack of food and excess of exertion. He seldom describes the symptoms of the sicknesses, and never any that remotely suggest leishmaniasis. The same is true of Cortes's account of the expedition, as written from Temuxtitan to the king in September 1526.

TRACHOMA

We have seen the statement that trachoma is today one of the most serious afflictions of the American Indians, among whom it is a frequent cause of blindness.

I have found no mention of this disease by the early historians, but that is not at all surprising, for had they seen its direful effects they would have considered it only blindness, or mentioned it as such, and we know that the causes of blindness are numerous and varied. Juan de Cárdenas stated in 1591[10] that blindness was common among the Mexicans, but he attributed it to wine, garlic, venery, dust, wind, beans, and smoke. Whether or not trachoma was a cause we cannot tell, but even if it were such at that time, seventy years after the conquest, the fact would prove nothing as to its existence before the conquest.

William Bosman[11] wrote that among slaves refused by traders were such as had film over their eyes. This may have referred to trachomatous pannus.

William Mackenzie[12] describes a severe and very acute epidemic of ophthalmia on the French slave ship *Le Rodeur*, in 1819. The disease broke out during the voyage, fifteen days after leaving Africa, and first among the Negroes, who, to the number of 160, were crowded together in the hold. When these unfortunate people were taken up on deck, because the fresh air seemed to have a favorable influence on the ophthalmia, many threw themselves overboard, so that the practice had to be abandoned. There was a great shortage of water on the trip, the drinking allowance being for a time but half a pint a day, later four ounces. Soon one of the sailors developed ophthalmia, and three days later the captain and almost the whole crew were taken down with the disease, so that it was only with the greatest difficulty that the ship could be brought to port. Of the 160 Negroes, 39 lost both eyes and 12 one eye each; of the 22 of the crew, 12 lost both eyes and 5 one eye each. This account suggests that ophthalmia also was a part of the price of slavery. In this instance again the black's relative immunity to a disease helps him to supplant the nonimmune. Naturally almost immune to trachoma, the Negro could and did suffer from it when it started under the horrible conditions obtaining on a slave ship that was undergoing a water famine. He thus became a transporter and spreader of it. Possibly, as in Egypt, it was here complicated and aggravated by gonorrheal infection. In ordinary conditions on land his immunity asserted itself; the Indian's nonimmunity made him a sacrifice.

However introduced to America, trachoma is today a terrible scourge to the Indians, but there is no record that it was ever so prevalent among them in their fighting days as to have materially influenced the progress of white settlement. It was another curse laid on the race, like poverty, hunger, and ignorance.*

* For further notes on trachoma see pp. 142-4.

Chapter XIII

IT REMAINS only to deal with a motley collection of diseases that are either common in America today or that, for one reason or another, may have been important during or after the conquest and may have been directly related to it. And so our story, or rather one single chapter in the whole long story of the effect of disease on history, closes.

The author's main task was not to write of all diseases, but only of those that either influenced the conquest of America itself, or, coming to the New World with the conquest, have largely affected its history since. The only other task confronting the author was to consider why certain other important or interesting sicknesses did not belong in either of these two classes.

The white man, by early in the eighteenth century, securely held both continents, north and south. His own fraternal quarrels as to who should be master in the new house grew more fierce. Old rivalries sharpened. There were fresh Indian wars, but the greatest of these were struggles in which the surviving red men took sides with one white master against another. The issue of the conquest was settled and behind it lasting results began to appear.

Among these results were permanently established diseases, most of them still important factors in life today and some of them of gigantic dimensions in social and economic terms. To this total the Indian contributed very little; the white man smallpox, measles, possibly typhus, possibly the venereal diseases, and surely some of the respiratory diseases; the Negro paid his way with a legacy of malaria, yellow fever, hookworm, probably dysentery, possibly syphilis, and numerous lesser maladies. There are those who hear only the thunder of the captains and the shouting; others see only the banners, the parchments, and the ledgers; but for still others there echo also down the corridors of time the groans and feverish tossing of the sick and the hungry and the weak. And a further question rises in one's mind. Granted the large effect of disease on the conquest of America, how did it happen that the white man suffered so relatively little? What was it that made this race better able to withstand the blows of illness than the Indian or the Negro? In the answer to this question may lie one of the clues to the future.

Meanwhile the strain and tumult of the conquest is long since past. Red, white, and black, men dwell today scarcely hearkening to the murmurs of old wars and the aching of old scars. Both the Indian and the Negro have increased in numbers in recent years, though not very many of either race are of pure blood any longer. The very causes of the original invasion have been forgotten. Minerals, not gold, have long since been produced in value exceeding all the cargoes of the galleons; oil alone has outflowed all the treasures of kings and conquistadores. The harvests of North America exceed all the produce of Europe, and where ships were wrecked or men and women perished of hunger there are roads and lighthouses and hospitals, and men have forgotten how frightening the wilderness could be.

F.D.A.

Landwehr: Miscellaneous Diseases

A large number of diseases have not been mentioned thus far because there is little or no evidence to show whether they were indigenous or introduced to America, or because they are unimportant in the history of the conquest.

A disease may be of vital importance to the person afflicted with it, of large importance to the race and to medicine, yet have practically no influence upon history. Cancer is an example. Often fatal to the individual, one of the great unsolved problems of medicine, apparently increasing in frequency, cancer is still so rare that it could not influence the history of any country, unless by causing the disability or death of a leading man.

Other diseases, such as dengue, may be widespread but do so little serious harm as to be unimportant in the large historical sense. The principal importance of dengue in relation to our subject is its symptomatic and epidemiologic resemblance to yellow fever, and such help as that fact affords us.

Another disease, tularemia, is apparently of American origin, certainly is best known in America, and is a serious disease in man and animals, but it is of recent recognition and there is no possible way in which we may know whether or not it existed at the time of the conquest.

Certain diseases, such as plague and cholera, are so obviously Old World diseases, such rare visitors to America, and so certain to excite interested comment when they occur, that we can be practically certain that they were not introduced during the conquest.

For the reasons given above and others equally good, it is not desirable that we try to discuss nearly all diseases. There are, however, certain ones other than those already considered that may be mentioned because we have some fairly reliable information regarding them, because they are American in origin, or because it is interesting to speculate in regard to them.

SUPPURATION

Among the very greatest afflictions of mankind in all parts of the world today is suppuration or infection by the germs that cause pus formation. It is doubtful if even syphilis, tuberculosis, or malaria is of greater importance. Such infections cause boils, abscesses, quinsy, osteomyelitis, septicemia or blood poisoning, most puerperal or childbed fevers, harmful infections of wounds and fractures, earache and mastoiditis and their complications, appendicitis and peritonitis, and many tragic things that made every surgical operation a menace to life until after Joseph Lister practiced and taught antisepsis. So universal are these infections or the opportunities for acquiring them that it is hard to conceive of a practical world without them. Did they exist in pre-Columbian America? We do not know and it is improbable that we ever shall know, but a few things suggest that they either did not exist or were very infrequent. The first of such things was the practice of trephining in ancient Peru. Trephining, or the removal of parts of the bony covering of the brain, is an operation that is very apt to result fatally if infection follows it. For this reason it was a major operation to be resorted to only for the purpose of saving life, and highly fatal until after the introduction of antisepsis. Yet the ancient Peruvians, who knew little of medicine in general, performed this operation frequently, with the crudest instruments of stone or copper, often repeatedly on the same individual, and very often successfully, as shown by smoothly healed bone margins or extensive formation of new bone. It would certainly seem that experience must have taught them that the operation (which was commonly done for depressed fractures and other head injuries) usually did more good than its avoidance. Had pus infections been common this would not have been true, as it was not true in Europe and the United States a century ago.

Bones of ancient Peru also show that its people did successful amputations, with recovery following.

The Indians of the northern United States and Canada habitually practiced as initiatory trials for young men such things as passing pieces of wood with attached thongs beneath the pectoral muscles, fastening buffalo skulls to the thongs, and having the young men drag the skulls until the muscles and skin tore and released the anchoring sticks. Such injuries should have resulted in very serious infections had pus-forming germs been common.

On the other hand, Indian burial places commonly yield a high proportion of skeletons of young women, suggesting that childbirth was a frequent cause of death. However, there are numerous risks in childbirth other than infection. All those incident to disproportion of size between mother and child, to deformities or obstruction of the maternal pelvis, to unusual presentation of the child, to unusual and dangerous insertions of the placenta, would be apt to result in death in a large proportion of cases, death hastened rather than retarded by the crude efforts to assist the sufferer.

Flores[1] says that suppuration, boils, and abscesses were well known and wisely treated by the ancient Mexicans, but the only evidence he advances in proof of his statements are quotations from Sahagun and the existence of native words for the troubles, both of which carry little weight for reasons already set forth (see chapter on malaria). In addition it is feared that Flores is somewhat like Hernandez, the sixteenth-century *protomédico*, prone to project his own knowledge of disease to the Indians.

The medical reader of Bernal Díaz del Castillo cannot but

be greatly impressed by the number of wounds suffered by Cortes's men and by the promptness with which they healed and the men returned to duty. Old Bernal stated that he had himself been wounded more than forty times. Carvajal tells us[2] that a detachment from Orellano's party descending the Amazon in 1542 was surrounded by a large party of Indians and all were wounded, one mortally, several seriously. "The Captain ordered that the wounded, of whom there were eighteen, be treated, and there was no means of treatment except a certain charm, and with the aid of our Lord all were well within fifteen days, except the one who died."

Sahagun writes of suppurations and abscesses and the methods of treating them, but there is no clear indication that these troubles were common, or even that they existed before the coming of the Spaniards.

There is a possibility that there was no suppuration in America before the coming of the Spaniards. There is no proof of it. There is good evidence that it was much less common than at present. Even so recently as fifty years ago it is related that operation wounds at Fort Washakie uniformly healed by first intention. General W. H. Arthur, Medical Corps, U.S.A., retired, explained this as follows: "I believe this was due to the fact that the remote, sparsely settled, dry country itself was sterile, that no pathogenic organisms had been introduced and that, though I was surgically dirty, I couldn't infect my cases. I do not remember ever having any pus all the time I was at that station."[3]

RICKETS, PELLAGRA, AND BERIBERI

We have seen that the Canadian Indians had scurvy the year of Cartier's first settlement and that they knew a remedy and showed it to Cartier. It is improbable that the Indians south of the Potomac often had this trouble, as they could get fresh food, animal or vegetable, at practically all times.

That all Indians occasionally suffered from famines we have also seen. It is probable that certain deprivation symptoms that have been regarded as diseases, such as hunger edema or dropsy, occurred at such times. Probably this was what Master George Percy referred to among the Jamestown settlers as "the swelling," which caused numerous deaths.

There is no evidence of other deficiency diseases until long after the whites came. The first known was rickets, the only one marking the bones. No bones of pre-Columbian Indians show it. Because of the Indian's open-air life, his abundant exposure to the sun, and his free use of animal fats, it is not likely that rickets was ever common before he became semicivilized, and his inability to refine his flour, together with his use of all kinds of food, would almost certainly prevent beriberi.

We know that both pellagra and beriberi exist in considerable parts of America today, and xerophthalmia, a disease of the eyes due to deficiency of the fat-soluble vitamin, is said to be rather common in children in Yucatan, usually as the result of a fat-deficient diet popularly used in the treatment of dysentery, which is very common.[4] To what extent these diseases prevailed before the conquest, if at all, is quite unknown. The same dietary deficiencies as now cause them could have produced them then.

ENDOCRINE DISEASES

There is a group of diseases, larger almost each year, that is due to disorders of the so-called ductless glands. These include goiter of various types, all of them diseases of the thyroid gland; Addison's disease and certain other troubles due to diseases of the suprarenal glands; *diabetes mellitus*, due to disease of the pancreas; *diabetes insipidus*, giantism, some forms of dwarfism, and adiposogenital disease, due to disorders of the pituitary gland; certain bone diseases and disorders of calcium metabolism due to disorders of the parathyroid glands; eunuchoidism, due to testicular deficiency; certain menstrual and metabolic disorders due to ovarian deficiency; and some other troubles of lesser frequency.

The old writers speak of the occurrence and treatment of goiter, but I have seen no accounts by which I can identify any of the other disorders named. However, they were not recognized in Europe at the time of the conquest, with the exception of giantism and dwarfism, the causes of which were unknown, and they could as well have been unrecognized in America. There is no sufficient proof that they did not exist.

ALLERGIC DISEASES

There is a considerable group of diseases, not all well understood, that seem to be due to personal peculiarities, usually to peculiar sensitization of the tissues to substances of extracorporeal origin. Such substances are usually of protein nature. The best-known examples of such diseases are the serum sickness that sometimes follows the injection of horse serum; the food idiosyncrasies shown by certain individuals to certain articles of food, one person being made violently ill by a trace of egg in any food, another by milk, another by fish, another by strawberries, etc.; asthma caused by horse dandruff, dog hair; hay fever due to ragweed and other pollens; and many cases of eczema.

There is frequent mention by the old writers on Mexican medicine of asthma and of eruptions, pustules, and crusts that may have been eczematous. All this group of diseases being due to sensitizations that may be brought about in various ways in healthy people, it is probable that the Indians suffered from them before the whites came, as well as afterward. There is no reason to think that the conquest had any influence in introducing or diffusing such diseases.

WEIL'S DISEASE (SPIROCHETAL JAUNDICE)

Adolf Weil in 1886 described an acute fever associated with jaundice, splenic enlargement, tendency to hemorrhages from the mucous membranes, and kidney inflammation, and often resulting in death. The disease was called by his name and was thought to be rare and something of a curiosity until World War I, when considerable outbreaks of it occurred in Gallipoli, Salonika, and Egypt. In 1915 Japanese investigators showed that it was due to a leptospiral infection. The germ *Leptospira icterohaemorrhagica*, which resembles somewhat the spirochete that causes syphilis, is found in the blood, urine, and sputum of the sick and as a harmless parasite of rats. Being harmless in the rat, the leptospira has probably long been a parasite of that animal and was introduced to America with it. While not important in relation to the conquest of America, the disease is of interest here because it was apparently found by Noguchi in tropical America and mistaken for yellow fever, for which reason he named the parasite that he found *Leptospira icteroides*. (See chapter on yellow fever.)

PINTA

Pinta or pinto is a contagious skin disease showing peculiar pigmented patches, at present believed to be due to the growth of certain fungi in the upper layers of the skin, although its nature and causes are not definitely determined, and interesting research in regard to it is now being carried on in Mexico. In some parts of that country it is very common, a recent census showing that among 21,586 persons examined in and about Oaxaca, there were 12,609 cases. The census recognized eight colors of spots on the skin, yellow, red, mulberry, black, lead-colored, mixed, white, and blue.[5] The disease is disfiguring, but not dangerous. It is important in this history merely because of its American origin. Cortes had probably seen it when, in one of his letters to the king, he wrote of individuals showing various colors.

PIEDRA

Piedra is a disease of the hair characterized by the growth on it of minute, hard, stony (*piedra*) nodules. The hairs become twisted, broken, and matted. The little nodules consist of masses of a parasitic fungus, *Trichosporum giganteum*. Like pinta, the disease is unimportant. It is peculiar to limited regions of Colombia and Guiana, so far as is known at present.

THE CHIGGER, OR SAND FLEA

Oviedo spoke of two diseases as indigenous to Santo Domingo, syphilis and niguas, the latter now known as chiggers or sand fleas. The females of this insect burrow into the skin of warm-blooded animals, including man, to live while developing their eggs, finally attaining the size of a small pea. Their presence causes much irritation, eventual ulceration, and sometimes crippling. The removal of the insects is an art in which some natives attain great skill.

This insect was limited to America until so recently as 1872, when it appeared in Africa. It may have been taken there by West Indian Negroes colonized in Liberia or Sierra Leone. In the sixty years since its introduction it has spread over all tropical Africa and some of the adjacent islands, including Madagascar.[6] It is a cause of suffering and inconvenience.

BAD BREATH

It is interesting, even if unimportant, to note that the advertising of popular medicine today, which has made halitosis a familiar word and a dreaded bogy and has capitalized the fear of it to make "big business," is scientifically on a par with

Aztec medicine. Flores tells us that bad breath (*mal odor de la boca*) was called by the Aztecs *camapotoniliztli*, a word even more impressive and mouth-filling than halitosis, and that they prescribed for it mouthwashes of decoctions of certain plants, *mecaxochitl* or *quimichpatli* (*Buddleia verticilata*). However, not having the advantages of either magazine or radio advertising, it is probable that the prescribers remained poor.

CHRONIC ARTHRITIS

Among the great crippling diseases of mankind is that chronic disease, or group of diseases, of the joints, not due to such definitely known infections as syphilis, tuberculosis, or gonorrhea, or to such clear-cut metabolic disorders as rickets and gout, but known under such varied names as chronic rheumatism, rheumatic gout, rheumatoid arthritis, osteoarthritis, arthritis deformans, spondylitis deformans, and chronic arthritis. Using the last name quoted and assuming that chronic arthritis is one disease and not many (an improbable assumption) we may say that it is the oldest known disease.

The sufferer from this disease, having but little comfort and few things to be proud of, may be able to take pride in the ancient and honorable lineage of his disability. Perhaps some dinosaur may have had a Hapsburg lip, but if so it has left no trace. Gout as an evidence of ancestry is as nothing, the "oldest profession in the world" deserves no higher social status because of its antiquity than it has been accorded by the common opinion of mankind. Relatively it has no antiquity.

It is to be noted that Moodie attributes chronic arthritis to the pre-Columbian American Indians, and in his book he pictures bones of such Indians from both North and South America that show the lesions very clearly. Dr. Ales Hrdlicka informs me that the pre-Columbian bones in the National Museum show this disease with a frequency quite comparable to its occurrence in America today.

Manifestly, a disease that antedates mankind antedates man's appearance in America, so if he came to America from the Old World, as seems probable, he could have brought with him the constitutional make-up, the metabolic defect, the dietary habits, the pathogenic germ, or the other necessary factor or factors for producing the disease. Certainly, chronic arthritis antedated the conquest in America and, so far as we can now see, it had no influence upon that event, nor did the conquest influence it. It was merely an older bond of relationship between the races than was their humanity itself, a touch of nature that makes the whole world kin.*

* For further notes on arthritis, miscellaneous diseases, and diseases in transition see pp. 244-9.

Chapter XIV

Epilogue

WE HAVE seen America conquered largely by disease, seen the Indian defeated not merely because he had no firearms, no horses, and no iron, but even more because he had no immunity to most of the diseases that the white man brought with him. So much is plain. But is it not true, even if not at once obvious, that the white man was a conqueror partly because he and smallpox, he and measles, he and alcohol were long-time acquaintances, ancient enemies whose combats had made them strong?

We have seen that from the Stone Age to the present man has had tuberculosis. During those thousands of years it has killed off all who could not develop a protective immunity. It is probable that all men become infected with tuberculosis at some time in their lives. It is obvious that most of us overcome the disease and survive to die from other infections or from degenerative processes. Again and again it has been shown that smallpox or measles introduced to a people to whom it was new worked frightful havoc. The introduction of malaria to Mauritius and the devastation wrought by it are matters of recent history.

In general, the peoples who have longest had alcohol—the Jews, Greeks, and Mediterranean peoples generally, the Hindus and Chinese—are not drunken, while those to whom drink is a relatively recent gift—the Slavs, Scandinavians, Germans, English, Irish, and their American progeny, and such more primitive peoples as the North American Indian and the Negro—are more prone to indulge to excess. This is probably somewhat like relative racial immunity to disease. Long use has weeded out the strains to which alcohol has been most poisonous. There is probably not a cellular or a serological immunity such as might be acquired to an infection, but rather a survival of such nervous systems as are less harmfully affected by drink.

It is not fantastic to think that perhaps the white race has been and is great because of the difficulties it has surmounted, the diseases and habits it has mastered or partly mastered in the past. It has traveled a long and difficult road in acquiring its present relative immunity to diseases; it has paid a tremendous price in lives sacrificed, but always the survivors have been able to pass on resistance to the progeny, and the time came when the race could see the Indians killed off by the smallpox and measles that scarcely hurt white men, see the Negroes dying more rapidly from most infections. However, there are diseases, yellow fever and malaria, against which the Negro possesses a better immunity than the white man. This fact is responsible for the much slower conquest and settlement of Africa by the whites. Known longer than America, rich in gold, animal life, soil, and cheap labor, it has until very recently remained the black man's continent. Only since the rise of modern medicine and hygiene, which enable the white to protect himself from the Negro's diseases, has white colonization really made any great progress in equatorial Africa.

And what of the yellow man? Those who have traveled in the Orient and smelled the odors of Araby, the scents of Cathay, and the breezes wafted across the rice fields of Japan, who have noticed the general dearth of sanitation in Asia and the unrivaled opportunities for ingesting a neighbor's dung, must wonder if the survival of Asian peoples is not largely due to immunity gained by the weeding-out process incident to agelong contact with the disease. The East has kept largely to itself during the past ages. The white man has dealt mainly with peoples who were his biological inferiors, in part at least, because of their lesser immunity to disease.

In the coming centuries is it machinery and science or immunity to disease that will most influence racial dominance?

There can be no doubt that every disease missed is a mercy to the individual. There can be doubt as to whether disease prevention by water purification, sewage disposal, tonsil enucleation, prohibition of alcohol, and other measures that remove the causes of disease are beneficial to the race in those long stretches of time that are dealt with by racial history. We may not know surely, and while that is the case, we must and will continue to act for the welfare of the individual or the social or political group, and allow the race to take care of itself. Possibly it can thrive only through adversity, most surely grow strong by overcoming, best keep well by acquiring immunity.

Appendix A

Technical Matter Allied with Text

CHAPTER IV: Sixteenth-Century Medicine

Remembering that Harvey's discovery of the circulation of the blood did not come until the seventeenth century, let us glance further at the Spanish medicine of the sixteenth. In order that it may be representative of the average or the best, I shall quote from writers whose positions assure on that score.

Francisco Lopez de Villalobos was a learned Jew who was born about 1473 and later rose to be personal physician to the King of Spain. He wrote much, among other things *El sumario de la medicina con un tratado sobre las pestíferas bubas*, in 183 pages of verse. Translations of extracts will be given, and if they seem hazy, the fault is not wholly the translator's, as the medical thought of that time was hazy, and the use of verse did not clarify it.

MEDICINE

This is the science by which all the dispositions of the human body are quickly known. It teaches us to distinguish by the senses and clear reasoning what parts are sound and what diseased, how to guard the health and what to avoid.

COMPLEXION

Medicine teaches us that complexion is that quality which arises and proceeds from the antagonism of contrary qualities, when one among them somewhat exceeds the others: and whenever in this play of qualities the four elements meet, their force and sharpness are broken, and the quality then remaining as a result constitutes the complexion and the temperaments.

COMPOSITION OF COMPLEXION

As it would be impossible for the qualities to be exactly equal or balanced, there is at times found more of moisture, at times more dryness, at times more cold or more heat, and at times there may be excess of moisture and of cold together; also cold and dry may be found, and hot and dry, and hot and moist appear sometimes, and rarest of all is equality.

THE FOUR HUMORS AND THEIR COMPLEXIONS

Medicine also teaches us of the humors, of the bile and phlegm and melancholy, and the blood, which nourishes all and with which the others mingle and to which they are accessory. Of these, bile is hot and dry, blood is hot and very moist, phlegm is moist and very cold, and melancholy (black bile) is cold and dry.

THE FOUR MOISTURES

Before the blood passes to nourish the body, it is changed into four moistures: First it is changed in trying to get out of the small veins to be infused into the members and porosities; second, it is changed after infusion into those same members, in order to moisten them; thirdly, it is changed within them, so as to cover and mix with every part; and fourthly, it is changed into the substance of the parts.

At times the moistures are healthy and natural, at times corrupted and damaged by changes of the animal virtues or by respiration of corrupted air.

THE MEMBERS

A member is a body composed of a mixture of humors. There are many members but the principal are the heart, the brain, the liver, and the organs of generation.

THE COMPLEXION OF THESE AND THE WHOLE BODY

The heart is very dry and hot, the brain cold and moist. The liver is hot and moist. Thus balanced, the body of man exceeds in heat and moisture, for in two of these is excess of heat and in only one is there strong cold. Likewise in two there is excessive moisture and in only one excess of dryness.

VIRTUES

These are the houses and principal places where the three virtues are perfected. In the heart are the vital, in the brain the animal, and in the liver the nutritive. The vital virtue is that by which we live, nutritive that by means of which we are nourished, and the other that by which we feel and move.

SPIRIT AND NATURAL HEAT

The proper instrument of these virtues and what carries them is spirit and heat. The spirit is a thin body and vapor which has its seat in the heart and the left side. It is this which pulses in the veins, which makes us to live and to eat, move and feel. This it is which brings the heat in chains to all the members to digest.

FEVER

Fever is a strange heat which is lighted in the heart, whence it is sent to the body by means of the spirit and the blood. It descends by the arteries and veins and thus offends the body by diverting its natural actions.

EPHEMERAL FEVER

This may be due to either external or internal causes. One internal cause is some grief. The remedy in this case is to make glad and give cordials, anoint with cold oils, and remove the grief.

QUARTAN FEVER

Quartan comes from black bile, and this from dry humors. If the blood be adust, the urine is red and comes from the blood after fever; if there be phlegm, there is less sweating and it is colder; if it be bile, it comes with cold and rigors, the pulse excited, the patient restless; if gloomy black bile, there are pains in the spleen and greater hardness, the urine is not concocted, and there is no sweat. The treatment should be purging, light diet, and moist and cold drugs.

THE DIVISIONS OF BILIOUS FEVER

If the bile putrefies in the remote veins, a tertian intermittent is engendered, and this is pure if bile alone is present. If there be a mixture of phlegm, the fever is continuous. If the putrefaction be in the veins near the heart, the fever is such as we call the causus; if distant, continued tertian results.

Lopez de Villalobos did not know when he wrote his summary of medicine in 1498 that either gonorrhea or syphilis was conveyed by sexual intercourse. Gonorrhea he regarded as an abnormal flow of semen and he said that nocturnal pollutions were due to the same cause and to be treated in the same way. (*"Gomorrea se dice cuando uno padece salirse la esperma sin su voluntad. . . . Las causas, las senas, la cura y el como daquesta [polucion] y gomorrea todos es uno."*) As for syphilis, he attributed it primarily to astrological influences (*"mala impression de los cuerpos celestes"*), while the cause within the body was adust humors in the liver and the veins. The reason that the disease showed first in the "shameful parts" was that these constituted the direct outlets for harmful materials from the liver, which formed adust humors and discharged through the urine. They corroded the tender flesh of these parts and caused ulcers. These humors reached the urine before they did the veins, for which reason the disease showed in the shameful parts many days before it did in the other organs.

Even in the last quarter of the sixteenth century Farfan[1] was ignorant of the usual method of spread of syphilis. He wrote that it came from many causes, among them corruption of phlegm or of black bile or of both, also from corruption of blood. Other causes were too much and too frequent conversation with women, which thinned and debilitated the liver and this in turn corrupted the blood. Another cause was union with women diseased in their shameful parts. "There are numerous other causes which need not be mentioned because they may all be summarized in the statement the disease is due to the mixture of phlegmatic and melancholic humors, so we must hasten to purge these humors, after due consideration of the complexion, virtues and disposition of the patient."

Dr. Juan de Cárdenas was born in Spain in 1563, went to Mexico as a child, and there received his education, that in medicine from Dr. Juan de la Fuente. He practiced in Mexico, Compostela, and Guadalajara, became professor in the University of Mexico, and wrote a book, *Primera parte de los problemas y secretos maravillosos de las Indias*, which was published in 1591 and was reprinted by the Museo Nacional de Arqueología, Historia y Etnología de México in 1913. His modern editor regarded him as typical of his age and wrote of him, "Throughout Cárdenas' whole book is reflected the vice which dominated the education of the period. He was a submissive son of the Aristotelian logic, always skilled in reasoning deductively, but without concern for the correctness of the premises on which he rested or of the results which he obtained. He was a poor observer but a tireless speculator."

The first book of his problems deals with climate, earthquakes, and natural phenomena; the second with metals, plants, fruits, and drinks. These things have complexions just as do diseases and persons, and as Galen taught that treatment was by opposites (a doctrine against which Hahnemann later rebelled, setting up his shibboleth of *similia similibus curantur*), it was proper to treat a cold, moist disease with a drug having a hot, dry complexion. Thus was tobacco, that holy herb, which was hot in the third degree, sovereign for diseases resulting from cold and abundance of phlegm, such as asthma, bilious purging, pain in the loins, chronic stomach pain, all sorts of obstructions and flatulence, swelling of the belly, impeded urination, and delayed labor. Maize gruel was a thing of such even balance as to be a healthful food for all complexions and diseases.

Cárdenas also said that some diseases were patent and manifest, while others were of a hidden or occult nature. As examples of the former he cites calenture, the whole of which consisted of excessive heat ("*Todo su ser consiste en un excesivo y demasiado calor*"); asthma, plainly due to too much phlegm in the chest; *esquilencia* (sore throat), due to inflammation in the throat; pain in the side, due to inflammation of the tissues covering the ribs on the inside. Among diseases of a hidden or occult nature he cites *cocoliztle*, which usually shows terrible injury of the liver and severe nosebleed, and which attacks only Indians, and not Spaniards. On the other hand, *landre* (bubonic plague) occurs in Europe and not in Mexico. Other diseases of occult nature were catarrh and smallpox. The fever that goes with occult diseases is not the whole thing, even though manifest. There are terrible suffering and intolerable anxieties that go with them and may kill even when the fever is slight. There is an occult quality, poison or malignant corruption of some sort. *Bubas* or syphilis is both manifest and occult, both hot and cold, and contagious. Everybody has it and there are seventy kinds of it, including gout, sciatica, headache, asthma, pain in the stomach, and other diseases of the sort.

Everybody also has stomach trouble; there is scarcely a man

that does not complain of it. It is nothing but a coldness or great lack of the natural heat of the stomach; in the language of the vulgar, a weakness and relaxation of the stomach, caused by lack of heat and excess of moisture. (This is reminiscent of Falstaff's medical lore. *Henry IV*, Part 2, Act 1, Scene 2.) Urinary diseases and *yjada* (pain in the flank) were very common in Spaniards and rare in Indians.

Rheuma included all diseases except fever. "Rheuma is the same as to say a running from one member to another, and if it be a running it can only be a humor, for these are the only things in the body which can run from one part to another; so that we can say that with the exception of fever, which is a general ill of the whole body, all the other special diseases are rheuma or running of a humor, gout, sciatica, pain in the side, toothache, sore throat, asthma, etc."

Cárdenas makes no mention of quotidian, tertian, quartan, or intermittent fevers, a fact evidential of their nonexistence or great rarity in Mexico at that time, in view of the many diseases that he does discuss.

Dr. Francisco Hernandez was the sixteenth-century physician who wrote most extensively on American *materia medica*. He was born in Toledo in 1514 and spent most of his life there. He became court physician to Philip II and in 1570 he was appointed "*protomédico de las Indias*" and went to Mexico, where he remained for seven years. He then returned to Spain, where he lived for another ten years, dying in 1587. His work (*Quatro libros de la naturaleza y virtudes medicinales de las plantas y animales de la Nueva España, Extracto de las obras del Dr. Francisco Hernandez, anotados, tradujidos y publicados en México el año 1615 por Fr. Francisco Ximenez*, etc.) was first published in 1615, and was reprinted at Morelia in 1888. He wrote not only of the plants of Mexico, as the title of his work suggests, but also of those of Peru, the West Indies, Florida, and the Philippines. He evidently advised the use of drugs according to their "complexions, their moisture, dryness, cold or heat." For example, he says of *salsifrax* (sassafras) that it is "of a hot and dry nature of about the third degree, and of subtle parts, so that it helps colic and bellyache, is a grand remedy for difficulty in urination and diseases of the kidneys; it resolves flatulence, opens obstructions and strengthens internal parts, cures asthma and other diseases of the chest arising from cold causes, prevents vomiting, aids digestion, relaxes the belly, helps much in female sterility, starts the menses, and is a great remedy for syphilis; it helps toothache and, by consuming the cause, cures rheuma, etc." *Chichicpatl*, he said, was good for tertians. It also stimulates the appetite, resolves and opens abscesses, cures bellyache, resists cold, lessens flatulence, cures itch of the head, kills lice, and preserves from pestilence. Several other drugs are recommended as good for intermittents, for chills or chilliness in fever. However, aside from the fact that the book first appeared almost a century after the introduction of Negro slavery, when malaria had obtained a foothold in the country, the fact that Hernandez spoke of a disease is no evidence that it existed in Mexico, as he spoke of many things that he must have known only in Spain.*

It is possible that Nicholas Culpeper, as so delightfully and sympathetically described by Kipling in his "A Doctor of Medicine," † was more representative of the seventeenth-century English physician than was Sydenham.

A few quotations from Culpeper's *A Key to Galen's Method of Physick*," [2] published a generation after Harvey's description of the circulation of blood, will serve to show us that some English medicine of this century showed little or no advance over that of Francisco Lopez de Villalobos or of Galen. The first section of this work is devoted to the discussion of medicines of the different

---

* Jourdanet, the French translator and editor of Sahagun's *Histoire générale des choses de la Nouvelle Espagne*, says of Hernandez in a footnote, "*On est justement surpris qu'Hernandez n'ait pu nommer aucune des affections que l'on connaissait alors en Europe sans le faire suivre de la longue énumération des substances dont les Méxicains se servait pour la combattre. Cette particularité curieuse du travail du médicin de Philippe II peut servir à donner la double idée du résultat considérable auquel les Indiens étaient parvenus en fait de connaissances pathologiques et thérapeutiques. Mais malheureusement rien de tout cela ne nous dit quelle était la nature des maladies les plus communes et surtout de celles qui ont été la base d'épidémies fréquentes dont le pays fut désolé à différentes époques de son histoire.*"

† Published in *Rewards and Fairies*.

complexions, "Herbs, Plants, and other Medicines manifestly operate, either by Heat, Coldness, Driness or Moisture, for the world being composed of so many qualities, they and only they can be found in the world, and the mixtures of them one with another."

The second section treats "Of the Appropriation of Medicines to the several Parts of the Body."

Cephalical Medicines may be found out from the Affections of the Brain itself. The Brain is usually oppressed with moisture in such afflictions: therefore give such medicines as very gently warm, clense, cut and dry. . . .

Ocular Medicines are two fold, viz. such as are referred to the Visive Virtue, and such as are referred to the eyes themselves. . . . [Doctors] say a Goat's liver conduceth much to make one see in the night, and they give this reason, Because Goats see as well in the night as in the day. . . . However, Astrologers know well enough that al Herbs, Plants, &c that are under the Dominion of either Sun or Moon, and appropriated to the head, be they hot or cold, they strengthen the Visive Virtue. . . .

But because such Medicines as conduce to the cure of Phthisicks (which is an Ulceration of the Lungs and the disease usually called the Consumption of the Lungs) are also reckoned among the Pectorals, it is not amiss to speak a word or two of them. In this Disease are three things to be regarded.
1. To cut and bring away the Concreted Blood.
2. To cherish and strengthen the Lungs.
3. To conglutinate the Ulcer.

The Heart is the seat of the Vital Spirit, the fountain of life, the original of infused heat, and of the natural affections of man.

So then these two things are proper to the Heart.
1. By its heat to cherish life throughout the Body.
2. To add vigor to the affections.

The heart is chiefly afflicted by too much heat, by Poyson, and by stinking vapors, and these are remedied by the second sort of Cordials.

Medicines appropriated to the Stomach are usually called stomachicals.

The infirmities usually incident to the Stomach are three.
1. Appetite lost.
2. Digestion weakened.
3. The retentive Faculty corrupted.

The Pallet is the Seat of tast, and its Office is to judg what Food is agreeable to the stomach, and what not, by that is both the Quality and Quantity of Food in the stomach discerned: the very same office the *Meseraik* Veins perform to the Liver. . . . And thus much for the Liver, the Office of which is to concoct Chyle (which is a white substance the stomach digests the food into) into Blood, and distributes it by the Veins to every part of the body, whereby the Body is nourished, and decaying flesh restored. . . .

In the breeding of Blood, are three Excrements most conspicuous, viz. *Urine, Choller* and *Melancholy*. The proper seat of Choller is in the Gall. The urine passeth down to the Reins or Kidneys, which is al one. The Spleen takes the thickest or Melancholy blood to itself. . . .

The Office of the Reins is, to make a separation between the Blood and the Urine: to receive this urine thus separated from the Blood, is the Bladder ordained, which is of a sufficient size to contain it, that so a man may go about his business and not be always pissing.

As for the nature of the Womb, it seems to be much like the Nature of the brain and stomach, for experience teacheth that it is delighted with sweet and Aromatical Medicines, and flies from their contraries. For example: A woman being troubled with the fits of the Mother, which is drawing of the Womb upward, apply sweet things as Civet, or the like, to the place of Conception, it draws it down again: but apply stinking things to the Nose, as Assafoetida, or the like, it expels it from it, and sends it down to its proper place.

In his "Premonitory Epistle" in his *London Dispensatory*[3] Culpeper justifies his faith in astrology and explains the physician's need for it in part as follows:

As the cause of Diseases is to be understood to be Natural, so is their Cures also to be effected in a natural way: and if you do but consider the whole Universe as one united Body, and Man an Epitomy of this Body, it will seem strange to none but Mad-men and Fools that the Stars should have influence upon the body of Man, considering he being an Epitomy of the Creation, must needs have a Celestial World within himself. . . .

As in the Celestial World he [the physician] ought very carefully to heed the Oppositions and great Conjunctions of the Planets, the Eclipses of the Luminaries, the Quarterly Ingresses of the Sun, and the Crisis of Diseases: so in the Elementary World he ought to heed the Seasons of the Year, whether they be hotter, colder, drier, moister than they should be: he ought to be very well skilled in Vegetables and Minerals, and how the Earth brings them forth, what is the office of the *Central Sun*, and what is the office of the *Celestial Sun*, what is the office of the *Central Moon*, what is the office of the *Celestial Moon* in the production of things here below, and how, and by what Mediums they perform it.

Fray Sahagun, whose *Historia universal de las cosas de la Nueva España* reveals a truly scientific curiosity, who is regarded by many as the father of modern ethnology, and who has given us the most valuable information we possess as to the diseases and medicine of the Aztecs, acquired his information in the following roundabout way. Going to Mexico soon after the conquest (1529), he made friends of many leaders and learned men among the Aztecs and later persuaded them to record for him in their picture writing the story, habits, customs, and learning of their people. Still later he had them translate the record into the Nahuatl language and he wrote the translation in that language but in Spanish characters. Some of his religious brethren recognized the value of his work and urged that it be published, but the higher church authorities feared that its publication might delay the conversion of the Indians to Christianity, as the work dealt so much with the old religion, mythology, and superstitions. The matter was therefore referred to the King of Spain for his decision and he ordered that all the writings be sent to Spain.

Sahagun himself translated a part of his work into Spanish, but so immersed was he in the Nahuatl tongue, or so unable to convey many ideas and words of Aztec usage into Spanish, that his text abounds in Nahuatl words, many of which have baffled the editors of later editions of his work. His whole work disappeared from view for more than two centuries, the Spanish translation being discovered in the latter half of the eighteenth century. The later Spanish, English, and French editions were all made from this, before the discovery in the latter half of the nineteenth century of

APPENDIX A

the Aztec version and the picture writing, and all are imperfect. The Aztec writing and pictures still exist in Spain and Florence (*Codice florentina*). During the presidency of Porfirio Díaz the Mexican government had facsimile copies made of them and published.

I was informed that Dr. Alcocer, whom I met and consulted in Vera Cruz, is the most reliable living authority on the Aztec language and has best translated Sahagun's sections on drugs and diseases, but has not yet published his work. Dr. Alcocer informed me that there is real information in Sahagun's work, but that it is most difficult to correlate it with modern medicine, because, first, the Aztecs had not the same understanding of medicine as the Europeans and did not "philosophize" about it in the same way, and second, because Sahagun, who was not a medical man, transformed what they told him into the priest's conception of the humoral medicine of his day, a medicine based upon a theory that bore little or no relation to facts.

I am indebted to Dr. Alcocer for a chapter on the diseases and remedies of the Aztecs, taken from the earliest memorials in Nahuatl collected by Sahagun, but not used in any translation of the latter's history.[4] The Nahuatl text is given paragraph by paragraph and each paragraph is followed by Dr. Alcocer's translation into Spanish.

This is distinctly simpler matter than has appeared in any of the published translations, and it shows at once the primitive state of Aztec medicine and Sahagun's efforts to translate it into his conception of the humoral theory. The so-called diseases, each of which is followed in the original and in Dr. Alcocer's translation by a remedy, were as follows: phlegm; bloody phlegm; white phlegm; yellow phlegm; flow, loss of blood, or hemorrhage; white flow; bloody diarrhea; diarrhea; gout, rheumatism, and paralysis; acute rheumatism; leprosy or disease of the gods; bullae of the skin, itch, and smallpox; abscesses, carbuncles, tumors, and buboes; cancer and chiggers; swelling; nausea and vertigo; phagedenic chancre; fevers with chill; dental fever; relapse of a disease; debility or lack of vigor of the hair; cough, catarrh, or cold; decayed teeth; inflammation or disease of the ears; flatulence or meteorism; eye diseases; crab lice; blindness, no remedy; cross-eyes; diseases of the urine or stone in the bladder; constipation; menstruation; fever of the country; nocturnal fever; excessive appetite; whooping cough; ringworm of the scalp; death, no remedy; headache; premature drying of the milk after labor; lightning stroke, no remedy; diseases of the chest; general fever. Dr. Alcocer states that some other conditions were listed but that they could not be identified because of the condition of the original manuscript. None of the prescriptions for treatment is believed to have much value. It is to be remembered that the mention of a disease in this list does not mean that the Aztecs knew it before the conquest. Smallpox, for example, is well known to have been introduced to Mexico and to the New World by the Spaniards.

Sahagun's description of Aztec medicine suggests that its value was very little, and that we cannot expect from it much assistance in the identification of diseases or in determining whether or not an identifiable disease existed before the coming of the whites.

CHAPTER VI: Notes on Typhus

It is not known what Cárdenas meant by his statement of terrible injury to the liver. There is no evidence and little probability that he did many autopsies, if any. Whether the statement as to the liver was based upon symptoms or upon some theory as to the state of the humors is not known. His teacher, Juan de la Fuente, did perform autopsies during the epidemic of 1565–67 and noted swelling (*hinchazon*) of the liver, but no "terrible damage." This epidemic of 1576–77 of which Cárdenas wrote was the sixth after the conquest, the first occurring in 1519. Indicative of the difficulties arising from the use of translations is the Aztec word *matlalzahuatl*, meaning typhus or *tabardillo*, as analyzed by different writers. Flores says that it is compounded of *matlauh*, meaning contagious, and *zahuatl*, meaning eruption. Reko says that it came from *mat-tlalh*, meaning blue, and *zahuatl*, meaning infectious. Nicolas León[5] says that it came from *matlatl*, a net, and *zahuatl*, itch, eruption, pimples, and that it meant an eruption like a net, which he explains by the resemblance of the symmetrically disposed spots to the knots of a net.

Nicolle, quoting from León, says that the word means red

(*rouge*) eruption. He apparently has taken the Spanish word *red*, used by León as meaning net, to be the same as the English red or French *rouge*. The only way to settle the matter seemed to be to consult Molina, whose Aztec dictionary was written when Aztec was still much more common in Mexico than was Spanish, and he does not give the word. More recently Dr. Alcocer of Vera Cruz has told me that the word signifies a bluish eruption, petechiae.[*]

Francisco Bravo, in the first medical book published on the American continent,[6] speaks at length of the disease, which he says had spread widely in Mexico, and says that it is the same disease with which he was familiar in Spain in 1553, when he was beginning the practice of medicine. His clinical description of it is pretty full and good, and the different amount of eruption and duration of fever in different cases shows pretty clearly that a minority of those he saw were probably typhoid, the majority clearly typhus. He emphasizes the almost general presence of lethargy, and although he does not use the word *modorra*, he describes the symptom. Bravo has been quoted [7] as saying that the disease passed to Mexico in Spanish ships, but Dr. Claudius F. Mayer and I have been unable to find this statement in his book. He does say that the disease was of much older standing in the Old World than Fracastorius had stated, and that it was the fever that Galen called *synochus* and the Arabians called the fever of putrefying blood. Farfan,[8] writing a few years later than Bravo (1579), regards the disease as the most common one in Mexico and treats of it at length, but adds little or nothing to Bravo's description of it.

At the time of the conquest, typhus fever was widespread and deadly in Spain and the rest of Europe, and as Nicolle says,[9] the soldiers who accompanied the conquistadores, like all mercenaries of the period, were proud but lousy ("*des porteurs orgueilleux de poux*").

In addition, it has been claimed that European and Mexican typhus differed clinically. Charles Nicolle, who in 1909 discov-

[*] Dr. George R. Minot comments: "Petechiae hardly can be called a bluish eruption. They are tiny, small hemorrhagic spots occurring in the skin."

ered that typhus was louse-borne, and who made a trip to Mexico in 1930 for the purpose of studying the disease there, stated [10] that he observed the following clinical differences: In the Mexican disease the eruption is more abundant ("*Cette éruption frappe parfois la paume des mains et la plante des pieds à la façon de l'exanthème d'une fièvre boutonneuse*"); there are less marked cerebral and cardiac symptoms. The disease is less grave, even among immigrants; convalescence is shorter. The tendency to hemorrhages, especially epistaxis, is infinitely more marked. He noted epistaxis in a fourth of the cases examined. This is not now the case in the Old World typhus, but from early accounts it was much more common in the sixteenth-century epidemics.

Carlos Govea[11] says that epistaxis often is so abundant as to put the patients in imminent danger of death, and in any case, they are so debilitated by the anaemia that their chances of recovery are lessened. ("*Suelen presentarse epistaxis de tal manera abundantes, que llegan a poner en inminente peligro de muerte a los pacientes, y en todo caso, quedan estos debilitados por la anemia, que les resta fuerzas para la lucha por la salud.*") We may accept it as fact that the disease is more apt to cause hemorrhage in Indians than is Old World typhus in whites, but the difference is not necessarily proof of nonidentity of the diseases.

Despite these slight differences, Nicolle found that the diseases were in general very much alike, and that they produce cross immunity; that is, an attack of either protects against infection with the other. But he thought that they were epidemiologically different in that the Mexican disease was found in wild rats and that the two diseases when inoculated into rats and guinea pigs reacted differently.

Much interesting work has been and is being done on typhus fever in very recent years, some of it apparently invalidating Nicolle's opinions as to the differences between Mexican and Old World typhus. It has been shown that both, as well as Brill's disease and the endemic typhus of our southern states, can be conveyed by fleas as well as by lice, and that the flea is apparently the more common vector in Mexico; that all behave alike in the rat and are in truth rat diseases, and are often kept alive by the rat in the absence of epidemics. Furthermore, very excellent experiments by Dr. Hermann Mooser of Mexico City indicate that all are the same disease. He kindly permitted me to copy from a manuscript then unpublished (since published in *Arch. Inst. Pasteur de Tunis*, July 1932, XXI, 1-19) his conclusion that *"Il n'y a donc plus de raisons valables pourquoi nous parlions de typhus méxicain, de Brill's disease et de typhus Européen: tous sont en fin de compte d'origine murine."* (There is no longer any good reason why we should speak of Mexican and European typhus and of Brill's disease: they are all the same thing and all of rat origin.) Believing this now proved, I have no doubt that typhus was brought to the New World by the whites and the rats that accompanied them.*

The rat was imported to America from Europe, and that this disease is practically harmless to and is carried by that animal is powerful evidence, if not positive proof, that the disease was also imported. Add to this the fact reported by Cárdenas and others that Indians suffered severely from tabardilla and the Spanish not at all. That is very strong evidence that the disease was new to the Indians but an ancient familiar to the Spaniards.

In view of the facts that the rat was introduced to America at a time (sixteenth and seventeenth centuries) when bubonic plague still lingered in Europe and was extensively epidemic in England, and that we now know this to be a rat-borne disease, it may seem strange that plague itself did not get to America. The most plausible explanation is that the Black Death had well-nigh died out in most of Europe by the time the rat had gained a foothold in America, and that it had also largely died out among the rats. If the rats on a ship bound for America were infected, they may have died off before the long voyage was completed, or, if there were infected survivors, they may not have left the ship, or if they left the ship, they may have met death from predatory animals or birds, or they may have died in such solitude that their fleas did not find another host. If plague broke out among the people on shipboard, it probably resulted in the loss of the ship. That the

* See Mooser, Castaneda, and Zinsser, *Journal of the American Medical Association*, July 15, 1931, LVII, 231-2; Hermann Mooser, *Medicina* (Mexico), Nov. 25, 1931, XI, 891-4; Mooser and Dummer, *Journal of Infectious Diseases*, Feb. 1930, XLVI, 170-2.

228   THE RANKS OF DEATH

disease did not reach America may not have been important so far as the Indians were concerned, as they were easily overcome by the more readily and more directly transmissible smallpox.

I suspect that at the time of the conquest typhus was in Spain about as it is today in North Africa. Reynaud, Soulier, and Ricard [12] say that exanthematic typhus has always existed in Africa Minor, always corresponding to years of misery (invasion of locusts and famine). The writings of Augustine and the Arabic authors are full of accounts of famines and epidemics of purple fever coming about once in twenty years. The disease usually spreads in winter, when the people crowd into their vermin-filled houses, but in the Saharan regions there are also outbreaks in summer, the natives being obliged by the heat of the sun to seek shelter during the day in the same narrow, crowded places. Most often the presence of the disease is recognized in a place through a "European reactor." Suddenly a doctor, an administrator, a police agent, or a teacher is stricken with typhus of severe grade and classical symptoms. Investigations then may show a large number of cases of various types of the disease in the native population. In the native, exposed since childhood in surroundings where cleanliness is unknown and vermin are habitual commensals, the disease generally shows only the abortive, ambulant form. The person afflicted is a convalescent or healthy carrier of the germ. This light ambulant form may be impossible of recognition. It is due to a partial immunity conferred by earlier attacks of the disease. In children typhus is remarkably mild, usually nothing more than a slight increase of temperature, a passing discomfort, and a discrete eruption. These benign forms assure the perennial presence of the disease, and are the starting points of epidemic explosions. In the Kabyles and Saharans that have had the disease in childhood, new attacks cause only 5 to 10 per cent of mortality; in city Moors, 15 to 30 per cent; in Europeans, 50 per cent or more.

CHAPTER VII: Notes on Malaria

The "kingdom of Quito" at the time of the conquest was almost the same as present-day Peru. Quito itself is 9,300 feet above sea level. Guayaquil, at sea level, was apparently free from malaria. Charles Darwin noted in 1836 that "In all seasons both inhabitants and foreigners suffer from severe attacks of ague. This disease is common on the whole coast of Peru, but is unknown in the interior." From the time of Carrión, who in 1885 inoculated himself with blood from a person having *verruga peruana* and who died of Oroya fever, the two were considered different manifestations of the same disease, and this is now believed to be fully established. The commission sent to Peru by Harvard School of Tropical Medicine said of Oroya fever, "The febrile symptoms and rigors usually increase in severity as the disease develops. The fever is very irregular, being usually remittent but sometimes intermittent," and, "The inhabitants of these regions stand in much fear of the febrile stage of Carrión's disease." These are much like Garcilaso's statements in regard to *chuchu*. As to the mortality of Oroya fever and the reasons for fear, the commission says:

In 1870 a severe outbreak took place among workmen building the Central Railway between Lima and Oroya, and it is estimated that at least 7000 individuals died. . . . Nourse reported that all the engineers superintending the building of the Trans-Andean Railway contracted verruga and that half of them died of it. Of forty sailors who had deserted from a British ship and gone to work on the railway, thirty died of the disease in the course of seven or eight months. In 1906 out of a force of 2000 men employed in tunnel work on the Central Railway, 200 are known to have died of the disease.

In the regions of its occurrence, Oroya fever is a much more fatal and feared disease than malaria, and more apt to have been the *chuchu* and *rupa* of the pre-Hispanic days.

CHAPTER VIII: The History of Yellow Fever

It is not worth while, at this late date, to thresh over the old chaff of speculation as to the epidemiology of yellow fever that antedates the work of the Army Medical Board headed by Major Walter Reed in Cuba in 1901. A very brief account of this splendid piece of work, which resulted in the complete control and almost complete abolition of yellow fever, will not be out of place here.

During the year 1898 there were 1164 cases of the disease in the Army, with a mortality of 144 cases, or 12.32 per cent. In 1899 there were 262 cases, with 55 deaths. The very great majority of these cases occurred in Cuba, a few in Porto Rico and the Southern States. In 1900 a great flow of emigration from Spain to Cuba supplied non-immune material for the disease and it prevailed more extensively in the island than for some years past. A new germ, Sanarelli's *Bacillus icteroides*, had been heralded to the world as the cause of yellow fever. General Sternberg, taught caution by the many mistakes which he had had to uncover in regard to similar previous announcements, as well as by his generally scientific attitude of mind, appointed the board to investigate the subject of yellow fever generally and of Sanarelli's bacillus in particular. The bacillus was disposed of in relatively short order. It was found in none of eighteen cases, eleven of which came to autopsy. But a happy concatenation of labors of other men speedily put the board upon the real trail of the mysterious vector which had made the disease so puzzling to the investigators of a hundred years. These important and interlinked labors were the following:

1. Ronald Ross, of the Indian Medical Service, had shown that malaria is carried by mosquitoes of the genus *Anopheles*. His work had been confirmed and elaborated in Italy.

2. The American administration in Cuba had cleaned up the city of Havana without in any way improving the yellow fever situation, thus apparently eliminating the possibility of its being a filth disease.

3. Surgeon Henry R. Carter, United States Marine Hospital Service, in May, 1900, published his very important observations on the epidemiology of the disease, especially the relation between the infecting, or imported, and the secondary cases, a relationship which, in the light of the work on malaria, pointed to an insect carrier for the disease, although Dr. Carter did not suggest this in his article.

4. Carlos Finlay, a resident of Cuba of Scotch and French ancestry, had nineteen years before published the reasoning by which he had reached the conclusion that yellow fever was mosquito-borne and that it was carried by the mosquito *Culex fasciatus* (later called *Stegomyia fasciata*, *Stegomyia calopus*, *Aedes aegypti*), for twenty years had talked his belief, had been re-

garded as an amiable crank, and had tried, as he thought successfully, as others thought, in vain, to transmit the disease by the insect's bite. His repeated failures in themselves seemed fair proof that he was wrong. Nevertheless, he was right and his rightness is one of the finest bits of sound reasoning from correct observation of which there is any record in the history of medicine. A great mind—too great perhaps to mix any malice with the satisfaction which must have come when, after twenty years, his so-called folly was recognized as the most profound wisdom. Walter Reed, having these interlocking facts, was also greatly intelligent in recognizing their importance and that they interlocked. The board set itself to test out Finlay's hypothesis in the light of the work of Ross and of Carter. It was also greatly fortunate that Finlay was still living in Havana, still riding his hobby, still the object of amusement to the knowing ones, still trying to prove what his observation and reasoning told him was true, and still, as for years past, breeding *Stegomyia* mosquitoes and trying to transmit yellow fever by their bites. He indicated the mosquito to the board and furnished its eggs.

There was at the time a small epidemic of yellow fever at Quemados, and thither the board proceeded on June 25, 1900, and at once began its investigations. No inoculation experiments were made until August 11th. The first nine attempts at inoculation failed to convey the disease, because, as afterward became apparent, the mosquitoes were non-infective for one of two reasons, either (1) they had bitten the yellow fever patient too late to obtain the virus with the blood, or (2) they had not been kept sufficiently long to complete the developmental phase which the virus undergoes in the insect. It is probable that a feeling that there was nothing in Dr. Finlay's hypothesis had begun to possess the members of the board, and when Dr. Carroll was bitten on August 27th by a mosquito which had bitten a yellow fever patient in the second day of the disease and had been kept for twelve days thereafter, he apparently did not expect to get the disease. At any rate, when he became sick on the afternoon of the 29th and on the 30th, he did not take his temperature or seek a diagnosis. On the 31st, he examined his blood for malarial parasites and failed to find them, and that evening his temperature was taken for the first time and was found to be 102°. The diagnosis of yellow fever was made on September 1st. The case was severe, but resulted in recovery. After the diagnosis was made, there was still no proof that he had acquired the disease from that mosquito.

The next case to develop the disease was Case II (xy), a soldier who accepted the bites in a spirit of disbelief and bravado. His case was diagnosed, "well-pronounced yellow fever." The third case, that of Dr. Jesse W. Lazear, resulted from the bite of a free mosquito in a yellow fever ward. "On September 13, 1900 (forenoon), Dr. Lazear, while on a visit to Las Animas Hospital, and while collecting blood from yellow fever patients for study, was bitten by a Culex mosquito (species undetermined). As Dr. Lazear had been previously bitten by a contaminated insect without effect, he deliberately allowed this particular mosquito, which had settled on the back of his hand, to remain until it had satisfied its hunger." In five days he sickened and in twelve days he was dead.

The board thereafter produced six more cases (all of which recovered) by mosquito inoculation, failed to produce it by most thorough experiments with fomites, and concluded:

1. The mosquito—*C. fasciatus*—serves as the intermediate host for the parasite of yellow fever.

2. Yellow fever is transmitted to the non-immune individual by means of the bite of the mosquito that has previously fed on the blood of those sick with this disease.

3. An interval of about twelve days or more after contamination appears to be necessary before the mosquito is capable of conveying the infection.

4. The bite of the mosquito at an earlier period after contamination does not appear to confer any immunity against a subsequent attack.

5. Yellow fever can also be experimentally produced by the subcutaneous injection of blood taken from the general circulation during the first and second days of this disease.

6. An attack of yellow fever, produced by the bite of the mosquito, confers immunity against the subsequent injection of the blood of an individual suffering from the non-experimental form of this disease.

7. The period of incubation in thirteen cases of experimental yellow fever has varied from forty-one hours to five days and seventeen hours.

8. Yellow fever is not conveyed by fomites, and hence disinfection of articles of clothing, bedding, or merchandise, supposedly contaminated by contact with those sick with this disease, is unnecessary.

9. A house may be said to be infected with yellow fever only when there are present within its walls contaminated mosquitoes capable of conveying the parasite of this disease.

10. The spread of yellow fever can be most effectually controlled by measures directed to the destruction of mosquitoes and the protection of the sick against the bites of these insects.

APPENDIX A

11. While the mode of propagation of yellow fever has now been definitely determined, the specific cause of this disease remains to be discovered.[13]

On the basis of these findings, Havana and the island of Cuba were promptly freed from yellow fever, the Isthmus of Panama was made habitable, and the canal dug; later the gulf, Caribbean, and Brazilian coasts and the Pacific coast of South and Central America were freed from the disease.

However, the cause of it was still unknown and the hunt for it was continued under great difficulties, as man was the only known animal to suffer from it. For some years it looked as though the American continent had been freed from the disease, as no cases were reported from any part of it. In these circumstances the search was transferred to Africa, susceptible animals were discovered, and information was gained that has thrown additional light on the cause, the pathology, and the epidemiology of the disease, and that also appears to have a bearing upon its history. The findings that testify as to history are discussed in Chapter VIII.

In a number of instances investigators of the history of yellow fever have assumed its presence at a given place or time because of mention, however casual, of the existence there or then of a fatal disease that caused some of the people to look yellow. Some of these have been discussed and it will be shown how slight is the evidence upon which they have been considered yellow fever. It is also to be noted that even in the hands of skilled physicians the diagnosis of yellow fever may be exceedingly difficult. There are excellent reasons for believing that much of what Benjamin Rush considered yellow fever in Philadelphia in 1793 was not really such, the most important being Rush's statement and belief that "the conquest of this disease" was the result of his method of treatment by violent purgation and bleeding. This is scarcely conceivable in regard to yellow fever, and it strongly suggests that those cases were dengue, malaria, or some mild disease that bore a resemblance to yellow fever. Such a belief is supported also by other evidence, especially:

(1) Rush's own statement[14] that "The yellow fever now pre-

vailing in our city differs very materially from that which prevails in the West Indies, and in several particulars from that of the year 1762."

(2) Adam Kuhn's statement[15] that of sixty patients of his own "The greater part were indisposed with remittent and intermittent fevers which always prevail among us at this season of the year, which all yielded readily to our mode of treating those diseases, except in one gentleman, who had been many years an invalid. Seven only of this number had the yellow fever."

(3) Rush's statement:[16]

> I shall not attempt to distinguish the yellow fever from the common bilious fever. They are only different grades of the same disease. The following appears to be the natural order of the scale of such fevers as are derived from marsh miasmata:
> 1. The yellow fever.
> 2. The common bilious remitting fever.
> 3. The intermitting fever.
> 4. The febricula of authors, or what are called "inward fevers" in the Southern States.*

A century and a quarter after Rush, the truly great and very modern Noguchi went astray on the laboratory and post-mortem diagnosis of yellow fever and announced the cause to be a leptospira.[17] He was apparently working with *Leptospira icterohaemorrhagica*, of infectious jaundice, as later work of the most scientific and painstaking character, on human beings and experimental animals, has wholly discredited the leptospira as a possible cause of yellow fever.

Many other excellent men and skilled diagnosticians have at

---

* It is to be remembered that Benjamin Rush was the leading practitioner, teacher, and writer of medicine of his day in America. Nevertheless, he was so wedded to his beliefs in regard to yellow fever that he engaged in the scandalous newspaper war with his colleagues about it, and he commissioned druggists, students, and Negroes to make up and distribute his powders, each containing ten grains of calomel and fifteen of jalap, to be administered every six hours for three doses. The methods used by this good man, the leader of his profession, were as unethical, unscientific, and unwise as those of the most arrant quack. That he was honest, conscious of superior virtue, excellent intentions, and high position, and full of enthusiasm, we may not doubt. Neither may we doubt that he was mistaken.

times gone astray in the diagnosis of this disease, and today, with susceptible animals with which to test the infectiousness or the immunizing powers of the blood of suspected cases, it is demonstrable that there are cases so mild that their nature could be shown in no other way.[18] Formerly, when diagnosis was based upon clinical signs and symptoms only, a case had to be very well marked, unless in the presence of an epidemic, to be recognized clinically. However, for so-called historical purposes, writers have often seemed willing to accept inconclusive proof as to the existence of some one sign or symptom, such as epidemic prevalence, jaundice, vomiting, or high mortality, as sufficient evidence of the existence of yellow fever. For example, Hippocrates' statement that black vomit (which might be due to cancer of the stomach or any of many other diseases) was of ill omen has been cited as evidence that he knew yellow fever; Thucydides' description of the plague of Athens, which was probably smallpox,[19] has been cited as the same disease, mainly because it was a fatal epidemic; and numerous outbreaks of other diseases (modorra at Darien in 1514, starvation and scurvy at Isabela in 1493 and in Cortes's army in Honduras in 1524) have been called yellow fever because somebody spoke of yellowness of skin.

The references to ancient history are not worth discussing, as they have no value here as evidence. The instances cited in Spanish America deserve consideration, even though knowledge of them is slight and vague, and though they have been called yellow fever merely because of mention of yellowness. Before we consider them as specific instances, it should be noted that the list of diseases that may cause jaundice is a long one. Among the more common and actually frequent causes of it are catarrh of the duodenum and the bile ducts; inflammation of the gall bladder; obstruction of the bile ducts by cancer or other tumor of the liver, the stomach, the pancreas, or the intestine, or by gallstones; injury of the liver by chemical poisons, such as chloroform, arsenic, antimony, cincophen, phosphorus, arseniated hydrogen or snake venom; certain infectious diseases, such as syphilis, dengue, Weil's disease or ictero-hemorrhagic jaundice, malaria, pneumonia, dysentery, liver abscess, and septicemia or pyemia; atrophy or severe chronic congestion of the liver, and eclampsia of pregnancy. A

Russian naval surgeon who was one of a small party that suffered from severe but not fatal scurvy informs me that three of the five men involved showed jaundice. This is analogous to the jaundice following hemorrhage into body cavities.

This is by no means a complete list of the causes of jaundice. James Lind wrote,[20] "I have perused many English accounts, both in manuscript and print, of this West Indian yellow fever, in most of which the authors agreed only in the common epithet of yellow, from the skins being frequently tinged with that colour. But the same appearance is also usual in almost all intermitting fevers, in some contagious fevers, and in many others, and so cannot properly be a distinguishing mark of this."

CHAPTER IX: Tuberculosis and the Modern American Indian

There is abundant evidence that tuberculosis has been a very important factor in the modern history of the American Indian. "Tuberculosis is without doubt the most serious disease among Indians. The high death rate from tuberculosis has been indicated . . . but the extent of the disease is not known with reasonable accuracy."[21] In 1908 Hrdlicka found ninety-one acceptable reports on tuberculosis applying to 107,000 Indian population. The proportion of the several forms of the diseases to the population was as follows:

Form of tuberculosis	Cases per 1,000 population
Pulmonary	9.7
Bone and joint	1.95
Glandular	15.

The Public Health Service in 1913 reported the following estimates of racial death rates from tuberculosis:

In whites, 1.73 per 1,000 population.
" Negroes, 4.85   "   "   "
" Indians, 5.06   "   "   "

The Bureau of the Census[22] reports the following statistics for the registration area of the United States:

APPENDIX A 237

All Indian deaths, 4,220; those due to tuberculosis, 461, or 11.1 per cent.

All Negro deaths, 186,898; those due to tuberculosis, 10,390, or 5.5 per cent.

All white deaths 1,168,269; those due to tuberculosis, 66,359, or 5.6 per cent.

A committee of the National Tuberculosis Association reported in 1923 that the Indian deaths from tuberculosis in the decade 1911–20 were from 26 to 35 per cent of all deaths of Indians; and that of 647,758 Indians examined in those years, 237,052, or 36 per cent, had tuberculosis.

Dr. Frederick L. Hoffmann[23] says that the American Indian is peculiarly subject to pulmonary tuberculosis and shows little resistance, once he is affected.

"Tuberculosis is about five times more common among Indians [of Canada] than among the general population." [24]

Surgeon Marshall C. Guthrie, chief medical director, U. S. Indian Bureau, says,[25] "The major problems from the health standpoint in the Indian country are, first: tuberculosis, second, factors which are responsible for the high death rate in infants and children, and, third, trachoma."

CHAPTER X: Further Notes on Hookworm

During the years 1910–15, hookworm surveys were made by state boards of health in eleven southern states. The rate of infection in 89,857 school children was 55.1 per cent. In 1920–23 another survey on 44,090 children showed but 27.8 infected. The decline was attributed to treatment and prevention.[26] J. F. Siler and C. L. Cole examined men from three militia regiments, finding the Fourth Texas Infantry, from northern Texas, to show 6 per cent of hookworm infection, the First Mississippi Infantry 32 per cent, and the First Alabama Cavalry 54 per cent. They also noted that men with hookworm came down with measles with twice the frequency of men free from that infestation, irrespective of their rural or urban origins, and that they developed complications with greater frequency. Charles A. Kofoid studied the relationship of infection by hookworm to the incidence of morbidity and mortality in 22,842 men of the U.S. Army at Camp Bowie, Texas, from October 1917 to April 1918, and concluded [27] that 3,079 or 13.5 per cent were infested with hookworm, and 19,828 or 86.5 per cent were not. The hookworm carriers showed an increase over the noncarriers of 27.9 per cent in men sick, 88.6 per cent in men attending sick call, and 76.5 per cent in admissions to hospital. They also showed an increased susceptibility to respiratory diseases. The mortality in ten organizations with hookworm infestation above 10 per cent was 1.5 per cent; in ten with hookworm below 10 per cent it was 0.8 per cent. An increase in one regiment of 284 per cent in hookworm, as compared with the rest of the division, was accompanied by an increase of 325 per cent in mortality from pneumonia. "Hookworm is one of a vicious circle of factors favoring inefficiency, morbidity and mortality among troops."

CHAPTER XI: Further Notes on Syphilis

Iwan Bloch, who quotes Díaz de Isla,[28] regards his work as *"der wichtigste Dokumente über den Ursprung der Syphilis."* For this reason and because of its intrinsic worth, the work deserves a consideration. Díaz de Isla is very definite and specific in his statements as to the history of the disease, and no one knowing syphilis can read his book and doubt that he was dealing with that disease and that he had had a vast experience with it. He described three "species" or stages of the disease and he uses the term *bubas* as synonymous with *boton* (button = French *chancre*) in describing the first stage.

This disease comes with some bubas or buttons: which diffuse their nature through all the body by an ebullition which is caused in the blood, as has already been said. These bubas do not cause pain nor itching, nor matter nor do they become ulcers. They may last [two months to] a year from the appearance of the buttons, and within that year ninety-eight of every hundred persons will get well of pure necessity without treatment, as if no disease had passed over them. This we may call the first species, because of its being the beginning of this disease and because it differs in other ways from the second and third species.

APPENDIX A

The second species follows the first, however, after a variable time, occasionally years, and this he treated with mercury. In some instances the third stage followed and it was apparently, from his description, a malignant cachexia, in the causation of which mercury, as well as very severe infection, may have played a part. His description of the manifestations of the various stages are very good and there can be no doubt of the seriousness of the disease. It was commonly of a very severe type now rarely seen, and its spread was doubtless promoted by the belief that its second species or stage was not transmissible. He considered the primary stage highly contagious ("*es mas contagiosa que ninguna enfermedad*"), and the second species, which certainly included many lesions that we should now consider tertiary, not at all so unless the mouth was sore. ("*La segunda especie no es contagiosa, ni se apega en ninguna manera: aunque toda la comunicación del mundo aya.*") His treatment was mercurial inunctions, guaiac, and a strict regimen. In view of the general state of medicine in his day and the apparent newness of the disease, Díaz de Isla produced a really remarkable work on syphilis. He definitely states that when the disease came from America no treatment for it was known, and that by experimentation with many medicines it was found that mercury in some way had more effect than any other.

Concerning the history of the disease, he wrote:

It pleased divine justice to give and send to us unknown diseases, never heard of and neither known nor found in the books of medicine, such as this serpentine disease, which was seen in Spain in the year of our Lord 1493 in the city of Barcelona, which city was infected and subsequently all Europe and the world in all known parts with which there was communication; which disease had its origin and birth from forever [*de siempre*] in the island which is now named Española, as shown by very large and certain experience. And as this island was discovered and found by the admiral don Xptoual Colon [Christopher Columbus], who was then carrying on trade and communication with it, and as the disease is in its own quality contagious, it easily attached itself and was then seen in the fleet, and as it was a disease never seen or known to the Spaniards, although they felt pains and other effects of the said disease, they attributed them to the work of the sea or to other causes according as they appeared to each one. . . . Then in the following year of 1494, the most

Christian King Charles of France who was reigning at the time, collected many people and passed into Italy: and at the time for entering there with his host he had many Spaniards in it infected with this disease, and then the camp began to be infected with the same disease, and as the French did not know what it was, they thought that the air of the land was causing it. The French called it the disease of Naples. And the Italians and Neopolitans, as they had never heard of such an affliction, called it the French disease, and from then onward as it spread each people gave it the name of the place from which (in their view) it had its origin. In Castile they called it bubas, in Portugal they gave it the name Castilian disease, in the Portuguese Indies it was named the Portuguese disease. . . .

Other writers quote Díaz de Isla as making certain statements in his 1542 edition, which I have not seen. For example, he is said to have named the pilot Pinçon of Palos as returning infected with the disease from Columbus's first voyage, and to have said that by 1504 he was given a written account of the treatment used by the Indians, from which he argued that they must have had long familiarity with the disease to have been able to find really useful methods of treatment with guaiac, mapuan, and tuna, as they were a people of only brutish intelligence. He is also quoted as saying that he had seen many animals infected with the disease and that laborers acquired it by using for irrigation purposes water in which the clothes of syphilitics had been washed, and children could acquire it from touching washed clothing that was drying in the sun. The last two statements can be truthfully applied to syphilis.

CHAPTER XII: Further Notes on Leprosy and Trachoma

The history of leprosy is very ancient, being traceable in Egypt to 4000 B.C., in India to the earliest times of which there is any record, in China to about 1500 B.C.[29] Concerning the Egyptian date, Munro says, "There was evidently abundant early and continuous communication between the interior of Africa and Egypt, that from the northern interior consisting of an influx of black servants or slaves." He later expresses the opinion that the disease may have been introduced to Egypt by Negroes.

That both leprosy and Negroes were present in Egypt before the Exodus and were both familiar to the Jews is shown by the statement that Moses married an Ethiopian woman, for which reason Miriam and Aaron took offense, and that Miriam became leprous.[30]

The leprosy of the Bible, like that of the Middle Ages, surely included diseases other than that which we call leprosy, although it also included this. Although lepers may show spots "white as snow," that alone does not justify the diagnosis. Moses' criteria (Leviticus 13 and 14) no longer suffice for the identification of the disease. Nevertheless, the history of leprosy is continuous through thousands of years, and like the history of malaria, epilepsy, and numerous other diseases; it has become more and more exclusive as knowledge has advanced.

Hirsch states[31] that the apparently rapid disappearance of leprosy at the end of the fifteenth and the beginning of the sixteenth centuries was not so much due to diminution in the amount of the disease as to improved diagnosis. "When a revision was undertaken in France and Italy, at the beginning of the sixteenth century, of the overcrowded lazar-houses, the fact came out that in many of them by far the most of the inmates, and in some of them the whole, were suffering from various chronic skin eruptions, and that only a minority were suffering from true leprosy."

There is a very recent example, well observed medically, of unusually rapid spread of leprosy among a people to whom it was quite new. Narau or Pleasant Island is a few miles south of the equator in longitude 167 degrees east. It is about twelve miles in circumference, rich in phosphate deposits, and has a population of 1,200 natives and 1,000 Chinese. Leprosy was first introduced in or about 1911 and by 1920 there had been introduced three cases and four had developed on the island. Thereafter all recognized cases in immigrants were excluded from landing. In October of 1920 an epidemic of influenza of pneumonic type swept the island, affecting all of the population and killing 30 per cent. Most of the survivors were left with health impaired and debilitated and leprosy spread rapidly, as shown by the following table:[32]

December 31	Lepers under observation
1920	4
1921	60
1922	242
1923	295
1924	346
1925	365
1926	336
1927	337
1928	218

These figures show that the disease is being brought under control, the result of active hygienic and medical measures. The percentage of infections here is one of the highest on record, but it is to be noted that the disease spread very slowly before the influenza epidemic, but four cases developing in nine years. In the next five years there were 365 cases. Possibly the hardships and sickness experienced by Negro slaves on the trip from Africa to America hastened the spread of leprosy in much the same way. Possibly the sufferings, sickness, and hardships of the Mexicans hastened its spread among them.

We know that trachoma has been present throughout all historical times in Egypt, and even today it is probably more common there than in any other country in the world. Long before Herodotus' day Egypt was famous for its eye diseases and its eye doctors, and according to that writer Cambyces' invasion of Egypt was prompted by an eye doctor who had been taken from his family and sent to Cambyces by Amasis, King of Egypt (525 B.C.).[33] Egyptian ophthalmia is mentioned in the Ebers papyrus and has been known in Europe from ancient times. It was well described by Celsus. There were extensive outbreaks of it in Europe after the Crusades and again after the Napoleonic and English invasions of Egypt in the early years of the nineteenth century.[34] Both the French and English armies became heavily infected.*

Jean Billant[35] shows that there was an earlier outbreak of the disease in and about Lyons in the latter part of the second century of our era, introduced by Roman soldiers brought there from Carthage. Later, the garrisoned cohort having been disbanded or destroyed by Septimus Severus because of mutiny (A.D. 197), there was further introduction by legionary soldiers, by merchants from the East, and by the first Christians, all of whom were Orientals. This knowledge, that the disease is ages old in Africa, more recent in Europe, and that there is a complete dearth of information enabling us to identify it in America until long after the conquest, and that it is now very prevalent among Indians, justifies the surmise that the disease was brought to America during or after the conquest.

Cuenod[36] says that Egypt has been the inexhaustible source of trachoma since the most ancient times and from there it has been carried by sailors, soldiers, pilgrims, and merchants to all the coast of North Africa, to Greece, Sicily, Corsica, Sardinia, Provence, and even to Ireland. He quotes Sodhy Bey as saying that 100 per cent of the lower classes of the population have the disease today, 90 per cent of the middle class, and that only the very small minority represented by the aristocracy is free from it. He emphasizes that the Musselman traders (who have for centuries controlled the slave trade) have progressively infected with trachoma all central Africa as far as French Equatorial Africa. Rowland P. Wilson[37] says it is perfectly clear that the ancient Egyptian surgeons and the Greeks recognized a difference between the acute ophthalmias and trachoma, which is essentially a chronic disease,

* Max Mayerhof in a paper read before the Royal Society of Medicine in London ("A Short History of Ophthalmia during the Egyptian Campaigns of 1798–1807," *British Journal of Ophthalmology*, XVI, 129–50) in 1931 states that, while trachoma has been present since Pharaonic times, "the ophthalmias affecting the French, Turkish and British armies in Egypt during the campaigns from 1798 to 1802 and in 1807 were—as far as the rather vague descriptions left by military surgeons allow them to be identified—the same as those which are still prevalent in Egypt. That is, a combination Koch-Weeks, gonorrhoeal and post-gonorrhoeal conjunctivitis with trachoma."

but that the difference was later lost sight of. The acute varieties are in Egypt usually due to either the gonococcus or the Morax-Axenfeld bacillus, and these cause about 75 per cent of the blindness. However, the trachoma virus flourishes more readily on an unhealthy conjunctiva and those mixed infections are potent causes in the spread of trachoma. This disease is pandemic in Egypt. In the villages 100 per cent of the indigenous population is affected. The age of onset is very early, as a general rule before the end of the first year.

CHAPTER XIII: Further Notes on Miscellaneous Diseases

Farfan[38] said (1579) that those portions of the body that are called congenital, that is, those that are developed especially from the father's seed, never heal their wounds by first intention, but that with the exception of such parts he hoped always for primary union, provided that all foreign bodies such as loose fragments of bone, bits of hair, arrows, earth, straw, and loose fragments of flesh were first carefully removed from the wound. I have been unable to find anything that indicates clearly just what parts Farfan referred to as congenital, but the following citations may bear upon the subject.

The Talmud says:[39]

Three co-operators are concerned in the making of man, God, the father and the mother. The father furnishes the white sperm, from which come the bones and tendons, the nails, the marrow of the head [brain] and the whites of the eyes: the mother furnishes the red sperm, from which come the skin and flesh and blood and hair and the black of the eyes: God gives the life and soul, the shine of the face, the sight of the eyes, the hearing of the ears, the speech of the mouth, the lifting of the hands, the going of the feet, the understanding and insight. When man's time comes to go out of the world God takes back his share, that of the parents remains behind. Then the father and mother weep and God says "Why do you weep, I have taken back only my own share." They then answer, "As long as your share remained with our child he was protected from worms and decay, but now he is given over to destruction."

APPENDIX A   245

Aristotle says:[40]

> While the body is from the female, it is the soul that is from the male, for the soul is the reality of a particular body. . . .
>
> The bones, then, are made in the first conformation of the parts from the seminal secretion or residue. . . .
>
> The sinews are formed in the same way as the bones and out of the same materials, the seminal and nutritious residue. Nails, hair, hoofs, horns, beaks, the spurs of cocks, and any other similar parts, are on the contrary formed from the nutriment which is taken later and only concerned with growth, in other words that which is derived from the mother, or from the outer world after birth.

ARTHRITIS

Sir Marc Armand Ruffer[41] has shown that the disease was very common in Nubia and upper Egypt "from the earliest periods down to the Christian era, that is for a period of eighty centuries at least. In lower Egypt, around Alexandria, it has been traced from the time of Alexander down to the time of Abou Menas, that is for another period of eight hundred years."

Paul Raymond goes further back and demonstrates the disease in the bones of European man of the Stone Age.[42] He says that it was a very common disease and that Rederer called it cave gout ("*goutte des cavernes*").

Even this, however, is recent history for this disease, as it is known[43] that it affected the great reptiles ages before man appeared upon the earth. Moodie says:

> The following brief tabular survey of *Spondylitis deformans* will show for one form of pathology the antiquity and nearly continuous history of one diseased condition, widely prevalent at the present time. The age given is in terms of the maximum years allowed the geological periods, to which must be added an enormous undetermined period of time of the Epi-Mesozoic interval . . .

		Estimated age in years
Comanchean evidences seen in various dinosaurs		110,000,000
Cretaceous " " " " "		86,000,000
Eocene " " " primitive ungulates		50,000,000

Miocene	"	"	" an Egyptian crocodile	15,000,000
Pliocene	"	"	" lumbar vertebrae of camel	1,800,000
Pleistocene	"	"	" cave bears, saber-tooth cat	750,000
Neolithic man				75,000
Ancient Egyptians				6,000
Pre-Columbian Indians in America				600

On the basis of the maximum estimate, it has been, since life existed in such form as to leave recognizable fossils, nearly 600,-000,000 years, and the pathology of spondylitis deformans has had its present characteristics for about one-sixth of that time.

DISEASES IN TRANSITION

TRYPANOSOMIASIS: Africa is the happy hunting ground for the trypanosome family. There infection with these flagellates has killed millions of men and domestic and wild animals, and has threatened depopulation and extinction of species in vast areas. As sleeping sickness or African lethargy, human trypanosomiasis was often introduced to America in slaves, but it did not spread for the reason that its carrier and intermediate host, the tsetse fly, does not occur in the Western world.

However, trypanosomal infections are by no means limited to Africa or the Old World. Many American animals harbor these parasites, sometimes without apparent harm, but there are two trypanosomal diseases in South and Central America that are of serious significance to man and livestock.

CHAGAS' DISEASE occurs in human beings. It is not very common but is very serious. The trypanosome causing it is apparently a natural and possibly a harmless parasite of the armadillo, from which it is conveyed to man, and also from man to man, by a blood-sucking insect, *Triatoma megista*. The disease has been known for a few years only, and almost exclusively among persons living under primitive and unhygienic conditions. It is apparently the result of the adaptation of the parasite of the armadillo, and possibly of other tropical American animals, to a human host. One manifestation of this disease is an enlargement of the thyroid gland, or goiter. Early Spanish and Portuguese writers describe this as common among some of the Brazilian Indians. Quite possibly the goiter they saw there was due to this disease.

A trypanosomiasis of horses and cattle, known in eastern South America and Panama as *mal de caderas* (disease of the hips) because it causes a paralysis of the animal's hindquarters before death, and in Panama also as *murrina*, bears some resemblance to surra, an Old World trypanosomiasis of animals, but is different clinically, and the parasite causing it has not been identified with that causing surra. However, a particularly interesting thing in regard to this disease is the fact that it has been shown by experiment in Panama that it is there transmitted to horses and cattle by the bites of vampire bats, and that the infected bats themselves die of the infection within a month.[44] This is a clear indication that the vampire bat has not always been a carrier of the disease. Had it been, it should have developed some species immunity before this. If the disease was introduced to America with horses or cattle, the vampire could not have had access to it for more than four hundred years, as there were no horses or cattle here before that. If the trypanosome be one adapted to the horse from another animal, as that of Chagas' disease has become adapted to man, then its original host must be one that vampires cannot or do not often bite. Any disease that is readily accessible to a carrier and that kills 100 per cent of the carriers ought to exterminate these within a rather short time.

Elmassian[45] gives reasons for believing that in Paraguay the causative trypanosome is a parasite of the capibara, that dogs acquire it from eating these animals, and that the dogs transmit it to horses by biting them. The dog, like the vampire, itself dies as a result of the infection, so the reasons cited above for believing that the vampire is only a recent carrier of the disease are applicable also in the case of the dog.

RELAPSING FEVER is in Europe and Asia a relatively mild louse-borne disease, long known and, like the louse-borne typhus, apt to occur in an epidemic after famine.

In central Africa and tropical America there occur relapsing fevers that are transmitted by ticks. The African and American forms do not produce cross immunity and are therefore probably not the same disease. Thus is lost a beautiful opportunity to convict the ticks in mutual guilt, although the same tick, *Ornithodorus*, is the carrier in each continent. Truth is a jealous mistress and sometimes, when less fascinating than speculation, very annoying.

Dr. H. C. Clark, director of the Gorgas Memorial Institute in Panama, informs me that there is much reason to believe that relapsing fever as found there is derived from animals, as the armadillo, opossum, and marmoset have all been shown to harbor a parasite that cannot be distinguished from the blood spirillum that causes this disease.

There are reasons for believing that other diseases of American wild animals have become or are becoming diseases of man or domestic animals since the conquest. ROCKY MOUNTAIN SPOTTED FEVER is an example. This disease was first described less than forty years ago and first attracted much attention some years later. It was at that time apparently limited to parts of Montana and Idaho. In Montana, where the writer first saw it in 1903, it was limited to the eastern slopes of the Bitterroot Mountains, the western side of the Bitterroot River. The eastern side of the river was quite free from it. The difference between the two sides of the river was that, in general, the western side, the land between the river and the crest of the mountain range, was wild, timbered, mostly uncultivated, abounding in wild life, frequented in most parts only by timbermen, hunters, and fisherman, and a few scattered ranchers, and the eastern side was fertile plain, well cultivated, prosperous, and more thickly populated. The disease is tick-borne, not at all contagious, bears much resemblance to typhus fever, and is caused by a similar organism, a rickettsia, but is quite distinct from that disease. Persons frequenting the west bank of the river to hunt or fish in the late spring or early summer were in great danger of acquiring the disease through the bites of ticks. Almost certainly the ticks acquired it from wild life, as there were not enough human cases to keep the disease going from year to year.

The disease was highly fatal in Montana, from 60 to 90 per cent of infected persons dying. Curiously, it was a mild disease in Idaho, where it was especially a disease of shepherds in the mountains, only 2 or 3 per cent dying. It has since spread to or been found in several other parts of the United States, including the vicinity of Washington, D. C., and it is everywhere milder than in the Bitterroot valley. This fact is as yet unexplained, but it may

APPENDIX A

be due to the disease in that particular part of the country getting to man from a different wild host than in the other parts.

As stated earlier in this chapter, tularemia is a disease of rabbits that has been but recently discovered, but cases of it have been identified in persons in most states of the union.

We may expect to learn of other diseases undergoing transition from American wild animals to man.

Appendix B

List of references specifically quoted or referred to in text

CHAPTER II

1. Peter Martyr, *De Orbe Novo*, I, 329.
2. Gonzalo Fernandez de Oviedo y Valdes, *Historia general y natural de las Indias, Islas, y Tierra Firme del Mar Oceano*, Libro XLI, Cap. IV.
3. *Ibid.*, Libro XLII, Cap. I.
4. "Cartas do Brazil, do Padre Manoel da Nobrega," *Cartas Jesuiticas*. Rio de Janeiro, Imprenta Nacional, 1886.
5. Padre Manuel Rodriguez, *El Marañon y Amazonas*, Lib. III, Cap. 3.
6. Gabriel Soares de Souza, *Tractado descriptivo do Brazil*.
7. Captain John Smith, *A Brief Discourse of Divers Voyages into Guiana*.
8. Antonio de Herrera, *Historia general de los hechos de los Castellanos en las Islas i Tierra Firme del Mar Oceano*.
9. Fray Toribio de Benavente Motolinía, "Historia de los Indios de la Nueva España," in Icazbalceta's *Colección de documentos para la historia de México*, 2 vols. Mexico, 1858.
10. Francisco Grana, *La Población del Perú a través de la Historia*. Lima, 1916.
11. Joaquin García Icazbalceta, *Colección de documentos para la historia de México*. Mexico, 1858.
12. Oviedo, *op. cit.*, Lib. III, Cap. VI.
13. Icazbalceta, *op. cit.*

14. Increase Mather, *Early History of New England*, etc., p. 110. Albany, 1864.
15. Master Thomas Heriot, printed with *Travels and Works of Captain John Smith*, Bradley ed., Pt. I, p. 323.
16. Ales Hrdlicka, "The Vanishing Indian," *Science*, XLVI, 266.
17. Bulletin No. 30, Bureau of American Ethnology.
18. Ernest Gruening, *Mexico and Its Heritage*. New York, Century Co., 1928.

CHAPTER III

1. George Bancroft, *History of the United States*, I, 109.
2. M. Penicault, "Annals of Louisiana from 1698 to 1721," in B. F. French's *Historical Collections of Louisiana and Florida*. New York, 1869.
3. Elizabeth Donnan, *Documents Illustrative of the History of the Slave Trade to America*. Washington, D. C., Carnegie Institution, 1930.
4. Jacobo de la Pezuela, *Historia de la Isla de Cuba*. Madrid, 1868.
5. Donnan, *op. cit.*
6. Ulrich Bonnell Phillips, *American Negro Slavery*. New York, Appleton, 1918.
7. *Practical Rules for the Treatment of Negro Slaves in the Sugar Colonies by a Professional Planter*. London, 1811. Also M. Dazille, *Observations sur les maladies des nègres*. Paris, 1776. Also James Thomson, *A Treatise on the Diseases of Negroes, as They Occur in the Island of Jamaica*. Jamaica, 1820.
8. J. F. X. Sigaud, *Du climat et des maladies du Brésil*. Paris, 1844.
9. Robert Southey, *History of Brazil*, I, 299. London, 1822.
10. William Bosman, quoted in Donnan, *op. cit.*, I, 438.
11. Donnan, *op. cit.*, I, 591-2.
12. *Ibid.*, I, 555-7.
13. Sir Robert W. Boyce, "Yellow Fever in West Africa,"

British Medical Journal, Dec. 3, 1910, and *Annals of Tropical Medicine and Parasitology*, V, 108.

CHAPTER IV

1. Fernando Colón, *La historia de Don Fernando Colón, en la que se da particular y verdadera relación de la vida y hechos de el Almirante D. Cristóbal Colón, su padre, y del descubrimiento de las Indias occidentales, llamados Nuevo Mundo, que pertenece al serenissimo Rei de España, que tradujo de Español en Italiano Alonso de Ulloa, y aora, por no parecer el original español, sacado del traslado italiano*, p. 80. Madrid, 1749.
2. *Colección de documentos ineditos relativos al descubrimiento, conquista y colonización de las antiguas posesiones españoles en America y Oceania*, XVII, 219–22. Madrid, 1872.
3. José Gabriel Navarro, "*La medicina y los médicos en Quito durante la epoca virreinal,*" *Revista de medicina*, VI, 430–40.
4. Herringham, "Life and Times of William Harvey," *Annals of Medical History*, March 1932, Vol. IV.
5. Polo de Ondegardo, "*Informaciones acerca de la religión y gobierno de los Incas,*" in Horacio H. Urteaga, *Colección de libros y documentos referentes a la historia del Perú*. Lima, 1916.

CHAPTER V

1. Letter from John Rolfe in John Smith, *The Generall Historie of Virginia, New England and the Summer Isles*, Bk. IV.
2. Captain John Smith, *Travels and Works*, Bradley ed., Bk. II, p. 608. Edinburgh, 1910.
3. Oviedo, *op. cit.*, Lib. XXII, Cap. II.
4. Père du Tertre, *Histoire générale des Antilles habitées par les Français*. Paris, 1667–71.
5. Robert Southey, *op. cit.*, III, 308–9.
6. Sir Patrick Hehir, "Effects of Chronic Starvation during the Seige of Kut," *British Medical Journal*, June 5, 1922, pp. 865–8.

APPENDIX B 253

7. *Ibid.*
8. Fray Juan de Torquemada, *Primera parte de los veinte i uno libros rituales i monarchia indiana, con el origen y guerras de los Indios occidentales, de sus poblaciones, descubrimiento, conquista, conversión y otras cosas maravillosas de la mesma tierra*, 1611.
9. *Medical Repository*, 1811, p. 85.
10. Donald Monro, *Observations on the Means of Preserving the Health of Soldiers*, II, 182. London, 1780.
11. Dr. J. P. Schotte, *A Treatise on the Synochus Atrabiliosa, a Contagious Fever Which Raged in Senegal in the Year 1788*. London.
12. See graph opposite p. 694, Pt. III, medical volume, *Medical and Surgical History of the War of the Rebellion*. Washington, D. C., Government Printing Office, 1870–83.
13. Fray Diego Duran, *Historia de las Indias de Nueva España y Islas de Tierra Firme. Escrito del siglo XVI*, Cap. XXX. Mexico, 1867.
14. Fernando Colón, *op. cit.*
15. Oviedo, *op. cit.*
16. Herrera, *op. cit.*, Decada I, Lib. V, Cap. III.
17. *Ibid.*
18. Adelantado Pascual de Andagoya, *Narrative of the Proceedings of Pedrarias Dávila in the Provinces of Tierra Firme or Castillo del Oro, and of the Discovery of the South Sea and the Coasts of Peru and Nicaragua*. Tr. Clements R. Markham. London, Hakluyt Society, 1885.
19. Oviedo, *op. cit.*, Lib. XXVI, Cap. XI.
20. Joaquin García Icazbalceta, *Bibliografía mexicana del siglo XVI*, p. 167. Mexico, 1886.
21. Cardenal, *Diccionario terminológico de ciencias médicas*.
22. Herrera, *op. cit.*, Dec. III, Lib. VI, Cap. I.
23. *Ibid.*, Dec. VI, Lib. V, Cap. I.
24. Pedro Pizzaro, *Relation of the Discovery and Conquest of the Kingdom of Peru*. Tr. P. A. Means. New York, Cortes Society, 1921.
25. Oviedo, *op. cit.*, Lib. XXIII, Cap. IV.
26. *Ibid.*, Lib. LXXIII, Cap. VI.

27. Herrera, *op. cit.*, Dec. V, Lib. IX, Cap. X: "*I dos Hombres, que ajusticiaron, se los comieron de la cintura abajo.*"
28. Álvar Núñez Cabeza de Vaca, "*Comentarios de Álvar Núñez Cabeza de Vaca, Adelantado y Gobernador del Rio de la Plata*," in *Historiadores Primitivos*.
29. Hendrick Ottsen, *Journael van de reis naar Zuid-Amerika (1598–1601) door Hendrick Ottsen, met inleiding uitgegeven door J. W. Ijzermann, met 3 Kaarten en 5 platen*. S. Gravenhagen, 1918.
30. Herrera, *op. cit.*, Dec. VII, Lib. III, Cap. XIV.
31. H. H. Bancroft, *History of Central America*, 3 vols. San Francisco, 1886.
32. *Mémoires historiques sur la Louisiane, etc., composés sur les mémoires de M. Dumont (de Montigny) par M. L. L. M.* Paris, 1753.
33. Réné Laudonnière, *Histoire notable de la Floride, située en Indes Occidentales*, etc. Paris, 1853.
34. George Bancroft, *op. cit.*, I, 97.
35. Captain John Smith, *op. cit.*, Ch. XI.
36. Governor William Bradford, *History of Plymouth Plantation*. Ed. William T. Davis. New York, Scribner, 1908.
37. Jacques Cartier, *Bref récit et succincte narration de la navigation faite en MDXXXV et MDXXXVI par le Capitaine Jacques Cartier aux îles de Canada, Hochelaga, Saguenay et autres. Réimpression figurié de l'édition rarissime de MDXLV avec les variantes des manuscrits de la Bibliothèque Impériale*, etc. Paris, 1863.
38. Samuel de Champlain, *Oeuvres*, 2nd ed., III, 170–2. Quebec, 1870.
39. James Lind, *A Treatise on the Scurvy*, p. 159. London, 1757.
40. William R. Riddell, "Sidelights on Diseases in French Canada before the Conquest," *New York Medical Journal and Record*, 1931, CXXXIV, 143.
41. Jesuit Relations, VIII, 292 n.

CHAPTER VI

1. Bernal Díaz del Castillo, "*La verdadera historia de los sucesos de la conquista de la Nueva España*," in Vedia's *Historiadores primitivos*, Tomo II, Cap. 124.
2. Francisco López de Gómara, *Historia general de las Indias*, Ch. 102.
3. Frailes Geronimos, *Colección de varios documentos para la historia de Florida*, etc. Letter addressed to the king.
4. Herrera, *op. cit.*, Dec. I, Lib. I, Cap. V.
5. Ruy Díaz de Isla, *Tractado contra el mal serpentino*, etc. Sevilla, 1539.
6. Pedro de Cieza de León, *La Crónica del Perú*.
7. Osgood, *American Colonies in the Seventeenth Century*, II, 429.
8. Increase Mather, *op. cit.*
9. Bradford, *op. cit.*
10. *Ibid.*, pp. 312–3.
11. Colony of Fiji, reports of commission, quoted by B. Scheube, "*Ueber den Ursprung der Syphilis*," *Janus*, 1901, VI, 649.
12. Fray Toribio de Benavente Motolinía, *op. cit.*
13. Sigaud, *op. cit.*, p. 111.
14. Riddell, *op. cit.*
15. Livingston Farrand, *The American Nation*, Vol. II, *The Basis of American History, 1500–1900*, p. 266.
16. Fielding H. Garrison, *An Introduction to the History of Medicine*, 4th ed.
17. August Hirsch, *Handbook of Geographical and Historical Pathology*, 3 vols. Tr. from 2nd German ed. by Charles Creighton. London, 1883–86.
18. Joaquin de Villalba, *Epidemiologia española, o historia cronológica de las pestes, contagios, epidemias y epizootias desde la venida de los Cartaginenses hasta el año 1801*. Madrid, 1801.
19. Juan de Aviñon, "*Sevillana medicina*," in Chinchilla, *Anales históricos de la medicina en general, y biográfico-bibliográfico de la española en particular*, 7 vols. Valencia, 1841–46.

20. Hieronymus Fracastorius, *De contagione et contagiosis morbis et eorum curatione*, Lib. III. Tr. W. C. Wright. New York, 1930.
21. Nicolas León, *Memorias y Actas del Congreso Nacional del Tabardillo*. Mexico, 1919.
22. Jesuit Relations, XXVIII, 203.
23. Ruy Díaz de Isla, *op. cit.*, Fol. XV.

CHAPTER VII

1. American Relief Administration Bulletin, Series II, No. 45, April 1926.
2. Dr. Antonio Barbieri, "*El paludismo en la República Argentina*," *La Semana Médica*, Sept. 8, 1910, p. 1368.
3. Angelo Celli, *La Malaria*, 4th ed., p. 57. Torino, 1910.
4. Edward Gibbon, *History of the Decline and Fall of the Roman Empire*, Vol. III, Ch. XLV.
5. Antonio Hernandez Morejon, *Historia bibliográfia de la medicina española*. Madrid, 1874.
6. Francisco A. Flores, *Historia de la medicina en México*. Mexico, 1886.
7. Fray Alonso de Molina, *Vocabulario de la lingua mexicana*, 1571. Facsimile ed. Leipzig, 1880.
8. Victor A. Reko, "*Infectionskrankheiten im alten Mexico*," *Aertzliche Rundschau*, 1931, XLI, 151–67.
9. Manuel Ramirez, *Estudio sobre las fiebres intermittentes del estado de Morelos*. Mexico, 1873. Also José Terres, "*El paludismo en México*," *Gac. Med.*, Mexico, 1893, XXIX, 252, 281, 326, 357; XXX, 17, 49, 93, 135, 162, 198. Also Carlos C. Hoffman, *Los Mosquitos anopheles, transmissores del paludismo en el Valle de México*, bulletin of Departimento del Salubridad Pública, 1929, No. 2, p. 11.
10. Victor C. Vaughan, *Epidemiology and Public Health*, I, 375. St. Louis, 1923.
11. Garcilaso de la Vega, Inca, *Comentarios reales de los Incas*, Pt. II, Lib. IX, Cap. XV. Madrid, 1733.
12. Pedro Pizarro, *op. cit.*
13. Oviedo, *op. cit.*, Lib. XLIII, Cap. III.

14. Pedro Cieza de León, *op. cit.*, Pt. II.
15. Herrera, *op. cit.*, Dec. V, Lib. I, Cap. I.
16. Pedro Sarmiento de Gamboa, *History of the Incas*. Tr. Sir Clements Markham. London, Hakluyt Society, 1907.
17. Garcilaso, *op. cit.*, Lib. II, Cap. XXIV.
18. Manuel Rodriguez, *op. cit.*
19. *Medical Report of the Rice Expedition to Brazil from the School of Tropical Medicine of Harvard University*. Cambridge, 1918.
20. *Medical Report of the Hamilton Rice Seventh Expedition to the Amazon, in Conjunction with the Department of Tropical Medicine of Harvard University, 1924–25*. Cambridge, 1926.
21. Baron Alexander von Humboldt, *An Account of the Cinchona Forests of South America*. London, 1821.
22. Clements R. Markham, *Peruvian Bark*. London, 1880.
23. Herrera, *op. cit.*, Decadas IV and VII. See also Luis Hernandez de Biedma in B. F. French, *Historical Collections of Louisiana*. Also in the same collection "A Narrative of the Expedition of Hernando de Soto into Florida by a Gentleman of Elvas," Evora, 1557, tr. from the Portuguese by Richard Hakluyt, London, 1880. Also Garcilaso, *La Florida del Inca, Historia del Adelantado Hernando de Soto*, Madrid, 1723.
24. Colonel P. M. Ashburn, *A History of the Medical Department of the United States Army*, Ch. 2. Boston, 1929.
25. Laudonnière, *Le second voyage des Français en la Floride*. Paris, 1853.
26. John Fiske, *Old Virginia and Her Neighbors*, II, 120. Boston, 1923.
27. S. P. James, "Some General Results of a Study of Induced Malaria in England," *Transcripts of the Royal Society of Tropical Medicine and Hygiene*, XXIV.
28. Dr. W. B. Blanton, *Medicine in Virginia in the Seventeenth Century*. Richmond, 1930.
29. Rev. Samuel Purchas, *Purchas His Pilgrimage, or Relation of the World and the Religions Observed in All Ages*, Bk. VIII, Ch. 5. London, 1616.

30. Blanton, *op. cit.*
31. Jesuit Relations, XLIII, 183.
32. *Ibid.*, LIII, 241.
33. Dr. S. P. Hildreth, "Climate and Early History of Diseases in Ohio," *Journal of the Proceedings of the Medical Convention of Ohio at Its Third Session.* Cleveland, 1839.
34. Supplement No. 88 to Public Health Reports, p. 21. Washington, D. C., Government Printing Office, 1931.
35. Sigaud, *op. cit.*, p. 130.

CHAPTER VIII

1. Dr. Henry R. Carter, *Yellow Fever, an Epidemiological and Historical Study of Its Place of Origin*, p. 307. Ed. L. A. Carter and W. H. Frost. Baltimore, 1931.
2. *Reference Handbook of Medical Sciences*, 1904, VIII, 322–32.
3. George Augustin, *History of Yellow Fever*, p. 1194. New Orleans, 1909.
4. M. Audouard, *Examen critique des opinions qui ont regné sur l'origine et les causes de la fièvre jaune.* Paris, 1826.
5. Dr. Chanca, "Secundo viage de Cristóbal Colón," in Navarrete's *Colección de viages*, Tomo I.
6. Almirante Cristóbal Colón, "Memorial que para los Reyes Católicos dió el Almirante Cristóbal Colón, en la ciudad Isabela, a 30 de Enero de 1494," in Navarrete, *op. cit.*, I, 225–41.
7. Carter, *op. cit.*, Ch. X.
8. Andagoya, *op. cit.*
9. Bernal Díaz del Castillo, *op. cit.*, Cap. CLXXX.
10. Fray Diego López de Cogolludo, *Historia de Yucatán, escrito en el siglo XVII*, 3rd ed., Tomo II, Lib. XII, Cap. XII. Mexico, 1868.
11. Sebastião da Rocha Pitta, *Historia da América Portuguesa*, 2nd ed. Lisbon, 1880.
12. J. P. Schotte, *op. cit.*
13. Carter, *op. cit.*, p. 250.
14. W. A. Sawyer, *op. cit.*

15. *Ibid.*
16. N. C. Davis and R. C. Shannon, "Transmission of Yellow Fever Virus," *Journal of Experimental Medicine*, 1932, LVI, 803.

CHAPTER IX

1. Edwin R. Baldwin, "History of Tuberculosis," in Osler, *Modern Medicine*, 3rd ed., I, 144.
2. Remy, *La Phthisiothérapy dans l'antiquité; Orientaux, Grecs, Arabes.* Lyon, 1910.
3. Rey Miqueu, *Contribution à l'étude de la phthisie pulmonaire dans l'Inde ancienne, d'après l'Ayurveda de Suçruta.* Paris, 1905.
4. Paul Raymond, "Les maladies de nos ancêtres à l'âge de la pierre," *Aesculape*, 1912, II, 121–3.
5. Sir Marc Armand Ruffer, *Studies in the Paleopathology of Egypt.* University of Chicago Press, 1921.
6. Reko, *op. cit.*
7. *Medical Repository*, 1800, III, 311. Also *Philadelphia Medical and Physical Journal*, 1806, p. 242.
8. Fray Augustin Farfan, *Tractado breve de anathomia y cirurgía, y de algunas enfermedades, que mas comunmente suelen hauer en esta Nueva España*, 2 vols. Mexico, 1579. Tract. VI, Cap. X, p. 249.
9. Jesuit Relations, LX, 175.
10. Georg Sticker, "Entwurf einer Geschichte der Ausstecken den Geschlechtskrankheiten," *Münchener Medizinische Wochenschrift*, 1931, LXXVIII, 793–4.
11. Herrera, *op. cit.*, Lib. X, Cap. XIV.
12. Bernal Díaz del Castillo, *op. cit.*, Cap. CXCII.
13. Gómara, *op. cit.*, Pt. II.
14. Graham Lusk, *The Elements of the Science of Nutrition*, 4th ed. Philadelphia and London, 1928.
15. Pedro de Cieza de León, *op. cit.*
16. Jesuit Relations, 1672–73, pp. 81–3.
17. *Ibid.*, XLVI, 255.

CHAPTER X

1. Herodotus, in Loeb Classics, Bk. VIII, par. 115.
2. A Professional Planter, *Practical Rules for the Treatment of Negro Slaves in the Sugar Colonies*. London, 1811.
3. Jesuit Relations, Vol. II, English translation.
4. *Ibid.*, III, 105, English translation.
5. *Ibid.*, XLVI, 143.
6. P. M. Ashburn, *A History of the Medical Department of the United States Army*.
7. Sir Patrick Manson, *Tropical Diseases*, 9th ed. rev.
8. Dr. Cabanés, "*Les Panacées d'autrefois*," *Bulletin de Thérapeutique*, 1898, CXXXVI, 33.
9. Dr. George C. Shattuck, *The Peninsula of Yucatan*. Washington, D. C., Carnegie Institution, 1933.
10. Bailey K. Ashford, Bulletin No. 2, Office of the Surgeon General of the Army, 1913–14.
11. Dr. Charles W. Stiles, "Economic Aspects of Hookworm Disease," *Trans. Intern. Cong. Hygiene and Demog.*, 1912, Washington, 1913, III, 757.
12. Dr. Victor G. Heiser, "Practical Results Obtained in the Philippines in Reducing the General Morbidity by the Elimination of Intestinal Parasites, Especially the Hookworm," *New York Medical Journal*, Feb. 13, 1909, LXXXIX, 330.
13. Père du Tertre, *op. cit.*
14. Jean Baptiste Labat, *Nouveau voyage aux isles de l'Amérique*. Paris, 1722.
15. Pouppé Desportes, *Histoire de maladies de St. Dominique*. Paris, 1770.
16. Professional Planter, *op. cit.*
17. James Thomson, *op. cit.*
18. David Mason, "On Atrophia a Ventriculo (Mal d'estomac) or Dirt Eating," *Edinburgh Medical and Surgical Journal*, 1833, XXXIX, 289.
19. F. W. Cragin, "Observation on Cachexia Africana or Dirt-Eating," *American Journal of Medical Science*, 1835, XVII, 356.

20. John Imray, "Observations of the Mal d'estomac or Cachexia Africana as It Takes Place among the Negroes of Dominica," *Edinburgh Medical and Surgical Journal*, 1843, LIX, 305.
21. Ulrich Bonnell Phillips, *op. cit.*
22. H. Rey, "*Des maladies parasitaires suivant les races et les climats,*" *Annales d'hygiène publique et de médecine légale*, Series 3, III, 489.
23. Samuel T. Darling, "Observations on the Geographical and Ethnological Distribution of Hookworms," *Parasitology*, XII, 217–33.
24. Arthur Loos, "Notes on Intestinal Worms Found in African Pygmies," *Lancet*, London, 1905, II, 430.
25. V. Linston, "Hookworm in the Chimpanzee," *Centralblatt für Bakteriologie, Parasitenkunde und Infectionskrankheiten*, XXXIV, 527.
26. Stiles and Hassell, *Key Catalogue of the Worms Reported for Man*, Hyg. Lab. Bull. No. 142. Washington, 1926.
27. Sir John Pringle, *Diseases of the Army*. London, 1774.
28. Fray Bernardino de Sahagun, *Historia general de las cosas de la Nueva España*, Vol. I, Lib. IV, Codice florentina, Lamina XCV, No. 341.
29. Hendrick Ottsen, *op. cit.*

CHAPTER XI

1. André Alcázar, *Chirurgiae libri sex*, Lib. V, Cap. 28. Salamanca, 1575.
2. Francisco A. Flores, *op. cit.*, I, 47.
3. Karl Sudhoff, "*Mal franzoso in Italien in der ersten Hälfte des 15 Jahrhunderts,*" *Zur historischen Biologie der Krankheitserreger*. Giessen, 1912. Also Georg Sticker, *op. cit.*
4. Hans Haustein, "*Die Frühgeschichte der Syphilis,*" *Archiv für Dermatologie und Syphilis*, 1930, CLXI, 255–388.
5. Julio C. Tello, *Antiquedad de la sifilis en Perú*. Lima, 1909.
6. Julio C. Tello and W. U. Williams, "Syphilis in Peru," *Annals of Medical History*, 1930, II, 515.

7. Professor G. Elliot Smith, introduction of Cyril P. Bryan's English translation of the German version of the Ebers papyrus. London, 1930.
8. Joseph L. Miller, "History of Syphilis," *Annals of Medical History*, II, 395.
9. Ed. Jeanselme, *Traité de la syphilis*, Vol. II. Paris, 1931.
10. Hieronymus Fracastorius, *Syphilis sive morbus gallicus*. Prose translation by Mario Truffi. St. Louis, Mo., 1931.
11. Karl Sudhoff, "History of Syphilis," *Essays on the History of Medicine*. Ed. Fielding H. Garrison. New York, Medical Life Press, 1926.
12. Burton Peter Thom, *Syphilis*. Philadelphia and New York, 1922.
13. Fray Bartolomé de Las Casas, *Historia de las Indias*, V, 233.
14. Oviedo, *op. cit.*, Lib. II, Cap. XV.
15. Don Fernando Colón, *op. cit.*, Cap. LXXIII.
16. Henry Beeuwkes, *American Relief in the Russian Famine*, American Relief Administration Bulletin, Series II, April 1926.
17. W. H. Gantt, "A Medical Review of Soviet Russia, IV: Change of Type and Incidence of Disease," *British Medical Journal*, Aug. 14, 1926, 303–7.
18. Keizo Dohi, *Beitrage zur Geschichte der Syphilis*. Tokyo, 1923.
19. Ferdinand Thugut, *Syphilis, ihre Ursprung und der Weg zu ihre Ausrottung*. Stuttgart, 1931.
20. Admiral E. R. Stitt, U.S.N., "Our Disease Inheritance from Slavery," *U.S. Navy Medical Bulletin*, 1928, XXVI, 801.
21. Captain C. S. Butler, U.S.N., "Syphilis and Yaws," *U.S. Navy Medical Bulletin*, 1931, Vol. XXIX, No. 4.
22. Otto Schöbl, "Coexistent Infection with Yaws and Syphilis," *Philippine Journal of Science*, 1931, Vol. XLVI, No. 2, p. 178.
23. Herodotus, *op. cit.*, Bk. I, par. 105.
24. *Vener. i Dermat.*, 1930, Nos. 10 and 11. Also *Vestnik. Khir.*, 1930, No. XX.
25. Hippocrates, *Epidemics*, Bk. III, p. 85 of Vol. 3 of Littre's translation. Paris, 1841.

26. Flavius Josephus, *Against Apion*, II, in Loeb Classics.
27. Aurelius Cornelius Celsus, *De Medicina*, Lib. VI, Caps. 2–8.
28. Jean Astruc, *Traité des maladies venériennes*, 3 vols. Paris, 1740.
29. Richard le Brun, *De la non-existence du virus venérien*. Paris, 1826.
30. Fielding H. Garrison, *An Introduction to the History of Medicine*, 4th ed. Philadelphia, 1929.
31. Galen, *Methodus medendi*, tr. Thomas Gale, Lib. V, Cap. 3. London, 1586.
32. Benjamin Rush, *A Natural History of Medicine among the Indians of North America*. Philadelphia, 1774.

CHAPTER XII

1. Hirsch, *op. cit.*, Vol. II.
2. M. Raymond, *Histoire de l'elephantiasis, contenant aussi l'origine du scorbut, du feu St. Antoine, de la vérole*, etc. Lausanne, 1767.
3. J. A. Thompson, "Leprosy in Hawaii," *Mittheilungen und Verhandlungen des internationalen wissenschaftlichen Lepra-Conferenz zu Berlin*, 1897.
4. Manson-Bahr, *Tropical Diseases*. London, 1929.
5. Justin Foley Donovan, "On Leprosy in Jamaica," *Lepra-Conferenz zu Berlin*, 1897.
6. T. Broes van Dort, "*La distribution et l'extension de la lèpre en Hollande et dans ses colonies*," *Lepra-Conferenz zu Berlin*.
7. A. Laveran, *Leishmaniosis, Kala-azar, Bouton d'Orient, Leishmaniosis américaine*. Paris, 1917.
8. Manson-Bahr, *op. cit.*
9. Victor A. Reko, *op. cit.*
10. Juan de Cárdenas, *op. cit.*, Cap. XII.
11. William Bosman, *op. cit.*
12. William Mackenzie, *Diseases of the Eye*, 4th ed. rev., p. 453. Philadelphia, 1855.

CHAPTER XIII

1. Flores, *op. cit.*, Vol. II, Ch. VIII.
2. Fray Gaspar de Carvajal, *Descubrimiento del rio de las Amazonas, según la relación hasta ahora inédita de Fr. Gaspar de Carvejal*, p. 36. Seville, 1894.
3. P. M. Ashburn, *A History of the Medical Department of the United States Army*, p. 118.
4. Álvar Carillo, "*La xeroftalmia, avitaminosis frequente en Yucatán*," La Revista Médica de Yucatán, April 1932, XVI, 224–30.
5. *Revista Mexicana de Biología*, XII, 74–85.
6. Manson-Bahr, *op. cit.*

APPENDIX A

1. Fray Augustin Farfan, *Tractado Breve de Anathomia y Chirurgia, y de algunas enfermedades, que mas comunmente suelen hauer en esta Nueva España*, 2 vols. Mexico, 1579.
2. Nicholas Culpeper, *A Key to Galen's Method of Physick*. London, 1658.
3. Nicholas Culpeper, *A Physicall Directory or a Translation of the London Dispensatory Made by the Colledge of Physicians in London*, etc., 6th ed. London, 1659.
4. Dr. Ignacio Alcocer, *Capitulo sobre enfermedades y remedios entre los Aztecas, sacada de los Primeros Memoriales coleccionados por Sahagun, y cuyo contenido no aprovecho en su Historia de las Cosas de la Nueva España.*
5. Nicolas León, *op. cit.*, p. 51.
6. Francisco Bravo, *Opera medicinalia*. Mexico, 1570.
7. Anastasio Chinchilla, *Anales históricos de la medicina en general, y biográfico-bibliográfico de la española en particular*. Valencia, 1845.
8. Farfan, *op. cit.*, Tractado VI, Cap. III.
9. Charles Nicolle and Hélène Sparrow, *Le typhus exanthématique méxicain*, Bull. de l'Institut Pasteur, XXIX, 946.
10. *Ibid.*
11. Carlos Govea, "*Algunas notas sobre prognostico en el

tabardillo," *Memorias y Actas del Congreso Nacional del Tabardillo*, p. 113. Mexico, 1909.
12. Reynaud, Soulier, and Ricard, *Hygiène et Pathologie Nord-Africaines*, I 415–25. Paris, 1932.
13. P. M. Ashburn, *op. cit.*, pp. 259–63.
14. Benjamin Rush, *An Account of the Bilious Remitting Yellow Fever as It Appeared in the City of Philadelphia in the Year 1793*, p. 150. Edinburgh, John Muir, 1796.
15. *Ibid.*, p. 151.
16. *Ibid.*, p. 125.
17. Hideyo Noguchi, various articles on the etiology of yellow fever and on *Leptospira icteroides* in *Journal of Experimental Medicine*, 1919 and 1920, Vols. XXIX, XXX, XXXI, XXXII.
18. W. A. Sawyer, "Recent Progress in Yellow Fever Research," *Medicine*, Dec. 1931, X, 509.
19. P. M. Ashburn, "Smallpox, the Plague of Athens," *Military Surgeon*, 1931, LXIX, 188–90.
20. James Lind, *An Essay on Diseases Incidental to Europeans in Hot Climates*. London, 1758.
21. *The Problem of Indian Administration*. Institute for Government Research, Johns Hopkins Press, 1928.
22. Mortality statistics, Bureau of Census, 29th annual report, 1928.
23. Dr. Frederick L. Hoffmann, *Health Progress of the American Indian*. Prudential Press, 1928.
24. Annual report, Department of Indian Affairs, Dominion of Canada, for the year ending March 31, 1928.
25. Dr. Marshall C. Guthrie, Public Health Report XLIV, No. 16, April 19, 1929.
26. W. D. Jacocks, "Hookworm Infection Rates in Eleven Southern States," *Journal of the American Medical Association*, 1924, LXXXII, 601.
27. *American Journal of Hygiene*, 1921, I, 79.
28. Iwan Bloch, *Der Ursprung der Syphilis*, p. 306. Jena, 1901.
29. W. Munro, "On the Etiology and History of Leprosy," *Edinburgh Medical and Surgical Journal*, 1876–77, Vols. XXII, XXIII, XXIV.

30. Numbers 12.
31. Hirsch, *op. cit.*
32. George W. Bray, *Proc. Roy. Soc. Med.*, 1930, Vol. XXIII, Part II, p. 1370, section on tropical diseases and parasitology.
33. Herodotus, *op. cit.*, Book III, par. 1.
34. Hofrath Ernest Fuchs, *Text-Book of Ophthalmology*, 7th ed., tr. Alexander Duane. Philadelphia and London, 1923.
35. Jean Billant, *Le trachome à Lugdunum, d'après les cachets d'oculistes romains*. Lyon, 1915.
36. Cuenod, "Trachome en Afrique," *Revue d'hygiène et de médecine préventive*, LIV, 81–4.
37. Rowland P. Wilson, "*Ophthalmia Aegyptica*," *Assoc. Journ. of Ophthalm.*, XV, 397.
38. Farfan, *op. cit.*, Tractado IV, Cap. II.
39. Julius Preuss, *Biblisch-Talmudische Medizin*, p. 449. Berlin, 1911.
40. Aristotle, *De generatione animalium*, Book II, Chs. 4 and 6. Clarendon Press, 1910.
41. Sir Marc Armand Ruffer, *Studies in the Paleopathology of Egypt*. University of Chicago Press, 1921.
42. Paul Raymond, *op. cit.*
43. R. I. Moodie, *Paleopathology*, p. 567. Urbana, University of Illinois Press, 1923.
44. L. H. Dunn, "Experiments in the Transmission of *Trypanosome hippicum*, Darling, with the Vampire Bat, *Desmodus rotundus*, Wagner, as a Vector in Panama," *Preventive Medicine*, 1932, VI, 415.
45. M. Elmassian, "*Mal de caderas*," *Anales del Instituto Nacional de Parasitologia de Paraguay*, Vol. I. Asuncion, 1928.

Appendix C

List of References

Acosta, Padre José de (1539–1600). *Historia natural y moral de las Indias*, etc. Reprinted from English translation of Edward Grimston, 1604. Notes and introduction by Clements R. Markham. London, Hakluyt Society, 1880.

Acuña, Padre Cristóbal de. Account of exploration of Amazon in 1639. See Rodriguez, Manuel.

Aichel, Dr. Otto. "Der Heilkunde der Ureinwohner Chiles (Mapuche) und ihre anthropologische Bedeutung," *Arch. für Geschichte des Medizin*, 1912, VI, 161.

Alcocer, Dr. Ignacio. Manuscripts.

Andagoya, El Adelantado Pascual de. *Narrative of the Proceedings of Pedrarias Dávila in the Provinces of Tierra Firme or Castillo del Oro, and of the Discovery of the South Sea and the Coasts of Peru and Nicaragua*. Tr. Clements R. Markham. London, Hakluyt Society, 1865.

Aristotle. *De generatione animalium*. Translated under the editorship of J. A. Smith and W. D. Ross. Clarendon Press, 1910.

Arnaldus de Villa Nova. *Practica medicine*, Liber quartus, 1497.

Ashburn, P. M. *History of the Medical Department of the United States Army*. Boston, 1929.

———. "Smallpox, the Plague of Athens," *Military Surgeon*, 1931, LXIX, 188–90.

Ashford, B. K. *Hookworm Disease in Porto Rico*, Bull. No. 2, S.G.O., War Dept., 1913–14.

Astruc, Jean. *Traité des maladies venériennes*, 3 vols. Tr. M. Astruc. Paris, 1740.

Audouard, M. *Examen critique des opinions qui ont regné sur l'origine et les causes de la fièvre jaune.* Paris, 1826.

Augustin, George. *History of Yellow Fever.* New Orleans, 1909.

Baldwin, Edwin R. "History of Tuberculosis," in Osler's *Modern Medicine*, 3rd ed., I, 144.

Balfour, Andrew. "A Medical and Sanitary Survey of Mauritius; Past, Present and Future," *Trans. Roy. Soc. Trop. Med. and Hyg.*, 1921–22, XV, 157.

Bancroft, George. *History of the United States.*

Bancroft, H. H. *History of Central America*, 3 vols. San Francisco, 1886.

Barbieri, Dr. Antonio. "*El paludismo en la República Argentina*," *La Semana Médica*, Sept. 8, 1910, p. 1368.

Beeuwkes, Dr. Henry. *American Relief in the Russian Famine, 1921–23*, American Relief Administration bulletin, Series 2, April 1926.

Biedma, Luis Hernandez de. "The Tremendous Voyage of De Soto," in B. F. French, *Historical Collections of Louisiana*, 2nd ed. Philadelphia, 1850.

Billant, Jean. *Le trachome à Lugdunum, d'après les cachets d'oculistes romains.* Lyon, 1915.

Blanchard, M. "*Géophagie et Ankylostomiase,*" *Bull. Soc. Pathol. Exot.*, XII, 322.

Blaev, Jan. *Blaev's Atlas*, 24 vols., folio. Utrecht, 1658.

Blanton, Dr. W. B. *Medicine in Virginia in the Seventeenth Century.* Richmond, 1930.

———. *Medicine in Virginia in the Eighteenth Century.* Richmond, 1932.

Bloch, Iwan. *Der Ursprung der Syphilis.* Jena, 1901.

Boccaccio, Giovanni. *The Decameron*, 2 vols. Tr. John Payne. New York, 1925.

Borden, Colonel W. B. Manuscript.

Boyce, Sir Robert W. "Yellow Fever in West Africa," *Annals Trop. Med. and Parasitol.*, V, 108.

Bradford, Governor William. *History of Plymouth Plantation.* Ed. William T. Davis. New York, Scribner, 1908.

Braun, Max. *Animal Parasites of Man*, 3rd ed. New York, 1909.

Bravo, Francisco. *Opera medicinalia*. Mexico, 1570.
Bray, George. "The Story of Leprosy at Narau," *Proc. Roy. Soc. Med.*, 1930, XXIII, Pt. 2, Sect. Trop. Dis. and Parasitology, p. 1370.
Breasted, James Henry. *The Edwin Smith surgical papyrus, published in facsimile and hieroglyphic translation, with English translation and commentary*, 2 vols. Chicago University Press, 1930.
Bryan, Cyril P. English of German version of the Ebers papyrus. London, 1930.
Buckle, Henry Thomas. Introduction to the *History of Civilization in England*.
Bureau of American Ethnology, Smithsonian Institution. Bulletins.
Butler, Captain C. S. "Syphilis and Yaws," *U. S. Navy Medical Bulletin*, 1931, Vols. XIX and XX.
Cabanés, Dr. "*Les Panacées d'autrefois*," *Bull. de Thérapeutique*, CXXXVI, 33.
Cabeza de Vaca, Álvar Núñez. "*Comentarios de Álvar Núñez Cabeza de Vaca, Adelantado y Gobernador del Rio de la Plata*," in *Historiadores Primitivos*.
———. "*Naufragios de Cabeza de Vaca y relación de la jornada que hizo a la Florida con el Adelanto Pánfilo de Narváez*," in Vedia's *Historiadores Primitivos*, Tomo I. Madrid, 1749.
Cardametis, J. P. *Rivista de Malariologia*, X, 209.
Cardenal, *Diccionario terminológico de ciencias médicas*.
Cárdenas, Juan de. *Primera parte de los problemas y secretos maravillosos de las Indias*. Mexico, 1591. Reprint, Mexico, 1913.
Carillo, Álvar. "*La xeroftalmia, avitaminosis frequente en Yucatán*," *La Revista Médica de Yucatán*, April, 1932, XVI, 224–30.
Carter, Dr. Henry R. *Yellow Fever, an Epidemiological and Historical Study of Its Place of Origin*. Ed. Laura A. Carter and W. H. Frost. Baltimore, 1931.
Cartier, Jacques. *Bref récit et succincte narration de la navigation faite en MDXXXV et MDXXXVI par le Capitaine Jacques Cartier aux îles de Canada, Hochelaga, Saguenay et autres.*

Réimpression figurié de l'édition rarissime de MDXLV avec les variantes des manuscrits de la Bibliothèque Impériale, etc. Paris, 1863.

Carvajal, Fray Gaspar de. *Descubriemento del rio de las Amazonas, según la relación hasta ahora inédita de Fr. Gaspar de Carvejal.* Seville, 1894.

Casas, Bartolomé de las. *Apologética historia de las Indias.*

———. *Historia de las Indias*, 5 vols. Madrid, 1875–76.

———. "*Viages del Almirante Cristóbal Colón*," in Navarrete's *Colección de viages.*

Castiglione, Arturo. *Storia della Medicina.* Milano, 1927. Also the French translation, *Histoire de Médecine.* Paris, 1931.

Catholic Medical Guardian. Editorial, IX, 1.

Cawadias, Alexandre. "Le paludism dans l'histoire de l'ancienne Grèce," *Bull. de la Soc. Française d'Histoire de la Médecine*, 1909, p. 159.

Celli, Angelo. *La Malaria*, 4th ed. Torino, 1910.

Celsus, Aurelius Cornelius (53 B.C.–7 A.D.). *De Medicina.*

Champlain, Samuel de. *Ouevres*, 2nd ed. Quebec, 1870.

Chanca, Dr. "*Segundo viage de Cristóbal Colón*," in Navarrete's *Collección de viages*, etc. Tomo I.

Cherrie, G. K. *Birds of Matto Grosso.* Bull. Am. Mus. Nat. Hist., LX, 1930.

Chinchilla, Anastasio. *Anales históricos de la medicina en general, y biográfico-bibliográfico de la española en particular*, 7 vols. Valencia, 1841–46.

Cieza de León, Pedro de (1519–60). *La Crónica del Perú.* Madrid, 1880.

Cilento, R. W. *Malaria with Special Reference to Australia and Its Dependencies.* Melbourne, 1924.

Cogolludo, Fray Diego Lopez de. *Historia de Yucatán, escrito en el siglo XVII*, 3rd ed. Mexico, 1868.

Colección de documentos inéditos relativos al descubrimiento, conquista y colonización de las antiguas posesiones españoles en America y Oceania, 41 vols. Madrid, 1864–84.

Colección de varios documentos para la historia de la Florida y tierras adyacentes. Londres, 1857.

Colón, Cristóbal. *"Memorial que para los Reyes Católicos dió el Almirante Don Cristóbal Colón, en la ciudad Isabela, a 30 de Enero de 1494,"* in Navarrete's *Colección de viages*, etc.

Colón, Fernando. *La historia de Don Fernando Colón, en la que se da particular y verdadera relación de la vida y hechos de el Almirante D. Cristóbal Colón, su padre, y del descubrimiento de las Indias occidentales, llamados Nuevo Mundo, que pertenece al serenissimo Rei de España, que tradujo de Español en Italiano Alonso de Ulloa, y aora, por no parecer el original español, sacado del traslado italiano.* Madrid, 1749.

Congreso nacional del tabardillo, Memorias y actas del. Mexico, 1919.

Cortes, Fernando. *"Cartas de relación,"* in Vedia's *Historiadores primitivos*, I, 1–155.

Councilman, W. T., and Lambert, R. A. *Medical Report of the Rice Expedition to Brazil.* Harvard University Press, 1918.

Cragin, F. W. "Observations on Cachexia Africana or Dirt-Eating," *Amer. J. Med. Sci.*, 1835, XVII, 356.

Craig, C. R. *The Malarial Fevers.* New York, 1910.

Creighton, Charles. *A History of Epidemics in Britain from A.D. 664 to the Present Time.* Cambridge, 1891.

Cuenod, M. *"Trachome en Afrique,"* Revue d'hygiène et de médecine préventive, LIV, 61.

Culpeper, Nicholas. *A Key to Galen's Method of Physick.* London, 1658.

———. *A Physicall Directory or a Translation of the London Dispensatory Made by the Colledge of Physicians in London*, etc., 6th ed. London, 1659.

Curran, William. "The Pathology of Starvation," *Med. Press and Circ.*, 1880, XXIX, 229.

Darling, Samuel T. "Observations on the Geographical and Ethnological Distribution of Hookworms," *Parasitology*, XII, 217–33.

Darwin, Charles. *Journal of Researches during the Voyage of H.M.S. "Beagle,"* 2nd. ed.

Dávila, Gil Gonzales. In *Colección de documentos inéditos del archivos*, etc., I, 333.

Davis, N. C., and Shannon, R. C. "Transmission of Yellow Fever Virus," *Am. Jour. Hyg.*, 1931, XIV, 715; also *Jour. Exp. Med.*, 1932, LVI, 803.

Dawson, Bernard. *The History of Medicine, a Short Synopsis.* London, 1931.

Dazille, M. *Observations sur les maladies des nègres.* Paris, 1776.

Desportes, Pouppé. *Histoire des maladies de St. Dominique.* Paris, 1770.

Díaz de Isla, Ruy. *Tractado contra el mal serpentino: que vulgarmente en España es llamado bubas, que fue ordenado en el ospital de todos los santos de Lisboa, fecho por Ruy Díaz de Ysla.* Seville, 1539.

Díaz del Castillo, Bernal. "*Verdadera historia de los sucesos de la Conquista de la Nueva España,*" in Vedia's *Historiadores primitivos,* Tomo II.

Dohi, Keizo. *Beitrage zur Geschichte der Syphilis, in besondere über ihren Ursprung und ihre Pathologie in Ostasien.* Tokyo, 1923.

Donnan, Elizabeth. *Documents Illustrative of the History of the Slave Trade to America,* 2 vols. Washington, Carnegie Institution, 1930–31.

Dort, T. Broes van. See *Lepra-Conferenz zu Berlin.*

Drake, Daniel. *A Systematic Treatise, Historical, Etiological, Practical, on the Principal Diseases of the Interior Valley of North America.* Cincinnati, 1850.

Dubon, Antonio. "*Resumen del primer censo del 'mal de pinto' en la República Mexicana,*" *Revista de Biología,* 1932, XII, 74–81.

Dumont de Montigny. *Mémoires historiques sur la Louisiane, etc., composés par M.L.L.M.* Paris, 1753.

Dunn, L. H. "Experiments in the Transmission of *Tr. hippicum,* Darling, with the Vampire Bat, *Desmodus rotundus,* Wagner, as a Vector in Panama," *Preventive Medicine,* 1932, VI, 415.

———. "Susceptibility of Bats to Infection with Horse Trypanosome, *Trypanosome hippicum,* Darling," *Preventive Medicine,* 1932, VI, 155.

Duran, Fray Diego. *Historia de las Indias de Nueva España y Islas de Tierra Firme. Escrito del siglo XVI.* Mexico, 1867.

Elmassian, M. "*Mal de caderas*," *Anales del Instituto Nacional de Parasitología de Paraguay*, I, 27, 63, 89. Asunción, 1928.

Farfan, Fray Augustin. *Tractado breve de anathomia y circurgía, y de algunas enfermedades, que mas comunmente suelen hauer en esta Nueva España*, 2 vols. Mexico, 1579.

Farrand, Livingston. *The American Nation*, Vol. II, *The Basis of American History, 1500–1900*.

Federmann, Nicolas. "*Belle et agréable narration du premier voyage de Nicolas Federmann d'Ulm, aux Indes de la Mer Océane, et de tout ce que lui est arrivé*," etc., 1537, in Ternaux's *Voyages, rélationes et mémoires*. Paris, 1837.

Finlay, Carlos J. "*El mosquito hipoteticamente considerado como agente de transmisión de la fiebre amarilla*," *Anales de la Real Acad. de Ciencias médicas, físicas y naturales de la Habana*, 1881, XVIII, 147.

Fiske, John. *Old Virginia and Her Neighbors*. Boston, 1925.

Flores, Francisco A. *Historia de la medicina en México*, 3 vols. Mexico, 1886–88.

Foussagrives et De Mericourt. "*Du mal-coeur ou mal d'estomac des nègres*," *Arch. de Méd. Navale*, I, 366.

Fox, Howard. "*Verruga Peruana*" (Carrion's Disease), *Jour. Am. Med. Assoc.*, Mar. 23, 1935, CIV, 985.

Fracastorius, Hieronymus (1478–1553). *De contagione et contagiosis morbis et eorum curatione*, Lib. III. Translation and notes by Wilmer Cave Wright. New York, 1930.

———. *Syphilis sive morbus gallicus*. Prose translation by Mario Truffi. St. Louis, 1931.

French, B. F. *Historical Collections of Louisiana*, 6 vols. Philadelphia, 1850–69.

Galen (Claudius Galenus). *Methodus medendi*, etc. Tr. Thomas Gale. London, 1586.

———. *Oeuvres anatomiques, physiologiques et médicales*. Paris, Ch. Daremberg, 1854–56.

Gamboa, Pedro Sarmiento de. *History of the Incas*. Tr. Sir Clements Markham. London, Hakluyt Society, 1907.

Gantt, W. H. "A Medical Review of Soviet Russia, IV: Change of Type and Incidence of Disease," *Br. Med. Journ.*, April 14, 1926, II, 303–7.

Garcilaso de la Vega, Inca. *Comentarios reales de los Incas.* Madrid, 1733.

———. *Historia del Adelantado Hernando de Soto,* etc. Madrid, 1723.

Garrison, Fielding H. *An Introduction to the History of Medicine,* 4th ed. Philadelphia, 1929.

Gentleman of Elvas, A. *Expedition of Hernando de Soto into Florida.* Published at Evora in 1559, translated from the Portuguese by Richard Hakluyt. London, 1600.

Ghilinus, Coradinus. "*De morbo quem Gallicum nuncupant,*" 1497. Tr. C. B. Barnard. *Janus,* April, 1930.

Gibbon, Edward. *History of the Decline and Fall of the Roman Empire.*

Gómara, Francisco López de. *Historia general de las Indias. Segunda parte, Crónica de la Conquista de Nueva España.* Zaragoza, 1552. Reprint, Madrid, 1922.

Gordon, M. H. "Cerebrospinal Fever," *Med. Research Coun. Rep.,* No. 50. London, 1920.

Govea, Carlos. "*Algunas notas sobre prognóstico en el tabardillo,*" *Memorias y Actas del Congreso Nacional del Tabardillo.* Mexico, 1909.

Graña, Francisco. *La Población del Perú a través de la Historia. Discurso de la apertura de la Universidad.* Lima, 1916.

Green, E. H. "Medical History of the Cases of the Survivors of the Lady Franklin Bay Expedition," *Med. Record,* 1884, XXVI, 253.

Gruening, Ernest. *Mexico and Its Heritage.* New York, 1929.

Guiteras, Juan. "Yellow Fever," *Ref. Handbk. Med. Sciences,* 1904, VIII.

Hammurabi, Code of, ed. R. F. Harper. Chicago, 1904.

Haustein, Hans. "*Die Frühgeschichte der Syphilis,*" *Archiv für Dermatologie und Syphilis,* 1930, CLXI, 255–388.

Hehir, Sir Patrick. "Effects of Chronic Starvation during the Siege of Kut," *Brit. Med. Jour.,* June 5, 1922, I, 865–68.

Heiser, Dr. Victor G. "Practical Results Obtained in the Philippines in Reducing the General Morbidity by the Elimination of Intestinal Parasites, Especially the Hookworm," *N. Y. Med. J.,* Feb. 13, 1909, LXXXIX, 329.

Henderson, James. *A History of Brazil,* etc. London, 1821.

Hernandez, Francisco. *Quatro libros de la naturaleza y virtudes medicinales de las plantas y animales de la Nueva España, anotados, etc., por Fray Francisco Ximenes.* Mexico, 1615. Reprinted Morelia, 1888.

Herodotus. English translations in Bohm's and in Loeb's Classical Libraries.

Herrera, Antonio de. *Historia general de los hechos de los Castellanos en las Islas i Tierra Firme del Mar Oceano, etc., en quatro decadas desde el año de 1492 hasta el de 1531,* Madrid, 1720.

Herringham. "Life and Times of William Harvey," *Ann. Med. History,* March 1932, Vol. IV.

Hildreth, S. P. "Climate and Early History of Diseases in Ohio," *Journal of the Proceedings of the Medical Convention of Ohio at Its Third Session.* Cleveland, 1839.

Hillery, William. *Observations on the Changes of the Air and the Concomitant Epidemical Diseases in the Island of Barbados.* London, 1759.

Hippocrates. *Works,* 2 vols. English tr. Francis Adams. London, 1849.

———. *Oeuvres,* 9 vols. French tr. E. Littre. Paris, 1839–61.

Hirsch, August. *Handbook of Geographical and Historical Pathology,* 3 vols. Tr. from 2nd German ed. by Charles Creighton. London, 1883–86.

Hoffman, Carlos C. *Los mosquitos anopheles, transmissores del paludismo en el Valle de México.* Boll. del Depart. de Salubridad Pública, 1929.

Hrdlicka, Ales. *Alaskan Eskimo,* 46th An. Rep. of Bur. of Amer. Ethnology.

———. "Diseases of Indians," *Washington Med. Annals,* IV, 372.

———. "Indians of Sonora, Mexico," *Amer. Anthropologist,* VI, 50–94.

———. *Physiological and Medical Observations among the Indians of Southwestern United States and Northern Mexico,* Bull. 34, Bur. of Amer. Ethnology, 1908.

———. "The Vanishing Indian," *Science,* XLVI, 266.

———. *Tuberculosis among Certain Indian Tribes,* Bull. 42, Bureau of American Ethnology, 1909.

Humboldt, Baron Alexander von. *An Account of the Cinchona Forests of South America*. London, 1821.

Icazbalceta, Joaquin García. *Biblografía mexicana del siglo XVI*. Mexico, 1886.

———. *Colección de documentos para la historia de México*, 2 vols. Mexico, 1858.

Imray, John. "Observations on the Mal d'estomac or Cachexia Africana as It Takes Place among the Negroes of Dominica," *Edinb. Med. and Surg. Journal*, 1843, LIX, 305.

Institute for Government Research, The. *The Problem of Indian Administration*. Baltimore, 1928.

International Health Board, Rockefeller Foundation. Annual Reports.

James, S. P. "Some General Results of a Study of Induced Malaria in England," *Trans. Roy. Soc. Trop. Med.*, 1931, XXIV.

Jeanselme, Ed. *La stupeur des contemporains lorsque apparut la syphilis à la fin du quinzième siècle*," *Aesculape*, 1931, XXI, 281.

———. *Traité de syphilis*, 3 vols. Paris, 1931–32.

Jerez (or Xerez), Francisco de. "*Verdadera relación de la conquista del Perú y Provincia del Cuzco*," etc., in Vol. II of Vedia's *Historiadores primitivos*.

Jesuit Relations and Allied Documents, 70 vols. Travels and explorations of the Jesuit missionaries in New France, 1610–1791. The original French, Latin, and Italian texts with English translation and notes. Ed. Reuben Gold Thwaites. Cleveland, 1896–1901.

Jones, W. H. S. *Malaria and Greek History*. University of Manchester, 1909.

Jones, W. H. S., Ross, R., and Ellett, G. G. *Malaria, a Neglected Factor in the History of Greece and Rome*. Cambridge, 1907.

Josephus, Flavius. *Against Apion*. Tr. in Loeb Classical Library.

Joutel, M. "Historical Journal of M. de la Salle's Last Voyage to Discover the River Mississippi," in French's *Historical Collections of Louisiana*.

Joyeux, Ch. "*Le Necator Americanus en Haute Guinée*," *bull. de la Soc. de Pathologie éxotique*, 1912, V, 843.

Kneeland, Jonathan. "Causes Tending to Promote the Extinction of the Aborigines of America," *Trans. Amer. Med. Assoc.*, 1864, XV, 253.

Kofoid, C. A., and Tucker, J. P. "On the Relationship of Infection by Hookworm to the Incidence of Morbidity and Mortality in 22,842 Men of the U.S. Army at Camp Bowie, Texas, from Oct., 1917 to April, 1918," *Am. J. Hyg.*, I, 79.

Labat, Jean Baptiste. *Nouveau voyage aux îles de l'Amérique*. Paris, 1722.

Laudonnière, Réné. *Histoire notable de la Florida, située en Indes Occidentales*, etc. Paris, 1853.

Laveran, A. *Leishmaniosis, Kala-azar, Bouton d'Orient, Leishmaniosis américaine*. Paris, 1917.

Le Brun, Richard. *De la non-existence du virus venérien*. Paris, 1826.

Leiper, R. T. "Distribution of the 'American' Hookworm," *Brit. Med. J.*, 1907, I, 683.

Lepra-Conferenz zu Berlin, Mittheilungen und Verhandlungen des internationalen wissenschaftlichen, 1897.

Le Roy de Mericourt, A. "*Brésil: Pathologie*," *Dictionnaire encyclopédique des sciences médicales*, 1st ser., Vol. X. Paris, 1876.

Lind, James. *An Essay on Diseases Incidental to Europeans in Hot Climates*. London, 1768.

———. *A Treatise on the Scurvy*. London, 1757.

Lindsay, J. W. "Dirt eating," *Brit. Med. Jour.*, 1913, II, 971.

Linston, V. "Hookworm in the Chimpanzee," *Centralblatt für Bakteriologie, Parasitenkunde und Infectionskrankheiten*, XXXIV, 527.

Loos, Arthur. "Notes on Intestinal Worms Found in African Pygmies," *Lancet*, London, 1905, II, 430.

López de Gómara, Francisco. See Gómara, Francisco López de.

López de Villalobos, Francisco. *Obras*. Madrid, 1880.

Lusk, Graham. *The Elements of the Science of Nutrition*, 4th ed. Philadelphia and London, 1928.

Mackenzie, William. *Diseases of the Eye*, 4th ed. rev. Philadelphia, 1855.

Magalhães, Pero de. *Historia de provincia Săcta Cruz: a que vulgarmēte chamamos Brasil*, etc., with English translation by John B. Stetson, Jr. New York, Cortes Society, 1922.

Maldonado, Angel. "La Berruga de los Conquistadores del Perú," *La Crónica Médica*, Lima, XLVIII, 313–345.

———. "Probable rol de algunas plantas lactescentes características de las quebradas verrucogenas y utogenas," *Crón. méd.*, Dec. 1930, XLVII, 381.

———. "Nuevo criterio para explicar la distribución geográfica de la enfermidad de Carrión," *Crón. méd.*, Feb. 1933, XXX, 41.

Manson, Sir Patrick. *Tropical Diseases*. See Manson-Bahr.

Manson-Bahr, Philip H. *Tropical Diseases*, 9th ed. of Manson. London, 1929.

Markham, Clements R. *Peruvian Bark*. London, 1880. Also various translations published by the Hakluyt Society.

Martyr d'Anghera, Peter. *De Orbe Novo*, 2 vols., tr. from Latin by F. A. McNutt. New York, 1912.

Mason, David. "*Atrophia Ventriculi*, *Mal d'estomac* or Dirt Eating," *Edinb. M. and S. Jour.*, 1833, XXXIX, 289.

Massey, A. Yale. "The Distribution of *Necator americanus*," *J. Trop. Med. and Hyg.*, XIII, 258.

Mather, Increase. *Early History of New England*, with introduction and notes by S. G. Drake. Albany, 1864.

Mayerhof, M. "A Short History of Ophthalmia during the Egyptian Campaigns of 1798–1807," *Brit. J. of Ophthalmology*, XVI, 120–50.

———. *Ueber die ansteckenden Augenleiden aegypteus, ihre Geschichte, Verbreitung und Bekampfung*. Cairo, 1909.

Maynarde, Thomas. *Sir Francis Drake, His Voyage*, 1595. London, Hakluyt Society, 1849.

Mazzini, Giuseppe. "I medichi e la medicine del Perú incaico," *Archeion*, 1931, XII, 408–22.

Medical and Surgical History of the War of the Rebellion, 7 vols. Washington, D. C., Government Printing Office, 1870–83.

Meira, R., and Paranhos, U. "L'ankylostomiasis au Brésil," *Soc. de pathologie comparée*, Feb. 11, 1913.

Mendez, Santiago. "The Maya Indians of Yucatan," *Indian Notes and Monographs*, ed. F. W. Hodge, IX, 143.

Miller, Joseph L. "History of Syphilis," *Ann. Med. Hist.*, II, 394.

Miqueu, Rey. *Contribution a l'étude de la phthisie pulmonaire dans l'Inde ancienne, d'après l'Ayurveda se Suçruta*. Paris, 1905.

Molina, Fray Alonso de. *Vocabulario de la lingua mexicana*, 1571. Facsimile ed. Leipzig, 1880.

Mollière, Humbert. *Un mot historique sur l'ipéca*. Lyon, 1889.

Monardes, Dr. *Primera, segunda y tercera partes de la historia medicinal de las cosas que se traen de nuestras Indias Occidentales*, etc. Seville, 1574.

Monro, Donald. *Observations on the Means of Preserving the Health of Soldiers*. London, 1780.

Montejo y Robledo. "*Procidencia americana de las bubas*," *Congreso internacional de Americanistas. Actas de la cuarta reunion, Madrid, 1881*. Tomo I, 334–416. Madrid, 1882.

Montesinos, Fernando. *Mémoires historiques sur l'ancien Pérou*. Paris, 1840.

Montigny. See Dumont de Montigny.

Moodie, H. L. *Paleopathology*. Urbana, Ill., University of Illinois Press, 1923.

Mooser, Hermann. Articles on typhus fever in *Medicina*, Mexico, XI, 891, and in *Arch. Inst. Pasteur de Tunis*, 1932, XXI, 1–19.

Mooser, H., Castaneda, M. R., and Zinsser, H. "Rats as Carriers of Mexican Typhus Fever," *J.A.M.A.*, XCVII, 231.

Mooser, H., and Dummer, Clyde. "Experimental Transmission of the Endemic Typhus of the Southeastern Atlantic States by the Body Louse," *J. Infec. Dis.*, 1930, XLVI, 170.

Morejon, Antonio Hernandez. *Historia bibliográfia de la medicina española*. Madrid, 1874.

Motolinía, Fray Toribio de Benavente. "*Carta a el Emperador Carlos V contra Fray Bartolomé de las Casas, Enero 5, 1555*," in *Colección de varios documentos para la historia de la Florida*, etc.

———. "*Historia de los Indios de la Nueva España*," in Icazbalceta's *Colección de documentos*, etc., q.v.

Munro, W. "On the Etiology and History of Leprosy," *Edinb. Med. J.*, 1876–79, Vols. XXII, XXIII, XXIV, XXV.

Navarrete, Martin Fernandez de. *Colección de los viages y descubrimientos que hicieron por mar los Españoles*, etc., 5 vols. Madrid, 1825.

Navarro, José Gabriel. "*La medicina y los médicos en Quito durante la epoca virreinal*," *Revista de medicina*, VI, 430–40.

Nicolle, Charles, and Sparrow, Hélène. *Le typhus exanthématique méxicain*. Bull. of Institut Pasteur, 1931, XXIX, 946.

Nobrega, Manoel da. *Cartas jesuiticas. Cartas do Brazil do Padre Manoel da Nobrega*. Rio de Janeiro, Imprenta nacional, 1886.

Noguchi, Hideyo. "On the Etiology of Yellow Fever, and on *Leptospira icteroides*," *Jour. Exper. Medicine*, 1919–21, Vols. XXIX, XXX, XXXI, XXXII, XXXIII.

Nott, Josiah Clark. "Yellow Fever," *New Orleans Medical Journal*, 1848, pp. 563–601.

Ondegardo, Polo de. "*Informaciones acerca de la religión y gobierno de los Incas, 1571*," in Horacio H. Urteaga, *Colección de libros y documentos referentes a la historia del Perú*. Lima, 1916.

Orvañon, Domingo. "Leprosy in Mexico." See *Lepra-Conferenz zu Berlin*.

Ottsen, Hendrick. *Journael van de reis naar Zuid-Amerika (1598–1601) door Hendrick Ottsen, met inleiding uitgegeven door J. W. Ijzermann, met 3 Kaarten en 5 platen*. S. Gravenhage, 1918.

Oviedo, Gonzalo Fernandez de —— y Valdés. *Historia general y natural de las Indias, Islas, y Tierra Firme del Mar Oceano*, etc., 4 vols. Madrid, 1851.

Ozanam, J. A. F. *Histoire médicale générale, et particulière des maladies épidemiques, contagieuses et épizootiques qui ont regné en Europe depuis les temps les plus réculés jusqu'a nos jours*, 2nd ed., 4 vols. Paris, 1835.

Penicaut, M. "Annals of Louisiana from 1698 to 1721," in French's *Historical Collections of Louisiana and Florida*. New York, 1869.

Pezuela, Jacobo de la. *Historia de la Isla de Cuba*, 2 vols. Madrid, 1868.

Phillips, Ulrich Bonnell. *American Negro Slavery*. New York, Appleton, 1918.
Pizarro, Gonzalo. "*Carta al rey, fecha en Tomebamba a 3 de Septiembre de 1542*," in Carvajal's *Descubrimiento del rio de las Amazonas*.
Pizarro, Pedro. *Relation of the Discovery and Conquest of the Kingdom of Peru*. Tr. P. A. Means. New York, Cortes Society, 1921.
"Planter, A Professional." *Practical Rules for the Treatment of Negro Slaves in the Sugar Colonies*. London, 1811.
Poncet, M. "*Des maladies qui ont regné dans le corps expeditionnaire du Méxique*," etc. *Rec. de mém. de méd., de chirurg. et de pharmacie militaires*, 3rd ser., IX, 81–208.
Prescott, William H. *Conquest of Mexico*.
——. *Conquest of Peru*.
Preuss, Julius. *Biblisch-Talmudische Medizin*. Berlin, 1911.
Pringle, Sir John. *Diseases of the Army*. London, 1774.
Prinzing, Friedrich, *Epidemics Resulting from Wars*. Ed. H. Westergaard. Oxford, 1916.
Procopius of Caesarea. *History of the Wars*. Loeb Classical Library.
Procurador de Honduras, El. In *Colección de documentos inéditos del Archivos de Indias*.
Purchas, Rev. Samuel. *Purchas His Pilgrimage, or Relation of the World and the Religions Observed in All Ages*, etc. London, 1616.
Ramirez, Manuel. *Estudio sobre las fiebres intermittentes del Estado de Morelos*. Mexico, 1873.
Ramirez de Fuenleal, El Obispo Sebastian. "*Carta al Rey*," in Icazbalceta's *Colección de documentos*, etc.
Raymond, M. *Histoire de l'elephantiasis, contenant aussi l'origine du scorbut, du feu St. Antoine, de la vérole*, etc. Lausanne, 1767.
Raymond, Paul. "*Les maladies de nos ancêtres à l'âge de la pierre*," *Aesculape*, 1912, II, 121–3.
Regnault, Felix. "*Du rôle du dépeuplement, du déboisement et de la malaria dans décadence de certaines nations*," *Revue scientif.*, 1914, LII, 46.

Reko, Victor A. "*Infectionskrankheiten im alten Mexiko,*" *Aerztliche Rundschau*, 1931, XLI, 151–67.

Remy, M. *Le phthisiothérapy dans l'antiquité; Orientaux, Grecs, Arabes.* Lyon, 1910.

Rey, H. "*Des maladies parasitaires suivant les races et les climats,*" *Ann. d'hyg. pub. et de méd. légale*, 1880, 3d ser., III, 489.

Reynaud, G. *Dissertation sur les fièvres remittent, pernicieuses qui régnèrent epidémiquement au Port-au-Prince française dans les hôpitaux des blessés pendant les mois de Germinal, Floréal et Prairéal an 11.* Paris, 1805.

Reynaud, Soulier, and Ricard. *Hygiene et pathologie Nord-Africaines*, 2 vols. Paris, 1932.

Riddell, William R. "Joseph Grünpeck of Brockhausen and His *Tractatus de pestilentiali Scorra sive Mala de Franzos*, 1496," *Arch. of Dermatol. and Syphilol.*, 1930, XXII, 431–61.

———. "Sidelights on Diseases in French Canada before the Conquest," *New York Med. Jour. and Record*, 1931, CXXXIV, 143.

Rocha Pitta, Sebastião da. *Historia da America Portuguesa desde o anno de mil e quinhentos do seu descobrimento até o de mil e setecentos e vinte e quatro. Segunda edição, revista e annotada por J. G. Goes.* Lisboa, 1880.

Rockefeller Foundation. Annual reports.

Rodriguez, Manuel. *El Marañon y Amazonas; Historia de los descubrimientos, entradas, y reducción de naciones, trabajos malagrados de algunos conquistadores, y dichosos de otros; assi temporales, como espirituales, en las dilatadas montanas y mayores rios de la América.* Madrid, 1684.

Rolfe, John. *Letters.* See *Works* of Captain John Smith.

Rosenau, M. J. *Preventive Medicine and Hygiene*, 5th ed. New York, 1927.

Ross, Sir Ronald. *Memoirs*, London, 1923.

———. *Studies on Malaria.* London, 1928. Also various journal articles on malaria.

Rossario, Giorgio. "Anophelism without malaria," *L'Igiene moderna*, 1931, XXIV, 199.

Ruffer, Sir Marc Armand. *Studies in the Paleopathology of Egypt.* University of Chicago Press, 1921.

Rush, Benjamin. *A Natural History of Medicine among the Indians of North America*. Philadelphia, 1774.

———. *An Account of the Bilious Remitting Yellow Fever as It Appeared in the City of Philadelphia in the Year 1793*. Edinburgh, 1796.

Sahagun, Fray Bernardino de. *Historia general de las cosas de la Nueva España*, etc., 3 vols., Bustamente edition. Mexico, 1829–30.

Sawyer, W. A. "Recent Progress in Yellow Fever Research," *Medicine*, 1931, X, 509.

Scheube, B. "*Ueber den Ursprung der Syphilis*," *Janus*, 1901, VI, 649, VII, 31.

Schöbl, Otto. "Coexistent Infection with Yaws and Syphilis," *Philipp. J. Sc.*, 1931, LXVI, No. 2, p. 177.

Schotte, Dr. J. P. *A Treatise on the Synochus Atrabiliosa, a Contagious Fever Which Raged in Senegal in the Year 1788*, etc. London.

Shannon, R. C. "Entomological Investigations in Connection with Carrion's Disease," *Am. J. Hyg.*, July, 1929, X, 79.

Shattuck, George C., and others. *The Peninsula of Yucatan: Medical, Biological, Meteorological and Sociological Studies*. Washington, Carnegie Institution, 1933.

Sigaud, J. F. X. *Du climat et des maladies du Brésil*. Paris, 1844.

Singer, Charles. *A Short History of Medicine*. New York, 1928.

Smith, G. E., and Ruffer, M. A. "Pottische Krankheit an einer aegyptischen Mumie aus der Zeit der 21 Dynastie (um 1000 v. Chr.)," *Zur historischen Biologie der Krankheitserreger*. Giessen, 1910.

Smith, Captain John. *Travels and Works of Captain John Smith*, 2 vols. Ed. Edward Arber. Edinburgh, 1910.

Soares de Souza, Gabriel. *Tractado descriptivo do Brazil em 1587. Ediçao castigada pelo estudo e exame de muitos codices existentes do Brazil, Hespanha e Franca, etc., por Francisco Adolpho de Varnhagen*. Rio de Janeiro, 1851.

Southey, Robert. *History of Brazil*, 3 vols. London, 1822.

Staden, Hans. *Véritable histoire et description d'un pays habité par des hommes sauvages, nus, féroces et anthropophages, situé dans le nouveau monde nommé Amérique*, etc., Vol. 3

of Terneaux's *Voyages, relations et mémoires*, etc. Paris, 1837.

Stegarda, Morris. "Psychological Tests of Maya Indians in Yucatan," *Eugenic News*, XVI, 120.

Sticker, Georg. "*Entwurf einer Geschichte der Ausstecken den Geschlechtskrankheiten*," *Münchener Medizinische Wochenschrift*, 1931, LXXVIII, 793–4.

———. "*Mittelamerikanische Krankheiten vor Columbus*," *Janus*, 1922, XXVI, 94–7.

———. "*Seuchenhafte Genickstarre zu Ende des fünfzehnten Jahrhunderts*," *Janus*, 1921, XXV, 105.

Stiles, Dr. Charles W. "Economic Aspects of Hookworm Disease," *Trans. Int. Cong. Hyg. and Demog.*, *1912*, III, 757. Washington, 1913.

Stiles, Dr. Charles W., and Hassell, Albert. *Key Catalogue of the Worms Reported for Man*, Hyg. Lab. Bull. No. 142. Washington, 1926.

Stitt, Admiral E. R. "Our Disease Inheritance from Slavery," *U.S. Med. Bull.*, 1928, XXVI, 801.

Stratton, Thomas. "Diseases of North American Indians," *Edinburgh Med. and Surg. Jour.*, 1849, LXXI, 209.

Strong, Richard P., et. al. *Report of First Expedition to South America, 1913*. Cambridge, 1915.

Strong, Richard P., and Shattuck, George C. *Medical Report of the Hamilton Rice Seventh Expedition to the Amazon, in Conjunction with the Department of Tropical Medicine of Harvard University, 1924–25*. Cambridge, 1926.

Sudhoff, Karl. "History of Syphilis," *Essays in the History of Medicine*. Ed. Fielding H. Garrison. New York, Medical Life Press, 1926.

———. "*Mal franzoso in Italien in der ersten Hälfte des 15 Jahrhunderts*," *Zur historischen Biologie der Krankheitserreger*, etc., 5 vols. Giessen, 1912.

Sydenham, Thomas. *The Whole Works of That Excellent Practical Physician, Dr. Thomas Sydenham*, etc., 2nd ed. corrected from the original Latin by John Pechey, M.D. London, 1697.

Tello, Julio C. *Antigüedad de la sifilis en Perú*. Lima, 1909.

Tello, Julio C., and Williams, H. U. "Syphilis in Peru," *Ann. Med. Hist.*, 1930, II, 515.

Terres, José. *"El paludismo en México," Gac. med.*, Mexico, 1893, XXIX, 252, 281, 326, 357; XXX, 17, 49, 93, 135, 162, 198.

Tertre, Père du. *Histoire générale des Antilles habitées par les Français.* Paris, 1667–71.

Thom, Burton Peter. *Syphilis.* Philadelphia and New York, 1922.

Thompson, J. Ashburton. See *Lepra-Conferenz zu Berlin.*

Thomson, James. *A Treatise on Diseases of the Negroes, as They Occur in the Island of Jamaica.* Jamaica, 1820.

Thugut, Ferdinand. *Syphilis, ihre Ursprung und der Weg zu ihre Ausrottung.* Stuttgart, 1931.

Torquemada, Fray Juan de. *Primera parte de los veinte y uno libros rituales i monarchia indiana, con el origen y guerras de los Indios occidentales, de sus poblaciones, descubrimiento, conquista, conversion y otras cosas maravillosas de la mesma tierra,* 3 vols., 1611.

Urteaga, Horacio H. *Colección de libros y documentos referentes a la historia del Perú.* Lima, 1916.

Vallery-Radot, R. *Vie de Pasteur.* Paris, 1900.

Van Swieten, Gerard L. B. *A Short Account of the Most Common Diseases Incident to Armies, with the Method of Cure.* Translated into English. London, 1762.

Vaughan, Victor C. *Epidemiology and Public Health.* St. Louis, 1923.

Vedia, Don Enrique de. *Historiadores primitivos de Indias,* 3 vols. Madrid, 1749.

Villalba, Joaquin de. *Epidemiologia española, o historia cronológica de las pestes, contagios, epidemias y epizootias desde la venida de los Cartaginenses hasta el año 1801.* Madrid, 1803.

Wesselhoeft, Conrad. "Early History of Malaria," *New Eng. Med. Gaz.*, 1916, LI, 341.

Wilson, R. P. *"Ophthalmia aegyptica," Ass. J. of Ophthalmol.*, XV, 397.

Winthrop, John. *Journal. History of New England,* 2 vols. New York, 1908.

Zarate, Augustin. *Historia del descubrimiento y conquista de la Provincia de la Perú y de las guerras y cosas senaladas en ella*, etc., 1555, in Vedia's *Historiadores primitivos*, Tomo II. Madrid, 1853.

Index

Aaron, 241
Abbas, Ali, 45
Abou Menas, 245
Abscesses, 201, 202
Acaporeta, Mexico, 161
Acidosis, 152
Acts, book of, 158
Acuña, Padre Cristóbal de, 114
Adams, Francis, 187
Adams, James Truslow, 22
Addison's disease, 204
Adiposogenital disease, 204
Adrian VI, Pope, 18
Aedes aegypti, 128, 135, 139, 140, 230
Aetius, 189
Africa, North, typhus fever in, 228
African sleeping sickness, 37, 40, 246
Ague, 120, 121, 123
Aguilar, Marcos de, 150, 151
Aguirre, P., 146, 171-2
Alabama, malaria in, 125
Alcazaba, Simón de, 58
Alcazar, André, 176
Alcocer, Dr. Ignacio, 193 n., 223-4, 225
Alcohol, relative racial immunity to, 210-1
Alegre, ———, 95
Aleppo boil, 194
Alexander the Great, 245
Alexander VI, Pope, 183
Algonquin Indians, 96
Allergic diseases, 205
Almagro, Diego de, 71
Amasis, King of Egypt, 242
Amazon River, 17-8
  smallpox along, 87
Amazon Valley, malaria in, 112-5
Americo-Liberians, 2
Amoebiasis, 40
Amoebic dysentery, 108, 155-6, 157, 162, 164-5
  see Dysentery
Ancurez, Pedro, 71
Andagoya, El Adelantado Pascual de, 67, 86, 132-3, 149
  on famine, 67-8
Aneurysm, 188-9
Anopheles mosquito, 100, 105, 126, 230
Antyllus, 189
Apion, 188

Appendicitis, 201
Arabian physicians, 3, 225
Argelata, Petrus d', 188
Argentina, 104
Aristotle, 45, 46
  quoted, 245
Army Medical Library, 181
Arteriosclerosis, 152
Arthritis, chronic, 208-9, 245-6
Arthur, General W. H., 203
Artieda, Padre Andrés de, 114
Asby (Asbie), John, 118, 159
Ashford, Bailey K., 165, 167, 169
Astatlan, Mexico, 161
Asthma, 205, 217, 218
Astrology, 3
Astruc, Jean, 176, 177, 179, 188
Asuncion, Paraguay, 10
Athens, plague of, 130, 235
Aubigny, Constable d', 180
Audouard, M., 130
Augustin, George, 130, 136 n.
Augustine, 228
Aurelius Cornelius Celsus, 188
Australia, population decrease due to disease, 25, 26
Avicenna, 45, 86
Avignon, statute concerning brothel in, 188
Avila, Gil Gonzales de, 133
Aviñon (Aviznon), Juan de, 93, 149
Aztec Indians, 9, 92, 95, 105, 182
  medicine of, 222-4

Bacillary dysentery, 155-6, 157, 159-60, 162, 164-5
  see Dysentery
Bacillus icteroides, 230
Bacon, Francis, 49
Bad breath, 207-8
Bagnall, Anthony, 119
Bahia, Brazil, 87
Balantidium coli, 164
Balboa, Vasco Núñez de, 13, 67, 133
Barbieri, Dr. Antonio, 103, 110
Barbot, James, on slaves' diet, 37
  on mortality among sailors, 38
Barre, ——— de la, 88
Bartels, ———, 144
Beeuwkes, Dr. Henry, 103

INDEX

Benavides, Dr. Pedro Arias de, 70
Beriberi, 203-4
Bibliografía mexicana del siglo XVI (Icazbalceta), 193 n.
Bibliothèque Nationale, 180
Bilibid prison, Philippines, hookworm in, 167-8
Billant, Jean, 243
Biloxi, La., famine at, 74-5
Bitterroot River as boundary of Rocky Mountain spotted fever, 248
Blaev, Jan, 135
Blanton, Dr. W. B., 121, 123
Bloch, Iwan, 176, 182, 238
Bogotá, Colombia, 10
Boils, 201, 202
Bolivia, 40
Borden, Colonel W. B., 120
Bosman, William, 196
Boyce, Sir Robert W., 39
Boyle, Robert, 50
Bradford, Governor William, 55, 88, 96
  on scurvy, 76-7
  on smallpox, 89-90
Bradley, A. G., 120
Bravo, Francisco, 225
Braxton, Colonel, 163
Brazil, 40, 91
  dysentery in, 162
  early settlement of, 16-8
  Jesuits in, 16, 17
  malaria in, 112-5
  smallpox epidemics in, 87
Brill's disease, 226-7
British conquest of America, 7-8, 10
British Museum, 180
Bronchitis, 60
Brooks, Edward, 118
Bruyas, Father, 123
  on epidemic among Iroquois, 153
Bubas, 181, 182, 217, 238-40
  see Syphilis
Buckle, Henry T., 2
Buenos Aires, Argentina, 10
Bureau of American Ethnology, 145
Butler, Captain C. S., 185
Byrd, Colonel William, 163

Cabanés, Dr., 163
Cabeza de Vaca, Álvar Núñez, 72, 160
Cabot, Sebastian, 71
Cachexia africana, 169
  see Hookworm cachexia
Calvin, Jean, 45 n.
Cambyces, 242
Camp Bowie, Texas, 238

Campbell, Captain, 74
Campeche, 13
Canada, Jesuits in, 19
  Negroes in, 40
  scurvy in, 78
  smallpox in, 87-8
Cancer, 142, 191, 200
Cannibalism, 69, 71, 72
Canon, The (Avicenna), 45
Cardenal, ———, 70
Cárdenas, Juan de, 94-5, 176, 182, 196, 217-8, 224, 227
  critique of, 216-7
Carib Indians, 4
Cariga, 69
Carrión, ———, 229
Carrión's disease, 111, 229
Carroll, Dr., 231
Cartagena, 10, 69
Carter, Dr. Henry R., 64, 120, 129, 132, 133, 136 n., 139, 140, 230, 231
  on scurvy and yellow fever, 137
Cartier, Jacques, 77-8, 87, 203
Carvajal, Fray Gaspar de, 16, 113, 203
Castenada, M. R., 227 n.
Catarrh, 217
Catholic Heroes and Heroines of America (Murray), 193 n.
Cayenne, 147
Celli, Angelo, 104
Celsus, 242
Central America, 4, 6 n., 9, 11
  state of before conquest, 4
Central states, malaria in, 124-5
Ceylon, malaria in, 104 n.
Chagas, Carlos, 115
Chagas' disease, 246-7
Champlain, Samuel de, 65, 79, 87
Chanca, Dr., 131-2
Chancroid, 177, 189
Charles V, Emperor, 183
Charles VIII of France, 179-80, 240
Charleston, S. C., 11
Chastellan, Father, 96
Chauliac, Guy de, 188
Chaves, Don Ezequiel, 193 n.
Chibchas, 9
Chigger, 207
Chile, 9, 26
China, effect of conquerors on, 1
Cholera, 35 n., 70, 200
Chontales Indians, 20
Chorea, 49
Christianismi Restitutio (Servetus), 45 n.
Cieza de León, Pedro de, 86, 111, 153
Cinchona, use of, 116
Circulatory system, 141

Cisneros, Don Fray Francisco Ximenes de, archbishop of Toledo, 18
Civil War, erysipelas in, 97
  incidence of scurvy in Union Army, 65
Clark, Dr. H. C., 248
Cogolludo, Fray Diego Lopez de, 134
Colds, common, 148-9
Cole, C. L., 237
Collingwood, Captain Luke, 35
Colombia, 9, 10, 40, 207
Colón, Cristóbal, see Columbus, Christopher
Colón, Fernando, 46, 67, 181
Columbus, Christopher, 9, 15, 46, 130-2, 180, 181-2, 239
  on sickness during second voyage, 132
  threatened by starvation, 66-7
Comentarios reales (Garcilaso), 51
Connecticut River settlement, smallpox at, 89-90
Conquest of America, threefold military nature of, 6
Constantinople, 183
  effect of fall of, 44
Cook, Captain James, 26
Corabaro, 15
Cortes, Andres, 47
Cortes, Hernando, 9, 13, 70, 83, 84, 107, 108, 109, 133, 149, 151, 152, 192, 193 n., 195, 203, 206-7, 235
Cosa, Julian de la, 69
Councilman, W. T., on malaria in Amazon Valley, 114-5
Council of Trent, 46 n., 183
Cragin, F. W., 169
Cramps, 158
Cromwell, Oliver, 49
Cuba, 9, 10, 13, 31, 85, 134, 135-6
Cuenod, M., 243
Cuitlahua, 84
Culex fasciatus, 128, 230, 232
  see Aedes aegypti
Culiacan, Mexico, 161
Culpeper, Nicholas, 219-22
Cuttyhunk, see Elizabeth's Isle

Darien, 60, 67-8, 132, 152, 235
  modorra in, 149-50
Dark Ages, as effected by Justinian plague, 25
Darling, Samuel T., on *Necator americanus*, 169-70
Darwin, Charles, 229
  on effects of disease, 25-6
Dazille, M., 32, 147
Defoe, Daniel, 164

De humani corporis fabrica libri septem (Vesalius), 45
De la Warre, Lord, 121
Dengue, 140, 200, 235
Denonville, Gouverneur de, 91
Dermer, Captain, 88
Descartes, René, 49
De Soto, Hernando, 117
Desportes, Pouppé, 168
Diabetes, 152
Diabetes insipidus, 204
Diabetes mellitus, 204
Diarrhea, 32, 60, 61, 133, 158, 165
Díaz, Porfirio, 223
Diaz de Isla, Ruy, 86, 97, 176, 180
  on bubas, 238-40
Díaz del Castillo, Bernal, 13, 55, 69, 83, 85, 107, 108, 111, 149, 151, 195, 202-3
  on death by modorra of Luis Ponce de León, 150
  on pleurisy and pneumonia, 147
  on sickness in Honduras, 133
Dibothryocephalus latum, 172
Dickens, Charles, 104 n.
Diphtheria, 95, 142, 143, 148, 177
Dirt eating, 168-9
  see Hookworm cachexia
Diseases of Negroes (Thomson), 171
"Doctor of Medicine, A" (Kipling), 219
Dohi, Keizo, 184
Dominicans, in New World, 18
Donnan, Elizabeth, 31
  quoted, 33
Donovan, Justin Foley, 193
Dort, T. Broes van, 194
Dover, Dr. Thomas, 163-4
Dover's powders, 164
Dracunculus medinensis, 174
Drake, Sir Francis, 6 n., 75
Dropsy, 204
Dry bellyache, 36
Du climat et des maladies du Brésil (Sigaud), 87
Ductless glands, 204
Dummer, Clyde, 227 n.
Duran, Fray Diego, 66
Dutch, minor landings of, 7
  struggles in West Indies, 7 n.
Dwarfism, 204, 205
Dysentery, 26, 32, 33, 34, 37, 39, 60, 61, 108, 120, 133, 136, 155-6, 157-65, 199, 235
  in Brazil, 162
  in Jamestown, Va., 159
  in Louisiana, 160

INDEX

Dysentery (Cont.):
  in West Indies, 162
  Negroes as carriers of, 158, 162

Earache, 201
Ebers papyrus, 242
Echinococcus, 172
Eczema, 205
Effertz, Dr. Otto, 107
Egypt, trachoma in, 242-3
  tuberculosis in, 145
Elizabeth of England, 49, 75
Elizabeth's Isle, 15
Ellett, G. G., 2, 103
Elmassian, M., 247
Encephalitis lethargica, 152
Endicott, ——, 96
Endocrine diseases, 204-5
English medicine in seventeenth century, 49-51
Enriquez, Viceroy, 95
Entamoeba histolytica, 157, 165
Epic of America, The (Adams), 22
Epilepsy, 241
Erysipelas, 97
Esdras, 46
Espinosa, Gaspar de, 9
Espira, Governor Jorge, 69
Eunochoidism, 205
Exercitatio anatomica de mortu cordis et sanguinis (Harvey), 48

Famine, 57-61, 65-79, 80, 120, 133, 150, 152, 204, 235
  among Huguenots in Florida, 75
  at Biloxi, La., 74-5
  during conquest of Peru, 70-1
  in Plymouth Colony, 77
  in Scotch settlement in Panama, 73-4
  in Virginia, 75
  on expeditions on Rio de la Plata, 71-2
  on Roanoke Island, 75-6
Farfan, Fray Augustin, 93 n., 148, 216, 225, 244
Faroe Islands, 90
Farrand, Livingston, on infectious diseases, 91-2
Fernando the Catholic, 93
Fiji Islands, 90
Filaria bancrofti, 173, 174
Filarial worms, 173-4
Filariasis, 40
Finlay, Carlos J., 129, 130, 136 n., 230-1
Fiske, John, 120
Flores, Francisco A., 92, 95, 107-8, 184, 202, 224

Florida, 6 n., 7 n., 9, 10
  famine in, 75
  Huguenots in, 75, 117-8
  malaria in, 116-8
Flower, G., 118
Fort Brady, Mich., 124
Fort Crawford, Wis., 124
Fort Gratiot, Mich., 124
Fort Howard, Wis., 124
Fort Mackinac, Mich., 124
Fort Niagara, 7
Fort Snelling, Minn., 124
Fort Washakie, 203
Fort Winnebago, Wis., 124
Fracastorius, Hieronymus, 45, 93-4, 225
Francis I of France, 183
Franciscans, in New World, 18
French conquest of America, 6-7, 8, 10, 11
"French disease," 16, 110, 182
  see Syphilis
Fuenleal, Sebastian Ramirez de, *see* Ramirez de Fuenleal, Sebastian
Fuente, Dr. Juan de, 216, 224

Galen, Claudius, 3, 45, 46, 48, 49, 50, 97, 144, 145, 189, 217, 219, 225
  see Humoral theory
Galileo, 49
Gamboa, Pedro Sarmiento de, 111
Gantt, W. H., 184
Garcilaso de la Vega, 51-2, 110, 111-2, 116, 229
Garnier, Father, 148
Garrison, Fielding H., xii, 92, 184
Geronimo brotherhood, *see* San Geronimo of Spain
Giantism, 204, 205
Gibbon, Edward, 104 n.
  on population decrease during reign of Justinian, 24
Gil Blas (Le Sage), 51
Goiter, 204, 205, 246
Gómara, Francisco López de, 83, 107, 149, 151
  on outbreak of smallpox in Mexico, 84-5
Gonorrhea, 175, 176, 177, 178, 186, 189
  conception of in sixteenth century, 215-6
Gordon, Bernard, 188
Gorgas, William Crawford, 127, 138
Gosnold, Captain Bartholomew, 15, 88, 118
Gout, 49, 217, 218
Govea, Carlos, 226
Gratrakes, Valentine, 50

INDEX

Great Lakes, role in French conquest, 6, 7
Greece, effect of malaria on, 2
  malaria in, 103
Grenville, Sir Richard, 75
Guadalupe, 59
Guatemala, 9
Guatemozin, 84
Guayaquil, Ecuador, 110
Guayaquil River, 110
Guest, L. H., 184
Guiana, 207
Guinea worm, 174
Guitierrez, Felipe, 69
Guthrie, Surgeon Marshall C., 237
Guzman, Nuño de, 161

Haiti, 9
Halitosis, 207-8
Hall, ——, 88
Hampden, John, 49
Handbook of Geographical and Historical Pathology (Hirsch), 104
Hannibal, 84, 103
Hapsburg, house of, 183
Harvey, William, 48, 49, 50, 213
Hassell, Albert, 170
Haustein, Hans, 178
Hawaii, 90
  leprosy in, 193
Headache, 217
Heart disease, 142, 152
Hehir, Major General Sir Patrick, 60
Heidelberg, 144
Heiser, Victor G., on hookworm in Bilibid prison, Philippines, 167-8
Helvetius, Dr., 163
Helvetius' powder, 163-4
Hemmeter, John C., 45 n.
Henry IV (Shakespeare), 218
Henry VIII, 183
Henry the Navigator, 31
Heriot, Master Thomas, on Roanoke Island settlement, 22
Hernandez, Dr. Francisco, 176, 202, 218-9, 219 n.
Herodotus, 158, 186, 242
Herrera, Antonio de, 67, 72, 85, 86, 94, 110, 111, 132, 149-50, 176
  on measles, 90-1
  on modorra on Pedrarias' expedition, 150
  on Tabasco, 20
Herringham, ——, 50
Hiebra River, 15
Hieronymite friars, 19

Hildreth, Dr. S. P., on malaria and typhoid epidemics in central states, 124
Hindus, tuberculosis among, 144
Hippocrates, 45, 46, 50, 97, 130, 144, 187, 235
Hirsch, August, 93, 104, 192
  on leprosy, 241
Hispaniola, 9, 10, 66, 85, 181
  at time of first settlement, 14
  introduction of slaves to, 30
Historia General de las Indias (Las Casas), 14
Historia universal de las cosas de la Nueva España (Sahagun), 222
Historia Verdadera de la Conquista de la Nueva España (Díaz), 13, 55 n.
Historiadores primitivos de Indias (Vedia), 160 n.
Hitler, Adolf, 101
Hoffmann, Dr. Frederick L., 237
Honduras, 9, 60, 90, 107, 133
  at time of first settlement, 15
Hookworm, 156-70, 199, 237-8
Hookworm cachexia, 32, 33
Hookworm Commission, see Rockefeller Sanitary Commission for the Eradication of Hookworm *and* International Health Board
Hrdlicka, Ales, 145, 146, 178, 208, 236
  on decrease of full-blooded Indians, 23
  on tuberculosis among Indians, 146
Huayna Capac, 86-7, 110-1, 112
Huguenots, famine in Florida among, 75
  no malaria in Florida and South Carolina among, 117-8
Humboldt, Baron Alexander von, 26, 116
Humoral theory, 3, 50, 145, 214
Hundred Years' War, 183
Huntington Library, San Marino, Cal., 180
Huron Indians, 87-8
Hymenolepsis nana, 172

Icazbalceta, Joaquin García, 70, 161 n., 193
Idaho, Rocky Mountain spotted fever in, 248
Ile de France, 147
Imray, John, 169
Incas, 9, 105
  medicine of, 51-4
India, effect of conquerors on, 1-2
Indians, decrease of after white settlement, 18-27

INDEX

Indians (*Cont.*):
  medicine of, 51-4
  state of before conquest, 3-4
  substitution of Negroes for, 40
Influenza, 148-9
Innocent III, Pope, 183
Innocent VIII, Pope, 183
Inoculation, practiced by Negroes, 32
International Health Board, Rockefeller Foundation, 165
Inquisition, Spanish, see Spanish Inquisition
Ipecac, use of, 163-4
Iroquois Indians, 88, 153
Isabela, Santo Domingo, 60, 67, 130-1, 235
Itaparica, 87
Itch, 33

James, S. P., 121
Jamestown, Va., 60, 75, 118, 204
  dysentery at, 159
  introduction of slaves to, 30
Jaundice, 131, 137, 206, 235-6
Jeanne I, Queen of the Two Sicilies, Countess of Provence, 188
Jeanselme, Ed., 176, 179, 180 n.
Jenner, Edward, 82
Jesuits in Brazil, 16, 17, 87, 116
  in Canada, 19, 79, 87-8, 91, 123, 153
Jogues, Father, 96
John of Gaddesden, 188
Jones, W. H. S., 2, 103
Josephus Flavius, 188
Jourdanet, ——, 219
Juan III of Portugal, 181
Justinian, 24
Justinian plague, 5, 24-5

Kala-azar, 194
Kepler, Johannes, 49
Key to Galen's Method of Physick, A (Culpeper), 219
  quoted, 220-1
Kidneys, inflammation of, 152
Kipling, Rudyard, 219
Kofoid, Charles A., 237-8
Kuhn, Adam, 234
Kut, siege of, 60-1

Labat, Jean Baptiste, 163, 168
Lake Nicaragua, 15
Lambert, R. A., on malaria in Amazon Valley, 114-5
Lamberville, Father, 159
Lane, Ralph, on climate and soil of Roanoke Island, 75

Lanfranc, 188
La Salle, Sieur de, 7, 160
Las Casas, Bartolomé de, 13, 14, 18-20, 67, 85, 132, 176, 181, 182
  on Hispaniola, 14
  on Lucayen Islands, 14
  on Nicaragua, 15
  on Tierra Firme, 14, 15
  partial responsibility for slavery of, 31 n.
Laudonnière, Réné, 118
Lazear, Dr. Jesse W., 232
Le Brun, Richard, 188
LeCointe, ——, 115
Leeuwenhoek, Anton van, 49
Leiper, R. T., 170
Leishmaniasis, 108, 191, 194-5
Le Jeune, Father, 87, 91
Leo X, Pope, 183
León, Nicolas, 95, 224-5
Leonine leprosy, 33
Lepra-Conferenz, Berlin, 192
Leprosy, 40, 177, 191-4, 195, 240-2
  in New Caledonia, 193
Leptospira icterohaemorrhagica, 206, 234
Leptospira icteroides, 206
Le Sage, Alain René, 51
Leviticus, 186, 241
Liber Regius (Ali Abbas), 45
Liberia, effect of disease on government of, 2
Library of Congress, 180
Lind, James, 63, 79
  on scurvy, 63-4, 137
  on yellow fever, 236
Lister, Joseph, 201
Littre, E., 187
Liver, cirrhosis of, 152
Liver abscess, 136, 137, 235
Lockjaw, 32
Lok, John, 38
Lopez, Dr. Pedro, 193 n.
Lopez, Pero, 151
López de Gómara, Francisco, see Gómara, Francisco López de
Lopez de Villalobos, Francisco, 143-4, 145 n., 147, 176, 213, 219
  quoted, 213-5
Louis XIII, 48
Louisiana, 64
  dysentery in, 160
  famine in, 74-5
  malaria in, 116-8
Lucayen Islands, at time of first settlement, 14
Luque, Hernando de, 71

Mackenzie, William, 196
Madison Barracks, N. Y., 124
Magalhães, Pero, on Brazil, 16-7
Mal d'estomac, 168-9
  see Hookworm cachexia
Malade imaginaire, Le (Molière), 51
Malali Indians, 72
Malaria, 2, 38, 39, 40, 49, 60, 68, 70, 97, 99, 103-26, 127, 128, 137, 142, 154, 175, 194, 199, 201, 210, 211, 228-9, 235, 241
  in Alabama, 125
  in Amazon Valley, 112-5
  in Canada, 123
  in central states, 124-5
  in Ceylon, 104 n.
  in Florida and Louisiana, 116-8
  in Greece and Rome, 103
  in Mexico, 107-9
  in Mississippi, 125
  in Panama, 104 n., 106-7
  in Peru, 109-12
  in Russia, 103
  in South Carolina, 125
  in Virginia, 118-23
  sixteenth-century knowledge of, 106
Malaria, a Neglected Factor in the History of Greece and Rome (Jones, Ross, Ellett), 103
Malaria in Ancient Greece (Jones), 103
Malhado Island, 160
Malpighi, Marcello, 49
Mansfield, Lord, 36
Manson, Sir Patrick, 166-7, 173
  on yellow fever, 134-5
Manuel of Portugal, 181
Maregraf, ——, 163
Markham, Clements R., 116, 133
Martha's Vineyard, 15, 88
Martin, Captain, 120, 121
Mason, David, 168
Mastoiditis, 201
Matheos, Hernan Perez, 181
Mather, Increase, 88, 89
  on smallpox among Indians, 22
Matto Grosso, 59
Maury, M. F., on Brazil, 17
Mayan Indians, 9, 105
Mayer, Dr. Claudius F., xii, 225
Mayerhof, Max, on trachoma in Egypt, 243 n.
Mayow, John, 50
Measles, 47, 80-2, 86, 90-2, 93, 98, 111, 142, 148-9, 154, 193, 198, 210, 211
Mendoza, Don Pedro de, 72
Meningitis, 70, 142, 143, 149
Mercado, 106

"Mercator Honestus," 37
Mercatus, 106
Mexico, 4, 9, 10, 13, 26, 40, 65
  depopulation of, 22
  malaria in, 107-9
  population statistics of, 23
  smallpox in, 82-6
  state of before conquest, 4
  typhus fever in, 95-6
Mexico City, 109
Michelangelo, 45
Miller, Joseph L., on absence of syphilis in Europe prior to discovery of America, 178-9
Milton, John, 49
Monday, Dr. H. A., 146
Minot, Dr. George R., xi, 61 n., 225 n.
Miqueu, Rey, 144
Miriam, 241
Mississippi, malaria in, 125
Mississippi River, role in French conquest, 6, 7
Modorra, 68, 132, 149-50, 235
  in Darien, 149-50
Molière, 51
Molina, Fray Alonso de, 107, 108, 125
Monardes, Dr., 110
Monro, Donald, on scurvy, 64-5
Montana, Rocky Mountain spotted fever in, 248
Montenegro, ——, 71
Monte-Rei, Conde de, 62
Montesinos, 46
Montezuma, 65, 84
Montpensier, Duke of, 180
Montreal, 7
Moodie, H. L., 208
  on arthritis, 245-6
Mooser, Dr. Hermann, 227
Morax-Axenfeld bacillus, 244
Morejon, Antonio Hernandez, 106
Morelos, Mexico, 109
Morgan, Henry, 59
Moses, 186, 241
Motolinía, Fray Toribio de Benavente, 20, 90
Munro, W., 192, 240
Murray, J. O'K., 193
Museo Nacional, Mexico, 146

Naples, siege of, 179-80
Narau Island, 193
  leprosy on, 241-2
Narrative of Missionary Enterprise (Williams), 26-7
Narváez, Pánfilo de, 59, 83, 84, 85, 117, 160

INDEX

Navarro, José Gabriel, on early American medicine, 47-8
Navarro, Padre, 16
Navidad, 66
Necator americanus, 165, 169-70
Negroes as carriers of dysentery, 158, 162
  as carriers of hookworms, 156
  as carriers of leprosy, 192, 194
  as carriers of trachoma, 196-7
  as carriers of yellow fever, 136-40
  diseases of, 32-40
  effects of on America, 3, 5
  hookworm among, 156, 168-70
  introduction to America of, 28-9
  medicine of, 51
  pneumonia and pleurisy among, 147
  schistosomiasis among, 173
Nephritis, 152
Nervous system, 141-2
New Caledonia, leprosy in, 193
New England, introduction of slaves to, 30
  role in British conquest, 7
New Orleans, 7, 12
New St. Andrew, 73-4
New Spain, 1670 boundaries of, 11
Newton, Sir Isaac, 49
New York, introduction of slaves to, 30
New Zealand, 26
Nicaragua, 90
  at time of first settlement, 14-5
Nicolle, Charles, 224-5, 225-7
Nicuesa, Diego de, 67, 68, 133
Nigua, 207
Ninan Cuyoche, 111
Nobrega, Padre Manoel da, on Brazil, 16
Noguchi, Hideyo, 206, 234
Nombre de Dios, Panama, 67, 68
North, Captain, 18
Nott, Josiah Clark, 129
Nouveau voyage aux isles de l'Amérique (Labat), 163
Nova Scotia, 6 n.

Oaxaca, Mexico, pinta in, 206
Ohio, 124
Ojeda, Alonzo de, 67, 68, 133, 151
Onchocerca volvulus, 174
Ondegardo, Polo de, 54
Ophthalmia, 33, 196-7
Orellano, Francisco de, 16, 72-3, 112-3, 203
Oriental sore, 194
Ornithodorus, 247
Oroya fever, 111, 112, 229
Orozco, Federico Gomez de, 193 n.

Orsuña, General Pedro, 113
Orvañanos, Domingo, on leprosy, 192-3
Osteitis, 144
Osteomyelitis, 144, 201
Ottsen, Hendrick, 72
Ovando, Nicolas, governor of Hispaniola, 30, 67
Oviedo, Gonzalo Fernandez de —— y Valdés, 58, 67, 72, 90, 132, 176, 181, 182, 207
  on depopulation of Hispaniola, 21-2
  on disease (yellow fever) at Isabela, Santo Domingo, 130-1
  on Honduras, 15

Panama, 9, 10, 11, 13, 47, 67
  conquest of disease in, 2
  malaria in, 104 n., 106-7
  modorra in, 149-50
Panama Canal, 106, 110, 127, 233
Paracelsus, 45
Parathyroid glands, 204-5
Paré, Ambroise, 45, 48
Patin, Guy, 48
Patterson, William, 73
Peccary, 172 n.
Pedrarias, 13, 68-9, 132-3, 150
Pedro I of Spain, 149
Pellagra, 203-4
Percy, Honorable George, 55, 204
  on disease in Jamestown, Va., 119
  on dysentery in Jamestown, Va., 159
Periosteitis, 144
Peripneumonia, 32
Peritonitis, 201
Pernambuco, 87, 134
Peru, 4, 9, 10, 40, 46
  communism in before conquest, 4
  famine during conquest of, 70-1
  malaria in, 109-12
  medicine of early, 51-4
  population decrease due to smallpox, 20
  smallpox epidemic in, 86-7
Peruvians, early notion of origin of, 46
Peter Martyr, quoted, 15
Philip II of Spain, 218
Philippines, conquest of disease in, 2
Phillips, Captain, 34, 37, 38
Phillips, Ulrich Bonnell, 32, 169
Physicall Directory or a Translation of the London Dispensatory ... (Culpeper), quoted, 221-2
Piedra, 207
Pilar, García del, 161
Pincon (Pinçon), Vicente Yanez, 181, 240

Pinta, 206-7
Piratininga, 33
Pison, ———, 163
Pituitary gland, 204
Pizarro, Francisco, 9
Pizarro, Gonzalo, 70-1, 72, 112-3, 153
Pizarro, Pedro, 111
Plague, 49, 200, 217, 227-8
Plata, Rio de la, 10
  famine on expeditions on, 71-2
Pleasant Island, *see* Narau Island
Pleurisy, 147, 177
Plymouth Colony, famine in, 77
  scurvy in, 76-7
  smallpox in, 88-90
Pneumonia, 60, 112, 142, 143, 147, 177, 235
Ponce de León, Juan, 117
Ponce de León, Luis, 149
  death of, 150-1, 152
Pontine Marshes, reclamation of, 104 n.
Popayan, Peru, 71
Pope, Alexander, quoted, 175
Porto Rico, 85
  hookworm in, 165, 167
Porto Seguro, Brazil, 16
Pott's disease, 144
Powell, Nathaniel, 119
Prescott, William Hickling, 83, 84 n.
Primera parte de los problemas y secretos maravillosos de las Indias (Cárdenas), 216
Pringle, Sir John, on worms, 171
Procopius, on Justinian plague, 24
"Professional Planter," 32, 158, 168
Prostate gland, enlarged, 152
Psammiticus, 186
Pueblo Indians, 9
Puerperal fevers, 201
Puerto Rico, *see* Porto Rico
Purchas, Reverend Samuel, 88
  on Jamestown, Va., 122-3
Puritans, 4
Pyemia, 235

Quebec, 7
  scurvy in, 77-9
Quemados, Cuba, yellow-fever epidemic at, 231
Quinsy, 201
Quito, kingdom of, 110, 228-9

Raleigh, Sir Walter, 75
Ramirez de Fuenleal, Sebastian, bishop of Santo Domingo, on effects of white settlement, 21
Rape of the Lock (Pope), 175

Rats, Lice, and History (Zinsser), viii
Raymond, M., 192
Raymond, Paul, 245
  on tuberculosis in prehistoric man, 144
Reed, Walter, 127, 129, 229, 231
Reformation, effect of, 44
Reko, Victor A., 95, 108, 148, 195, 224
Relapsing fever, 247-8
Remy, M., 144
Renaissance, Spain during, 43-5
Respiratory system, diseases of, 141-54
Rey, H., 169
Reynaud, G., 228
Rhazes, 45
Rheuma, 218
Rheumatism, 47
Ribault, Captain, 75
Ricard, ———, 228
Rickets, 203-4
Riddell, William R., 79, 91
Rio de Janeiro, 87
Riolan, Jean, 48
Roanoke Island, colonization of, 75
  famine on, 75-6
Roberval, Sieur de, 78
Robinson Crusoe (Defoe), 164
Rocha Pitta, Sebastião da, 134
Rockefeller, John D., 165, 167
Rockefeller Foundation, 165-7, 168
Rockefeller Sanitary Commission for the Eradication of Hookworm, 165
Rocky Mountain spotted fever, 248-9
Rodriguez, Padre Manuel, on Brazil, 17
Rodriguez, Padre Simão, 16
Rolfe, John, on introduction of slavery, 30
  on Jamestown, Va., 122
Roman Campagna, reclamation of, 104 n.
Rome, effect of malaria on, 2, 103
Rosa Anglica (John of Gaddesden), 188
Ross, Ronald, 2, 103, 230, 231
Rougemont, Philippe, 78
Roundworms, 171
Rubios, Dr. Palacios, 18
Ruffer, Sir Marc Armand, 145, 245
Rush, Benjamin, 158, 171, 189, 233-4
Russia, 4, 57
  malaria in, 103
  venereal disease in, 184, 186-7

Sahagun, Fray Bernardino de, 146, 171, 176, 182, 202, 219 n., 222-4
  on typhus fever, 94-5
St. Augustine, Fla., 10
St. Helena, 26
St. James, 189

St. Lawrence River, role in French conquest, 6, 7
St. Paul, 158
Salamis, battle of, 158
Salem plantation, typhus in, 96-7
Saliceto, Gulielmus de, 188
Sanarelli, ——, 230
Sand flea, 207
Sandwich Islands, see Hawaii
San Geronimo of Spain, order of, 18-9, 85
San Lazaro Hospital, Mexico City, 193 n.
San Marino, Cal., 180
San Salvador, 87
Santa Marta, Colombia, 10
Santiago, Chile, 10
Santo Domingo, 9, 10, 66, 85, 181-2
Scarlet fever, 26, 49, 91, 92
Schistosoma mansoni, 172-3
Schistosomiasis, 172-3
Schöbl, Otto, on syphilis and yaws, 185-6
Scholasticism, 3, 44, 45
Schotte, Dr. J. P., 36, 136
  on prevention of scurvy, 65
Sciatica, 217, 218
Scotch, settlement in Panama of, 73-4
Scurvy, 33, 36, 57-60, 61 n., 62-5, 72, 76-7, 80, 120, 121, 137, 203, 235, 236
  in Canada, 77-9
  in Massachusetts, 76-7
Scythians, possible syphilis among, 186
Selkirk, Alexander, 164
Semashko, Dr., 184
Septicemia, 201, 235
Septimus Severus, 243
Serveto, Miguel, see Servetus, Michael
Servetus, Michael, 45
Seventeenth-century medicine, 49-51
Sévigné, Mme de, 163
Shakespeare, William, 49
Shattuck, George C., 85, 165
  on malaria in Amazon Valley, 115
"Short History of Ophthalmia during the Egyptian Campaigns of 1798–1807" (Mayerhof), 243 n.
Sigaud, J. F. X., 33, 72, 87, 91, 126
Siler, J. F., 237
Simulium damnosum, 174
Sixteenth-century medicine, 43-8, 105-6, 213-24
Sixtus IV, Pope, 48
Slave ships, conditions aboard, 35
  mortality on, 31-2
Slaves, diet of, 36-7
  examination of, 33-4

Slaves (*Cont.*):
  introduction to America of, 28-9, 30-41
  quarantine of, 39-40
Smallpox, 20, 22, 32, 33, 34, 35, 37, 45, 47, 70, 90, 91, 93, 94, 96, 97-8, 99, 111, 142, 154, 162, 193, 194, 198, 210, 211, 217, 224, 228, 235
  in Canada, 87-8
  in conquest of Mexico, 82-6
  in Brazil, 87
  in Peru, 86-7
  in Plymouth, 88-90
Smith, Buckingham, 160 n.
Smith, Sir Grafton Elliot, 145, 178
Smith, Captain John, 13, 55, 76, 118, 120, 121, 122, 159
  on Amazon Valley, 18
  on diet, 58
  on disease in Jamestown, Va., 119
Smithsonian Institution, 145 n., 178, 195
Soares de Souza, Gabriel, on Brazil, 17
Sodhy Bey, 243
Soulier, ——, 228
South Carolina, malaria in, 125
Southey, Robert, 33
Spanish conquest of America, 9-14
Spanish Inquisition, 4, 44, 183
Spanish medicine in sixteenth century, 42-8
Spirochetal jaundice, see Weil's disease
Spondylitis deformans, 245-6
  see Arthritis
Starvation, see Famine
Stegomyia calopus, 230
Stegomyia fasciata, 128, 139, 230
  see *Aedes aegypti*
Sternberg, General, 230
Sticker, Georg, 151 n., 179, 183, 184
  on modorra, 149
Stiles, Charles Wardell, 165, 167, 169, 170
Stitt, Admiral E. R., 185
Stomach trouble, 217-8
Strong, Richard P., on malaria in Amazon Valley, 115
Sudhoff, Karl, 179, 180, 184
Sudley, Thomas, on disease in Jamestown, 119
Sulfa drugs, 142
Sumario de la medicina con un tratado sobre las pestiferas bubas (Lopez de Villalobos), 213, 215-6
  quoted, 213-15
Suppuration, 201-3
Suprarenal glands, 204
Surgeon General's Library, 181 n.

Susruta, 144
Sweating sickness, 49
Swedes, minor landings of, 7
Sydenham, Thomas, 49-50, 55, 92, 120, 144, 145 n., 185
Syphilis, 32, 40, 78, 85, 97, 108, 129, 175-90, 192, 193, 195, 199, 201, 206, 207, 217, 235, 238-40
   conception of in sixteenth century, 215-6
   in Russia, 186-7

Tabasco, 9, 13, 20
Tadoussac, 7, 19, 153
Taenia saginata, 172
Taenia solium, 172
Tahiti, 26
Talmud, quoted, 244
Talteluco, Mexico, 84
Taos, N. M., 11
Tapeworm, 155, 172
Taranta, Valescus de, 188
Tello, Fray Antonio, 161
Tello, Julio C., 178
Tenesmus, 158
Tenochtitlan (Mexico City), 9
Tertre, Père du, 59, 168
Texeira, Captain Pedro, 114
Thom, Burton Peter, 184
   on disease among French troops at Naples, 180
Thomson, James, 32, 168
   on worms, 171
Thucydides, viii, 130, 235
Thugut, Ferdinand, 185
Thyroid gland, 204, 246
Tierra Firme, at time of first settlement, 14, 15
Todkill, Amos, 119
Torquemada, Fray Juan de, 95
   on scurvy, 62-3
Trachoma, 191, 196-7, 237, 242-4
   in Egypt, 242-3
Tractado contra el mal serpentino (Díaz de Isla), 180
Traité de la syphilis (Jeanselme), 179
Treatise on the Scurvy (Lind), 63, 137
Trent, Council of, 46 n., 183
Trephining as practiced in Peru, 201-2
Treponema pallidum, 185
Treponema pertenue, 185
Triatoma megista, 246
Trichina, 172
Trichosporum giganteum, 207
True History of the Conquest of New Spain (Díaz), 13, 55 n.
Trypanosomiasis, 37, 40, 246

Tuberculosis, 142, 143, 144-7, 154, 175, 177, 201, 210
   and modern American Indians, 236-7
Tularemia, 200, 249
Typhoid fever, 32, 92, 95, 96, 120, 124, 142, 157, 158, 160 n., 177, 180, 225
Typhus fever, 47, 60, 66, 70, 80-2, 92-7, 98, 111, 157, 198, 224-8
   in Mexico, 95-6
   in North Africa, 228
   in Salem plantation, 96-7

Uruguay, 104

Valdes, Diego Rodriguez de ⸺ y de la Vanda, on Guinea worm, 174
Vampire bat, 247
Van Swieten, Gerard L. B., 171
Vaughan, Victor C., 109-10
Vedas, 144
Vedia, Don Enrique de, 160 n.
Vela, Viceroy Blasco Nuñez, 153
Velazquez, Diego, 84
Venereal diseases, 32, 38, 198-9
   see Chancroid, Gonorrhea, Syphilis
Venezuela, 10, 11
Vera Cruz, 107
Veragua River, 15
Verruga, 111
Vesalius, 45
Villalba, Joaquin de, 93
Villalobos, Francisco Lopez de, see Lopez de Villalobos, Francisco
Vinci, Leonardo da, 45
Virginia, famine in, 75
   malaria in, 118-23
   role in British conquest of, 7

Washington, George, 148
Weil, Adolf, 206
Weil's disease, 206, 235
Wesson, ⸺, 77
West Indies, 4, 6 n., 7 n., 11, 40
   depopulation of, 22
   dysentery in, 162
   introduction of slaves to, 30
White, John, 75
White, Captain William, 18
White dysentery, 34-5
Williams, Reverend J., on intercourse between whites and natives, 26-7
Williams, W. U., 178
Wilson, Rowland P., 243
Windham, Captain Thomas, 38
Wingfield, Captain, 119
Worms, 32, 34, 36, 37, 40, 155-74

Xalisco, Mexico, 161
Xerophthalmia, 204
Xerxes, 158
Ximenes, Gonzalo, 69

Yaws, 32, 33, 40, 185

Yellow fever, 38, 39, 40, 60, 66, 67, 70, 97, 106, 127-40, 142, 194, 199, 200, 206, 211, 229-36
Yucatan, 134, 149, 165, 204

Zinsser, Hans, viii, 227 n.

www.ingramcontent.com/pod-product-compliance
Lightning Source LLC
Chambersburg PA
CBHW071804300426
44116CB00009B/1204